THE WRIT- SELECTIONS

Shaping Our Lives

THE WRITER'S SELECTIONS

Shaping Our Lives

Third Edition

Kathleen T. McWhorter
Niagara County Community College

HOUGHTON MIFFLIN COMPANY
Boston   New York

Senior Sponsoring Editor: Mary Jo Southern
Development Editor: Kellie Cardone
Editorial Assistant: Peter Mooney
Senior Project Editor: Fred Burns
Senior Manufacturing Coordinator: Priscilla Bailey
Marketing Manager: Annamarie L. Rice

Cover image: Copyright © 1999 Jane Nelson, Artville, LLC.

PHOTO CREDITS: **Page 31:** © Richard Glaubman; **Page 78:** photo by Chris Curry/Hedge-hog House, N.Z.; map created by Parrot Graphics; **Page 80:** © Didrik Johnck/Corbis Sygma; **Page 175:** Lester Sloan, Gamma-Liaison/Getty Images; **Page 190:** Oprah Winfrey; **Page 229:** Edward Keating/© New York Times Pictures.

Acknowledgments for reprinted material appear beginning on page 265.

Printed in the U.S.A.

Library of Congress Control Number: 2002101701

ISBN: 0-618-23256-7

1 2 3 4 5 6 7 8 9-CRS-06 05 04 03 02

Contents

Preface   xi

Essential Reading and Writing Skills   1

The Reading Process   2

The Writing Process   6

1. Decisions That Shape Our Lives   18

Brainstorming About Decisions   19

"The Chosen One" LAURA CUNNINGHAM   20
*An adoptive mother discovers the joy and torment of being forced
to choose between two babies.*

"Arming Myself with a Gun Is Not the Answer"
BRONWYN JONES   25
*A college professor who was threatened by a stalker considers
whether to buy a gun for self-protection.*

"Life Is So Good." GEORGE DAWSON AND
RICHARD GLAUBMAN   29
*A ninety-eight-year-old man decides to learn to read by attending
adult education classes.*

"Saying Good-bye to Eric" JENNIFER S. DICKMAN   35
*A young woman describes how the tragedy of her boyfriend's
permanent debilitating injuries helped her make a career decision.*

"Evan's Two Moms" ANNA QUINDLEN   39
*A well-known syndicated columnist presents her views on
same-sex marriages.*

"Hello, Goodbye, Hey Maybe I Love You?"
JOSHUA KURLANTZICK   43
*Presented here is a new, fast-paced method of meeting people in
which participants decide in approximately seven minutes whether
they wish to date an individual.*

"The Gift of Sacrifice" BLANCA MATUTE
[STUDENT ESSAY]   47
*A young woman from Honduras learns to understand and live with
the consequences of leaving her family and moving to the United
States.*

Making Connections   49

Internet Connections   49

2. Events That Shape Our Lives   51

Brainstorming About Events   52

"The Scholarship Jacket" MARTA SALINAS   53
*A high school teacher tries to deny a scholarly student her
rightful reward.*

"Ragtime, My Time" ALTON FITZGERALD WHITE   59
*A young man describes an incident of racial profiling that
changed his life.*

"A Letter to My Daughter"   SIU WAI ANDERSON   64
*In a loving letter, a mother tells her infant daughter how and why
she is important to her.*

"To Mr. Winslow"   IAN FRAZIER   69
There are many ways to pay homage to a life cut short by tragedy.

"Breaking Glass"   JONATHAN ROSEN   73
*The custom of stamping on a glass at the conclusion of a Jewish
wedding ceremony becomes particularly meaningful to the author
as he connects his own wedding to his father's past.*

"Blind to Faith" KARL TARO GREENFELD   77
*Despite numerous hardships, a blind mountain climber struggles
to conquer Mt. Everest.*

"Desert Storm and Shield"   SCOTT STOPA
[STUDENT ESSAY]   85
*Being in the middle of a war zone, a young man learns what is
important in life.*

Making Connections   87
Internet Connections   87

3. Work That Shapes Our Lives   89

Brainstorming About Work   90

"Mr. Mom's World" DAVID CASE   91
*A new trend in childrearing — stay-at-home dads — is examined in
this essay.*

"Working Students Need to Look for Career Experience"
SABRA CHARTRAND   97
*This essay describes the benefits of part-time jobs and suggests how
to find them.*

"The Family Farm"   DAVID MAS MASUMOTO   101
*Working on his family's farm becomes a meaningful experience for
a college graduate.*

"Disney's Head Trips"   JANE KEUNZ   105
Surprising working conditions exist at Disney World.

"*Mojado* Like Me" JOSEPH TOVARES 109
Posing as a laborer, an Hispanic documentary producer confronts prejudice he thought he left behind.

"What Are They Probing For?"
BARBARA EHRENREICH 116
A well-known journalist explores the issue of drug and personality testing as part of the application process for low-paying jobs.

"A Seafood Survey" ROBERT WOOD
[STUDENT ESSAY] 120
An employee at a fish market reports the strange questions his customers ask.

Making Connections 123
Internet Connections 123

4. Cultures That Shape Our Lives   124

Brainstorming About Culture 125

"Primary Colors" KIM MCLARIN 126
A mother writes about how society reacts to her light-skinned daughter.

"Black *and* Latino" ROBERTO SANTIAGO 130
Being both black and Puerto Rican causes an identity crisis in a young man from Harlem.

"Fifth Chinese Daughter" JADE SNOW WONG 134
A young woman makes a decision that goes against her family's cultural values.

"Through Tewa Eyes" ALFONSO ORTIZ 138
Learn the symbolic meaning of summer and winter as explained through the rituals performed by the Tewa Indians.

"Dumpster Diving" LARS EIGHNER 143
A young man survives by picking medicine, food, and clothes out of Dumpsters.

"Silenced Voices: Deaf Cultures and 'Hearing' Families"
RICHARD APPELBAUM AND WILLIAM J. CHAMBLISS 147
Being deaf means more than not hearing sounds; it means belonging to an entire culture in and of itself.

"Cultural Education in America" JONATHAN WONG
[STUDENT ESSAY] 151
After attending college in the United States for one month, a young man from Hong Kong describes numerous conflicts between his culture at home and the American lifestyle.

Making Connections   153
Internet Connections   154

5. Others Who Shape Our Lives   155

Brainstorming About Others   156

"Shopping Can Be a Challenge" CAROL FLEISCHMAN   157
*A blind woman describes how people react to her when she
goes shopping.*

"The Promised Land" BILL COSBY   161
*A famous comedian discusses why his parents' marriage of more
than fifty years is special.*

"Our Wounded Hearts" ALLISON BERNARD   165
*A woman describes her efforts to rescue her uncle, a heart attack
victim, from an unhealthy lifestyle.*

"Poppa and the Spruce Tree" MARIO CUOMO   170
*Remembering his father's determination, a former governor finds
the strength to continue his failing political campaign.*

"Food from the 'Hood" LESTER SLOAN   174
*A group of high school students devises projects that bring college
scholarships to inner-city youths.*

"Bill Gates: Computer Wizard" MICHAEL SCHALLER,
VIRGINIA SCHARFF, AND ROBERT D. SCHULZINGER   178
*Bill Gates revolutionized America with his invention of Windows
computer software.*

"Do unto Others" DAVID POLMER
[STUDENT ESSAY]   182
*A college student explains how his beliefs about sportsmanship
have changed since his childhood.*

Making Connections   185
Internet Connections   185

6. Media That Shape Our Lives   186

Brainstorming About the Media   187

"Oprah Winfrey" DEBORAH TANNEN   188
*A noted authority on human communication examines Oprah
Winfrey's rise to fame and her impact on talk shows.*

"My First Story" PATRICE GAINES   193
*Criticism motivated this young black writer to pursue her goal of
becoming a successful journalist.*

"Music 'n Moods" Carolyn Gard   197
The beneficial effects of music on emotions are described in this essay.

"Advertising: Institutionalized Lying" Donna Woolfolk
Cross   202
Advertising can be inaccurate and misleading to the public.

"Can TV Improve Us?" Jane Rosenzweig   206
This essay explores television as an agent of social change.

"How Much 'Reality' TV Can We Survive?"
Todd Leopold   211
*This essay discusses the newest trend in television programming —
reality TV — and examines reasons for its popularity.*

"Sporting the Fan(tasy) of Reality TV" Colleen Diez
[Student Essay]   217
A college student explains the popularity of reality TV programs.

Making Connections   219
Internet Connections   219

7. Technology That Shapes Our Lives   221

Brainstorming About Technology   222

"The Seven Sustainable Wonders of the World"
Alan Thein Durning   223
*In addition to the true seven wonders of the world, there are, in this
author's opinion, seven simple wonders of the world that help solve
everyday problems.*

"Stepping Through a Computer Screen, Disabled Veterans
Savor Freedom" N. R. Kleinfield   227
*A virtual reality program helps paraplegics to move and phobics to
overcome their fears.*

"Log to Learn" Jodie Morse   233
*A journalist registers for an online college course and describes her
experiences.*

"Inventing the Future" Thomas J. Frey and
Darby L. Frey   240
*Technological advances may produce surprising new inventions in
the near future.*

"Dr. Dolphin" Richard Blow   245
*Swimming with dolphins, in water or on a computerized program,
can affect brain waves and help people to become healthier.*

"The Case for Selling Human Organs"
Ronald Bailey   253
This essay examines the controversial issue of human organs for sale.

"Human Interaction"   Christine Choi   258
[Student Essay]
*This student argues that computers should not replace human
contact and interaction.*

Making Connections   260
Internet Connections   261

Glossary   263

Acknowledgments   265

Index of Authors and Titles   269

Preface

The Writer's Selections: Shaping Our Lives is a thematic reader developed to meet the specific needs of beginning writers. Using readings as springboards for student writing is a well-recognized and established approach to the teaching of writing, but the readings in most anthologies are inappropriate for developing writers in terms of length, difficulty, and subject matter. Furthermore, beginning writers often lack sophisticated reading skills, and can find these readings troublesome and frustrating. We have all heard comments such as, "You mean I have to read all this just to write a one-page paper?" or "I just got lost trying to read it, so how could I write about it?" Instructors who use readers often find themselves spending more class time explaining the reading and less time teaching writing skills than they would like. *The Writer's Selections: Shaping Our Lives* addresses these concerns by offering brief, accessible, engaging readings and providing structured apparatus that focuses and directs students and thus stimulates writing.

Thematic Organization

Reading exposes us to ideas that can, as the book's subtitle suggests, shape or change our lives. The seven chapters in this text explore some major factors that shape our lives: decisions, other people, events, cultures, media, work, and technology. Each is a category relevant to students' daily experience — a category about which they can think and write. As students read about how people's lives have been shaped by these factors, they may become more fully aware of the impact of such factors on their own lives.

The Reading Selections

The 49 reading selections, chosen with the needs, interests, and learning characteristics of beginning writers in mind, offer instructors choices, but do not leave students with the complaint that most of the book was left unassigned. The readings have the following characteristics:

- **Short.** The readings range in length from very brief, three to four paragraphs, to a maximum of two to five pages. Students will regard them as realistic, "do-able" assignments.
- **Readable.** The readings are within the skill range of most beginning writers; they are thought-provoking but lack burdensome vocabulary or a complicated writing style. An occasional

longer, more challenging reading is included for instructors to assign to prepare students for readings typically assigned in freshmen composition courses.

- **Engaging.** The readings will spark interest and stimulate thought. Many are personal narratives to which students can relate immediately; others are issue-oriented, about topics such as media bias, computers, false advertising, the effects of music, part-time jobs, and inventions of the future. The readings are timely, sometimes humorous, and within the realm of the students' experience.

- **Representative of a Wide Range of Sources.** There is a wide sampling of writers, including Asian, Hispanic, Native American, and black writers chosen from a range of periodicals, newspapers, and books. Student writing is well-represented, with one student essay included in each chapter.

The Apparatus

The Writer's Selections: Shaping Our Lives is a collection of essays, but it is also an instructional tool. Its apparatus is intended to guide students through the reading, prompt their thinking, and prepare them to write about the reading.

Reading and Writing Process Introduction

Because beginning writers need instruction in how to read and write more effectively, the book opens with an overview of the reading and writing processes. This section guides students through each process, offering numerous skills and strategies for becoming better writers and readers. Preceding this introduction are two four-color inserts that present the reading and writing processes in a visually appealing format.

Chapter Features

Each chapter opens with an introduction that briefly explores the chapter theme and guides students through preliminary "brainstorming" that makes the theme real and personal. Each chapter concludes with a "Making Connections" section containing writing assignments that link two or more of the readings in the chapter. An "Internet Connections" section guides students in discovering online sources related to chapter topics. Each of these features encourages students to synthesize ideas and to use sources to support their ideas.

Features Accompanying Each Reading

- **Headnote.** A brief introduction precedes the reading; it focuses the students' attention, identifies the source, and establishes a context for the reading.
- **Reading Strategy.** This section offers practical advice on how to approach each essay. It suggests a particular reading or review technique that will improve the students' comprehension and recall of each essay.
- **Vocabulary Preview.** A list of challenging words used in the reading together with their meanings is given before the reading. Since students preview the words and their meanings before reading, their comprehension of the essay will be strengthened.
- **Finding Meaning.** These questions guide the students in grasping the literal content of each essay. Answering these questions enables students to assess their understanding. Students either confirm that they understand the key points or realize that they have not read as carefully as necessary, in which case a closer reading is encouraged.
- **Understanding Technique.** This section offers questions designed to guide students in analyzing the writer's methodology. For example, students may be asked to evaluate a writer's thesis statement; assess the effectiveness of a title, introduction, or conclusion; or study how the writer uses topic sentences or transitional words and phrases.
- **Thinking Critically.** These questions engage students by provoking thought, sparking lively discussion, and fostering critical analysis. They may be used as collaborative activities or as brainstorming sessions to generate ideas about the reading.
- **Writing About the Reading.** Journal writing assignments encourage students to explore their ideas and write about them in a journal format. Paragraph-length assignments offer writers the opportunity to explore a focused topic. Essay-length assignments give students experience in narrowing a topic and developing a short essay. Assignments often provide prompts that offer advice on how to approach the assignment or what to include.
- **A Creative Activity.** This activity is intended to stimulate interest and creativity by offering light, spontaneous writing assignments that, alternately, may be used as collaborative learning activities.

Changes to the Third Edition

- **Thirteen New Readings.** Ten new professional readings and three new student essays were added to this edition. New topics include racial profiling, organ donation and sale, stay-at-home fathers, climbing Mount Everest, reality TV, online learning, and speed dating.
- **Revised Skill Instructional Section.** The introduction to the book has been revised and retitled "Essential Reading and Writing Skills." Additional cross references to the reading and writing success tips featured in the four-color inserts have been added.
- **New Internet Connections Section.** Each chapter now concludes with an Internet activity that demonstrates the relevance of chapter content, allows the students to explore their own ideas using electronic sources, and culminates in a writing assignment.

Ancillary Materials

The Writer's Guide. *The Writer's Guide* is a brief handbook that may be used in conjunction with *The Writer's Selections*. The two books may be ordered together for a discounted cost. *The Writer's Guide,* organized around questions that student writers frequently ask, provides a concise, easy-to-use reference for the five-step writing process as well as a practical review of grammar and mechanics.

Instructor's Resource Manual. This manual provides practical suggestions for teaching writing along with individual discussions of each reading in the book.

Expressways, Third Edition. Available in DOS, Windows, and Macintosh versions, **Expressways,** Third Edition software is an interactive tutorial program that allows students to complete a range of writing activities and exercises at their own pace.

Dictionary Deal. The *American Heritage College Dictionary* may be shrink-wrapped with the text at a substantial savings.

Acknowledgments

I appreciate the excellent ideas, suggestions and advice of my colleagues who served as reviewers:

Kirk Adams, *Tarrant County Junior College,* TX
Teh-Min Brown, *Las Positas College,* CA

Mark Connelly, *Milwaukee Area Technical College,* WI
Bette Daudu, *Montgomery College—Takoma Park Campus,* MD
Judith Hanley, *Wilbur Wright College,* IL
Judy Hathcock, *Amarillo College,* TX
Linda S. Houston, *Ohio State Agricultural Technical Institute,* OH
Ann Judd, *Seward County Community College,* KS
Michael A. Knoll, *Fisher College,* MA
Jane Lasky-MacPherson, *Middlesex County College,* NJ
Daniel Lowe, *Community College of Allegheny County,* PA
Mary McCormick, *Portland Community College,* OR
Susan McCray, *Jefferson Community College,* KY
Eleanor Montero, *Daytona Beach Community College,* FL
Julia Nichols, *Okaloosa Community College,* FL
Michael A. Orlando, *Bergen Community College,* NJ
Don Ross, *Lamar University—Port Arthur,* TX
Audrey J. Roth, *Miami-Dade Community College,* FL
Linda Tappmeyer, *Southwest Baptist University,* MO
Robert W. Walker, *Daytona Beach Community College,* FL
Mary Beth Wilk, *Des Moines Area Community College,* IA
Deanna Yameen, *Quincy College,* MA

The entire staff at Houghton Mifflin deserves praise and credit for their assistance. In particular I wish to thank Mary Jo Southern for her support of the project and Danielle Richardson and Kellie Cardone for their valuable assistance in planning the third edition. Finally, I thank my students who have helped me to select appropriate, meaningful readings.

USE PREVIEWING
TO GET STARTED

Previewing is a quick way of finding out what a reading will be about *before* you read it. Try previewing the brief reading at the right using the steps listed below.

How to Preview

1. Read the title.

2. Read the introductory note.

3. Check the author's name.

4. Read the introductory paragraph.

5. Read the dark print headings (if any).

6. For readings without headings, read the first sentence of a few paragraphs per page.

7. Glance at any photographs or drawings.

8. Read the last paragraph.

Why Preview?

Previewing has several benefits:

1. It gives you a mental outline of the reading *before* you read it.

2. Reading will be easier because you have a mental outline; your comprehension will improve.

3. You will be able to remember more of what you read.

4. You will find it easier to concentrate.

Friends All of Us
Pablo Neruda

A Nobel Prize–winning poet's backyard lesson in brotherhood

One time, investigating in the backyard of our house in Temuco [Chile] the tiny objects and minuscule beings of my world, I came upon a hole in one of the boards of the fence. I looked through the hole and saw a landscape like that behind our house, uncared for, and wild. I moved back a few steps, because I sensed vaguely that something was about to happen. All of a sudden a hand appeared—a tiny hand of a boy about my own age. By the time I came close again, the hand was gone, and in its place there was a marvelous white sheep.

The sheep's wool was faded. Its wheels had escaped. All of this only made it more authentic. I had never seen such a wonderful sheep. I looked back through the hole but the boy had disappeared. I went into the house and brought out a treasure of my own: a pinecone, opened, full of odor and resin, which I adored. I set it down in the same spot and went off with the sheep.

I never saw either the hand or the boy again. And I have never again seen a sheep like that either. The toy I lost finally in a fire. But even now, in 1954, almost 50 years old, whenever I pass a toy shop, I look furtively into the window, but it's no use. They don't make sheep like that any more.

I have been a lucky man. To feel the intimacy of brothers is a marvelous thing in life. To feel the love of people whom we love is a fire that feeds our life. But to feel the affection that comes from those whom we do not know, from those unknown to us, who are watching over our sleep and solitude, over our dangers and our weaknesses—that is something still greater and more beautiful because it widens out the boundaries of our being, and unites all living things.

That exchange brought home to me for the first time a precious idea: that all of humanity is somehow together. That experience came to me again much later; this time it stood out strikingly against a background of trouble and persecution.

It won't surprise you then that I attempted to give something resiny, earthlike, and fragrant in exchange for human brotherhood. Just as I once left the pinecone by the fence, I have since left my words on the door of so many people who were unknown to me, people in prison, or hunted, or alone.

That is the great lesson I learned in my childhood, in the backyard of a lonely house. Maybe it was nothing but a game two boys played who didn't know each other and wanted to pass to the other some good things of life. Yet maybe this small and mysterious exchange of gifts remained inside me also, deep and indestructible, giving my poetry light.

KNOW WHAT TO LOOK FOR AS YOU READ

If you know what to look for as you read, you'll find reading is easier, goes faster, and requires less rereading. Use the list below to guide you in reading the essays in this book.

What to Look For

1. THE MEANING OF THE TITLE.

In some essays, the title announces the topic of the essay and may reveal the author's viewpoint toward it. In others, the meaning of the title becomes clear only after you have read the essay (as with the sample essay on the right).

2. THE INTRODUCTION.

The opening paragraph of an essay should be interesting, give background information, and announce the subject of the essay.

3. THE AUTHOR'S MAIN POINT.

This is often called the *thesis statement*. It is the one big idea that the entire essay explains. Often it appears in the first paragraph, but in the sample essay at the right, it does not.

4. SUPPORT AND EXPLANATION.

The essay should explain, give reasons, or offer support for the author's main point.

5. THE CONCLUSION.

The last paragraph should bring the essay to a close. Often, it will restate the author's main point. It may also suggest directions for further thought.

Friends All of Us
Pablo Neruda

A Nobel Prize–winning poet's backyard lesson in brotherhood

One time, investigating in the backyard of our house in Temuco [Chile] the tiny objects and minuscule beings of my world, I came upon a hole in one of the boards of the fence. I looked through the hole and saw a landscape like that behind our house, uncared for, and wild. I moved back a few steps, because I sensed vaguely that something was about to happen. All of a sudden a hand appeared—a tiny hand of a boy about my own age. By the time I came close again, the hand was gone, and in its place there was a marvelous white sheep.

The sheep's wool was faded. Its wheels had escaped. All of this only made it more authentic. I had never seen such a wonderful sheep. I looked back through the hole but the boy had disappeared. I went into the house and brought out a treasure of my own: a pinecone, opened, full of odor and resin, which I adored. I set it down in the same spot and went off with the sheep.

I never saw either the hand or the boy again. And I have never again seen a sheep like that either. The toy I lost finally in a fire. But even now, in 1954, almost 50 years old, whenever I pass a toy shop, I look furtively into the window, but it's no use. They don't make sheep like that any more.

I have been a lucky man. To feel the intimacy of brothers is a marvelous thing in life. To feel the love of people whom we love is a fire that feeds our life. But to feel the affection that comes from those whom we do not know, from those unknown to us, who are watching over our sleep and solitude, over our dangers and our weaknesses—that is something still greater and more beautiful because it widens out the boundaries of our being, and unites all living things.

That exchange brought home to me for the first time a precious idea: that all of humanity is somehow together. That experience came to me again much later; this time it stood out strikingly against a background of trouble and persecution.

It won't surprise you then that I attempted to give something resiny, earthlike, and fragrant in exchange for human brotherhood. Just as I once left the pinecone by the fence, I have since left my words on the door of so many people who were unknown to me, people in prison, or hunted, or alone.

That is the great lesson I learned in my childhood, in the backyard of a lonely house. Maybe it was nothing but a game two boys played who didn't know each other and wanted to pass to the other some good things of life. Yet maybe this small and mysterious exchange of gifts remained inside me also, deep and indestructible, giving my poetry light.

ANNOTATE:
READ WITH A PEN IN HAND

What Is Annotation?

Annotating is a way of keeping track of your impressions, ideas, reactions, and questions AS YOU READ. It is also a way of marking key phrases, sentences, or paragraphs to return to. When you are ready to discuss and/or write about the reading, you will find your annotations helpful. Study the sample annotations on this page to see how it is done.

How did he know?

How to Annotate

Here is a partial list of the things you might want to annotate:

1. Questions that come to mind as you read

2. Key events that you may want to refer to again

3. Particularly meaningful expressions or descriptions

4. Important ideas you may want to find again

Why? What has happened in his life?

5. Sections where you need further information

6. Sections where the author reveals his or her feelings or reasons for writing

How can he feel affection for people he doesn't know?

7. Striking examples

8. Key supporting information—dates, statistics, etc.

What happened?

9. Your personal reactions (agreement, anger, amazement, shock, surprise, humor)

10. Ideas you disagree with

Thesis explains why he writes poetry.

Timesaving Tip: Devise a code system. Bracket key ideas, underline key events, circle unusual expressions, etc. Consider using color to distinguish types of annotations.

Friends All of Us
Pablo Neruda

A Nobel Prize–winning poet's backyard lesson in brotherhood

One time, investigating in the backyard of our house in Temuco [Chile] the tiny objects and minuscule beings of my world, I came upon a hole in one of the boards of the fence. I looked through the hole and saw a landscape like that behind our house, uncared for, and wild. I moved back a few steps, because I sensed vaguely that something was about to happen. All of a sudden a hand appeared—a tiny hand of a boy about my own age. By the time I came close again, the hand was gone, and in its place there was a marvelous white sheep.

The sheep's wool was faded. Its wheels had escaped. All of this only made it more authentic. I had never seen such a wonderful sheep. I looked back through the hole but the boy had disappeared. I went into the house and brought out a treasure of my own: a pinecone, opened, full of odor and resin, which I adored. I set it down in the same spot and went off with the sheep.

I never saw either the hand or the boy again. And I have never again seen a sheep like that either. The toy I lost finally in a fire. But even now, in 1954, almost 50 years old, whenever I pass a toy shop, I look furtively into the window, but it's no use. They don't make sheep like that any more.

I have been a lucky man. To feel the intimacy of brothers is a marvelous thing in life. To feel the love of people whom we love is a fire that feeds our life. But to feel the affection that comes from those whom we do not know, from those unknown to us, who are watching over our sleep and solitude, over our dangers and our weaknesses—that is something still greater and more beautiful because it widens out the boundaries of our being, and unites all living things.

That exchange brought home to me for the first time a precious idea: that all of humanity is somehow together. That experience came to me again much later; this time it stood out strikingly against a background of trouble and persecution.

It won't surprise you then that I attempted to give something resiny, earthlike, and fragrant in exchange for human brotherhood. Just as I once left the pinecone by the fence, I have since left my words on the door of so many people who were unknown to me, people in prison, or hunted, or alone.

That is the great lesson I learned in my childhood, in the backyard of a lonely house. Maybe it was nothing but a game two boys played who didn't know each other and wanted to pass to the other some good things of life. Yet maybe this small and mysterious exchange of gifts remained inside me also, deep and indestructible, giving my poetry light.

ASK CRITICAL THINKING QUESTIONS

To get the full meaning out of the essay and to make writing about the reading easier, ask yourself questions during and after reading that will help you think critically and analyze the reading. Here are some useful questions along with sample answers applied to the "Friends All of Us" reading.

Critical Reading Questions and Answers

1. **Q.** What types of evidence or reasons does the author use to explain or support the thesis statement? Was adequate support provided?

   A. Neruda uses an event (the exchange of toys), personal experience, and personal reactions to support his thesis.

2. **Q.** Did the author present a one-sided (biased) view of the topic or were both sides of the issue examined?

   A. Neruda's view was one-sided; he was presenting his personal viewpoint.

3. **Q.** What big issues (big questions about life) does this essay deal with? Do you agree or disagree with the author's viewpoint toward these issues?

   A. The essay deals with human relationships, brotherhood, and the common bond among people.

4. **Q.** Why did the author write the essay?

   A. Neruda wrote to explain how an event helped him understand human relationships and to explain how he sees poetry as a gift to others.

5. **Q.** What key message about "Shaping Our Lives," the theme of this book, does Neruda convey in this essay?

   A. Neruda shows how a simple event —the exchange of toys—can have an impact on one's life.

6. **Q.** What further information, if any, did you need?

   A. More information is needed about the persecution and trouble Neruda experienced.

Friends All of Us
Pablo Neruda

A Nobel Prize–winning poet's backyard lesson in brotherhood

One time, investigating in the backyard of our house in Temuco [Chile] the tiny objects and minuscule beings of my world, I came upon a hole in one of the boards of the fence. I looked through the hole and saw a landscape like that behind our house, uncared for, and wild. I moved back a few steps, because I sensed vaguely that something was about to happen. All of a sudden a hand appeared—a tiny hand of a boy about my own age. By the time I came close again, the hand was gone, and in its place there was a marvelous white sheep.

The sheep's wool was faded. Its wheels had escaped. All of this only made it more authentic. I had never seen such a wonderful sheep. I looked back through the hole but the boy had disappeared. I went into the house and brought out a treasure of my own: a pinecone, opened, full of odor and resin, which I adored. I set it down in the same spot and went off with the sheep.

I never saw either the hand or the boy again. And I have never again seen a sheep like that either. The toy I lost finally in a fire. But even now, in 1954, almost 50 years old, whenever I pass a toy shop, I look furtively into the window, but it's no use. They don't make sheep like that any more.

I have been a lucky man. To feel the intimacy of brothers is a marvelous thing in life. To feel the love of people whom we love is a fire that feeds our life. But to feel the affection that comes from those whom we do not know, from those unknown to us, who are watching over our sleep and solitude, over our dangers and our weaknesses—that is something still greater and more beautiful because it widens out the boundaries of our being, and unites all living things. That exchange brought home to me for the first time a precious idea: that all of humanity is somehow together. That experience came to me again much later; this time it stood out strikingly against a background of trouble and persecution.

It won't surprise you then that I attempted to give something resiny, earthlike, and fragrant in exchange for human brotherhood. Just as I once left the pinecone by the fence, I have since left my words on the door of so many people who were unknown to me, people in prison, or hunted, or alone.

That is the great lesson I learned in my childhood, in the backyard of a lonely house. Maybe it was nothing but a game two boys played who didn't know each other and wanted to pass to the other some good things of life. Yet maybe this small and mysterious exchange of gifts remained inside me also, deep and indestructible, giving my poetry light.

WRITING SUCCESS
Strategy
#1

WORKING THROUGH PROBLEMS IN YOUR WRITING

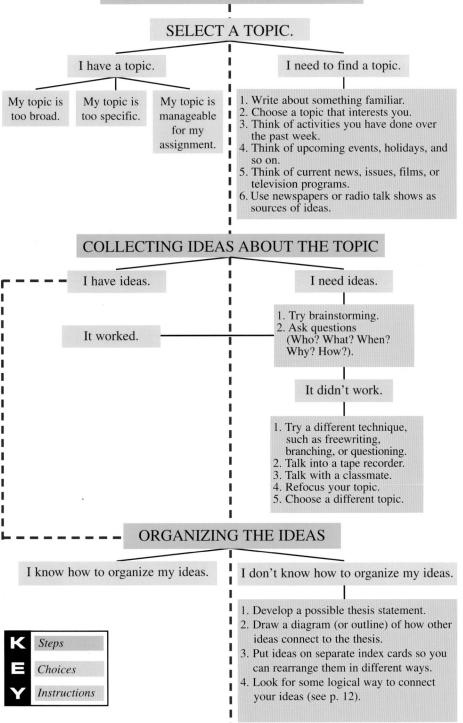

I HAVE A WRITING ASSIGNMENT.

SELECT A TOPIC.

I have a topic.

I need to find a topic.

My topic is too broad.

My topic is too specific.

My topic is manageable for my assignment.

1. Write about something familiar.
2. Choose a topic that interests you.
3. Think of activities you have done over the past week.
4. Think of upcoming events, holidays, and so on.
5. Think of current news, issues, films, or television programs.
6. Use newspapers or radio talk shows as sources of ideas.

COLLECTING IDEAS ABOUT THE TOPIC

I have ideas.

I need ideas.

It worked.

1. Try brainstorming.
2. Ask questions (Who? What? When? Why? How?).

It didn't work.

1. Try a different technique, such as freewriting, branching, or questioning.
2. Talk into a tape recorder.
3. Talk with a classmate.
4. Refocus your topic.
5. Choose a different topic.

ORGANIZING THE IDEAS

I know how to organize my ideas.

I don't know how to organize my ideas.

1. Develop a possible thesis statement.
2. Draw a diagram (or outline) of how other ideas connect to the thesis.
3. Put ideas on separate index cards so you can rearrange them in different ways.
4. Look for some logical way to connect your ideas (see p. 12).

KEY
Steps
Choices
Instructions

WRITING SUCCESS
Strategy
#1
(continued)

WRITING A FIRST DRAFT

I wrote a draft and I like it.

I'm having trouble getting started.

1. Don't try to write the paper in order, from beginning to end; write any part to get started.
2. Just write ideas in sentence form; worry about organizing them later.
3. Write fast and keep writing; don't worry about anything except continuing to write.
4. Dictate into a tape recorder.

I don't like my draft.

1. Let it sit a day; come back when your mind is fresh.
2. Analyze each part (see pp. 15–17); determine which parts are weak.
3. If the draft doesn't seem to say much, collect more ideas about your topic.
4. Refocus your topic; it may be either too broad or too narrow.

REVISING THE DRAFT

I know what to revise.

I don't know what to revise.

1. Let it sit a day; return with a fresh mind.
2. Use a revision checklist (see inside front cover).

PROOFREADING

I know how to find my errors.

I'm not sure I will find all my errors.

Spelling Errors

Punctuation Errors

Grammar Errors

1. Use the spelling checker, if you are using a computer.
2. Read your paper backward, from the last sentence to the first.

Read your paper several times, each time checking for a different type of error.

Read your paper aloud, listening for pauses; punctuation is usually needed at the pauses.

K *Steps*
E *Choices*
Y *Instructions*

FOLLOW AN ORGANIZING PLAN FOR YOUR ESSAY

To make your essay easy to read and understand, you should follow an organizing plan. An essay has specific parts, and each part serves specific purposes for both the reader and the writer.

ESSAY

Note: There is no set number of paragraphs that an essay should contain. This discussion shows six paragraphs, but in actual essays, the number will vary greatly.

PARTS TO INCLUDE

WHAT EACH PART SHOULD DO

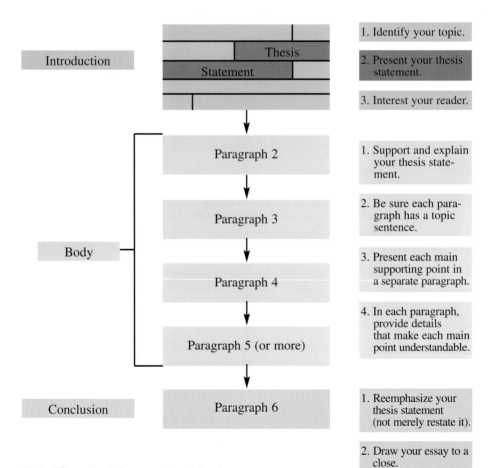

Introduction

Thesis Statement

1. Identify your topic.

2. Present your thesis statement.

3. Interest your reader.

Paragraph 2

Paragraph 3

Body

Paragraph 4

Paragraph 5 (or more)

1. Support and explain your thesis statement.

2. Be sure each paragraph has a topic sentence.

3. Present each main supporting point in a separate paragraph.

4. In each paragraph, provide details that make each main point understandable.

Conclusion

Paragraph 6

1. Reemphasize your thesis statement (not merely restate it).

2. Draw your essay to a close.

Note: Throughout the essay, transitional words, phrases, and sentences work to lead the reader from idea to idea.

SPEND TIME ORGANIZING EACH PARAGRAPH

Before you write each paragraph of your essay, plan what you will say and the order in which you will say it.

PARAGRAPH

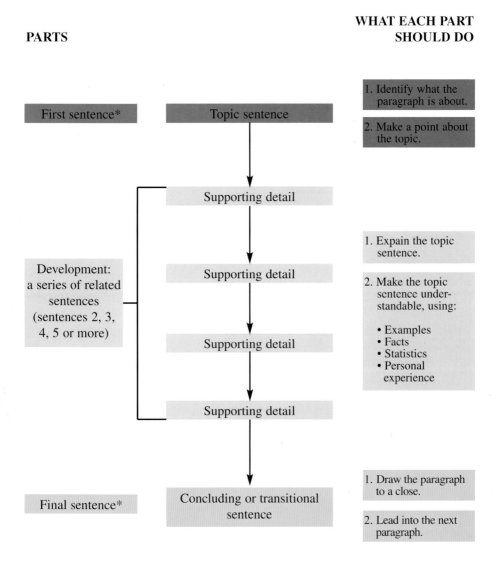

PARTS

WHAT EACH PART SHOULD DO

First sentence*

Topic sentence

1. Identify what the paragraph is about.

2. Make a point about the topic.

Supporting detail

Development:
a series of related sentences
(sentences 2, 3, 4, 5 or more)

Supporting detail

1. Explain the topic sentence.

2. Make the topic sentence understandable, using:

• Examples
• Facts
• Statistics
• Personal experience

Supporting detail

Supporting detail

Final sentence*

Concluding or transitional sentence

1. Draw the paragraph to a close.

2. Lead into the next paragraph.

Note: The topic sentence is often placed first, but it may appear elsewhere in the paragraph. For emphasis, writers sometimes even place it last in the paragraph.

Essential Reading and Writing Skills

Many people, events, and ideas influence our lives. This collection of readings explores seven major factors that influence our lives: decisions, events, work, cultures, others, media, and technology. You will read about how other people's lives have been shaped by these factors. By learning how these factors affect others, you will begin to realize more fully how they shape the course of your own life.

As you read these selections about factors that shape our lives, you will be shaping your own reading and writing skills. You will read a variety of articles and essays, some by professional writers and others by student writers from different colleges across the country. You will discover new ideas and new ways of looking at things. As you read, you will encounter a wide range of writing styles, ways of approaching a topic, and methods of organizing ideas. These will give you ideas for your own writing and will also make you a versatile reader who can adapt to a wide range of reading materials.

Following each reading, you will work with different writing tasks that include journal writing as well as paragraph, essay, and creative activity assignments. These assignments will give you an opportunity to explore your ideas about the topic of the reading and to explore how your life is shaped by decisions, events, work, cultures, others, media, and technology. As you complete these writing tasks, you will have the opportunity to plan, organize, write, and revise your ideas. The following section explains and gives examples of each of these steps. This text also contains two useful reference sections, "Reading Success Strategies 1–4" and "Writing Success Strategies 1–3," preceding this page. These sections lead you, step-by-step, through reading a selection and writing about it. These sections are perforated so you can remove them easily from the book and refer to them frequently as you work through readings and complete writing assignments. For example, until you are familiar with the steps in previewing, keep Reading Success Strategy

1

#1 handy for quick reference. Refer to Reading Success Tips #2–4 as you read, annotate, and evaluate assigned readings. Before you begin a writing assignment, use the flowchart in Writing Success Strategy #1 to guide you through the process. Refer to Writing Success Strategy #2 to help you organize your essay and Writing Success Strategy #3 to help you write effective paragraphs.

THE READING PROCESS

Reading is a means of understanding and responding to an author's message. In this book you will read a wide variety of essays, each written by a different author. As you read each essay, first focus on what the author says and then, once you've understood the message, think about and react to the ideas the essay presents. This introduction will help you to read essays by offering some practical advice on how to get involved, understand the author's message, read and think critically, remember what you have read, and get ready to write.

Getting Involved with the Reading

If you are interested in and involved with an essay, it will be easier to read, as well as easier to react to and write about. Use the following suggestions to get involved with each essay you are assigned.

Choose the right time and place to read.   Be sure to read at a time when you can concentrate—when you are not tired, weary from working on other assignments, hungry, or feeling stressed. Choose a place that is quiet and free of distractions—one in which nothing will compete for your attention.

Preview the essay.   Begin by studying Reading Success Strategy #1, "Use Previewing to Get Started," to become familiar with what the essay is about before you read it. Refer to this color insert frequently until you are familiar with the previewing process. Previewing will enable you to read the essay more easily because you will know what to expect and how the essay is organized.

Connect the topic of the essay with your own experience.   Try to discover what you already know about the topic of the essay. At first, you may think you know little or nothing about it, but for most of the essays in this book, you do have some knowledge of or experience with the topic. For example, suppose an essay is about managing stress. At first, you may not think you know much about it, but all of us have experienced stress and have learned how to deal with it. What do you do when you are under pressure? How do you react? What do you do to

cope with or escape the pressure? These questions are probably bringing ideas to mind. Here are two ways to jump-start your memory on a
given topic:

- Ask as many questions as you can about the topic. Suppose your
  topic is radio talk show hosts. You could ask questions such as,
  Why are they popular? What kinds of personalities do they have?
  Who is the most popular? Why do they sometimes insult people?
  Why do people agree to talk with them? Who chooses the topics
  they discuss? Questions such as these will get you interested in the
  reading and help you maintain interest as you read.
- Brainstorm a list of everything you know about the topic. Suppose the topic is the treatment of AIDS. Make a list of the things
  you know. You might list people you know who were treated, information you have read about experimental drugs, and so forth.

**Read the discussion questions or writing assignments before
reading the essay.**   If you know what you will be expected to discuss
and write about after reading, you will find it easier to keep your mind
on the reading.

Getting the Author's Message

Before you can discuss or write about a reading, you have to be sure
you have understood what the author was saying. At times, this is easy.
But sometimes, depending on the author, the style of writing, and the
topic, it is not so easy. Here are some suggestions to use to be sure you
are getting the author's message. (See Reading Success Strategy #2.)

Understand Essay and Paragraph Organization

Begin by studying the chart in Writing Success Strategy #2. Once you
are familiar with the way essays and paragraphs within essays are organized, you will find them easier to understand. This chart describes
how you should organize essays and paragraphs as you write; however,
it also explains how other writers organize essays and paragraphs as
they write. You are probably beginning to see that as you improve your
skills in writing essays and paragraphs, you will also find that your skill
in reading them increases. As you read, be sure to identify:

- The **thesis statement**
- The **topic sentence** of each paragraph and how it supports the
  thesis statement
- The key supporting **details** that the author provides

Many students find it helpful to underline or highlight these parts as
they find them.

Reading Success Strategy #2, "Know What to Look for As You Read," identifies and illustrates the key parts of the essay. Refer to this color insert often as you read. It will focus your attention on what is important to know and remember.

Use Questions to Guide Your Reading

Be sure you can answer the following questions about each essay you read. These questions together produce a condensed summary of the content of the essay.

Who (or what) is the essay about?

What happened? (What action took place?)

When did the action occur?

Where did the action occur?

Why did the action occur?

How did the action occur?

These questions focus your attention on the literal, or factual, meaning of the essay. You will also want to ask critical questions that help you respond to, react to, and evaluate the essay. Refer to Reading Success Strategy #4 for a list of useful questions.

Read with a Pen or Highlighter in Hand

Begin by reading through Reading Success Strategy #3. To write about a reading, you will need to refer to it frequently; however, you should not have to reread the entire essay each time you want to locate a key point. (Rereading an essay *is* useful at times, and sometimes it is necessary if you are to understand the essay fully, but you should not have to reread to find particular information.) To avoid unnecessary rereading, underline or highlight important parts of the essay, parts you would like to reread, key statements, parts about which you have questions, and parts you think you may want to refer to as you write.

In addition to marking or highlighting key parts, you should also make marginal notes. These are called annotations. Think of annotations as a way of recording your thoughts as you read and as a means of "talking back" to the author. Reading Success Strategy #3, "Annotate: Read with a Pen in Hand," describes and illustrates how to annotate. Refer to this color insert often to remind yourself of the kinds of annotations that are useful to make.

Deal with Difficult Vocabulary

Before each reading, a list of vocabulary words is given, along with a brief definition of each word as it is used in the reading. Be sure to look through this list *before* you read, checking the meaning of each word that is unfamiliar. Highlight or place an asterisk (*) next to each unfamiliar word. While reading, you may need to refer back to the list, since no one expects you to remember a definition after reading it only once.

In addition to the words listed, you may find other unfamiliar words in the essay. If you come across an unfamiliar word while reading, finish reading the sentence it is in. Often, you will be able to figure out enough about the word from the way it is used in the sentence to continue reading without losing meaning. Since you will have a pen in your hand, mark or circle the word so that you can check its exact meaning later. If you cannot figure out what the word means from the way it is used, then you will need to work on it further. First try pronouncing it aloud; often hearing the word will help you find out its meaning. If you still do not know it, take the time to look it up in a dictionary. (Keep one nearby for convenient reference.) Once you find the meaning, circle the word and write its definition or a synonym in the margin—you may want to refer to it again as you discuss or write about the reading.

Reading and Thinking Critically

Begin by studying Reading Success Strategy #4. To write about an essay, you must understand the author's message, but you must also react to and evaluate that message. You must be able to do more than summarize what the author said. You must analyze, interpret, judge, and respond to the ideas presented. Reading Success Strategy #4 lists six useful questions and illustrates how to find clues to their answers in the reading. Refer to this color insert often to get in the habit of reading and thinking critically.

Annotating, as described above, will also help you read and think critically. By "talking back" to the author, you will find yourself adopting a challenging, questioning attitude that promotes critical thinking.

Remembering What You Read

Reading an essay once does not guarantee that you will remember it; in fact, the odds are that you will not remember it in detail unless you take certain steps after you read it. Use the following techniques to increase your recall of material that you have read.

Underline or highlight and annotate as you read.   As noted above, underlining and highlighting are useful ways to locate information without rereading; annotating is an effective way to record your ideas and reactions to the reading. Each of these techniques, however, also will help you remember what you read. To underline or highlight or annotate, you have to *think* about what you are reading. The thinking process aids recall.

Review the reading as soon as you finish.   While it is tempting to close the book and reward yourself for finishing an assignment, doing so is a mistake. Instead, spend three or four minutes reviewing what you have just read. These few minutes will pay high dividends in the amount you will be able to remember later. Review the reading by following the same steps you used to preview the reading (see p. xx). This postreading will fix ideas in your mind, clarify others, and show you how ideas are connected.

Write a summary.   Many students find it helpful to write a summary of an essay right after they finish reading it. Writing the summary is another way to review key points and prevent memory loss. Additionally, your summary will be useful later as a means of refreshing your memory without rereading and as a handy reference during class discussions.

Getting Ready to Write

You can take many steps to make writing about an essay easier. Several of these you have learned already. Underlining, highlighting, annotating, and summarizing prepare you to write about what you have read. Each identifies important ideas that may be used as starting points for writing. Here are a few additional tips.

Write an outline or draw a diagram.   As you write, the organization will become clearer and you will be reviewing the content.

Keep a notebook or journal.   Use it to record your ideas, reactions, feelings, and responses to the reading.

Discuss the reading with classmates.   You may discover new ideas or find that your own ideas become clearer once you express them in conversation.

THE WRITING PROCESS

Writing is a means of expressing your ideas. Writing Success Strategy #1 describes this process in detail. Study it before continuing with this section. Throughout this book you will be asked to write essays in which you discuss your ideas about a reading or ideas suggested by it. This introduction will help you get started by showing you the steps that most writers follow to produce a well-written essay. The five steps are

1. Generating ideas
2. Organizing ideas
3. Writing a first draft
4. Revising and rewriting
5. Proofreading

If you use each of these steps, writing will become easier for you. You will avoid the frustration of staring at a blank sheet of paper. Instead, you will feel the satisfaction of putting your ideas into words and making headway toward producing a good essay.

As you work through this introduction and complete the questions that follow each reading, note unfamiliar terms about the writing process and check the Glossary on pages 263–264.

Generating Ideas

The first step before writing is to generate ideas about your topic. You can use four techniques to do this:

1. Freewriting
2. Brainstorming
3. Branching
4. Questioning

These four techniques can help you overcome the common problem of feeling that you have nothing to say. They can unlock ideas you already have and help you discover new ones. Each of these techniques provides a different way to generate ideas. Feel free to choose from among them, using whichever technique seems most effective for the task at hand.

Freewriting

Freewriting involves writing nonstop for a limited period of time, usually three to five minutes. Write whatever comes into your mind, whether it is about the topic or not. If nothing comes to mind, you can just write, "I'm not thinking of anything." As you write, don't be concerned with grammar, punctuation, or spelling, or with writing in complete sentences. Words and phrases are fine. Focus on recording your thoughts as they come to you. The most important thing is to keep writing without stopping. Write fast; don't think about whether your writing is worthwhile or makes sense. After you finish, reread what you have written. Underline everything that you might be able to use in your paper. Above is a sample of freewriting on the topic of playing the lottery.

Freewriting is a creative way to begin translating ideas and feelings

Playing the lottery is a get rich quick dream.
Many people play it, but hardly anyone wins. Most
people think they have a chance to win. They do
have a chance, but it is a very small chance. So
why do people continue to play? Some people are
lucky and they win small amounts often and this
keeps them going. My grandfather is like that.
He wins a couple of dollars every month—
sometimes more. But he has never won anything
big. I wonder how much money a state makes from
each lottery draw. I think lotteries take advantage
of poor people. They really don't have the money
to waste on a lottery, but the advertising draws
them in. In New York state the slogan "All it
takes is a dollar and a dream" is very misleading.
Some people are addicted to playing, I don't think
they could stop playing if they wanted to. At
least the money earned from state-run lotteries
should directly help those who play.

into words, without being concerned about their value or worrying about correctness. You'll be pleasantly surprised by the number of usable ideas this technique uncovers. Of course, some of your ideas will be too broad; others might be too personal; still others may stray from the topic. In the freewriting above, there are several usable sets of ideas: addiction to lotteries, reasons people play, misleading advertising, and use of revenues from lotteries.

Brainstorming

Brainstorming is a way of developing ideas by making a list of everything you can think of about the topic. You might list feelings, ideas, facts, examples, or problems. There is no need to write in sentences; instead, list words and phrases. Don't try to organize your ideas, just list them as you think of them. Give yourself a time limit. You'll find that ideas come faster that way. You can brainstorm alone or with friends. You'll discover many more ideas with your friends because their ideas will help trigger more of your own. When you've finished, reread your list and mark usable ideas. Here is an example of ideas generated during a brainstorming session on the topic of stress.

Sample Brainstorming

pressure	headaches, neck aches
things not under control	feel tired and rushed
feel like you're losing it	can ruin your day
little things bother you	avoid problems
how to get rid of or control	everybody experiences it
daily hassles add up	stressed-out people are crabby
need to relax	big problems make it worse
need to learn to manage my time	avoid stressful situations
feeling put upon	keep a balanced outlook

Stress is too broad a topic for a short essay, but there are several groups of usable ideas here: symptoms of stress, causes of stress, and ways to control stress. Any of these topics would make a good paper.

Branching

Branching is a visual way of generating ideas. To begin, write your topic in the middle of a full sheet of paper. Draw a circle around it. Next, think of related ideas and write them near your center circle. Connect each to the central circle with a line. Call these ideas the primary branches. Your topic is like a tree trunk, and your ideas are like primary limbs that branch out from it. Below is an example of a branching diagram that one student drew on the topic of the value of sports.

BRANCHING DIAGRAM I

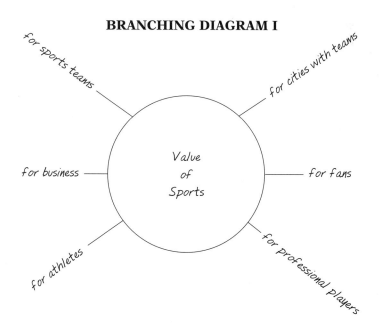

You can connect other related ideas to the main branches with smaller, or secondary, branches. In the next example, the student looked at his first branching diagram and decided to focus on one of the narrower topics (the value of sports for athletes) he had put on a primary branch.

BRANCHING DIAGRAM II

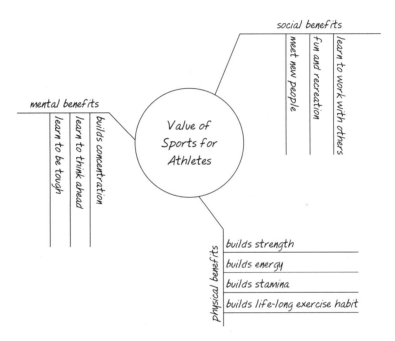

The student used "value of sports for athletes" as the trunk; then he created primary branches: mental benefits, social benefits, and physical benefits. Then he drew secondary branches onto each of the primary ones, and he could have kept going. If you use this technique, you can branch from your branches until you run off the paper. But there's no need to develop secondary branches for every main branch. Choosing one branch that interests you or that you're familiar with and ignoring all the other possibilities is fine. When you have finished branching, use a different color pen to mark those branches that seem usable for your paper.

Questioning

Another way to generate ideas about a given topic is to ask questions. The questions *what? why? where? when? how?* and *who?* are an effective way to explore any topic. As with freewriting and brainstorming, write any question that comes to mind. Don't worry if it seems silly, and don't stop to evaluate whether it is really related to the topic. If you can think of answers, include them as well, but don't limit yourself to questions for which you know the answers. When you have finished, reread what you have written and underline questions or answers that you might be able to use in writing your paper. Here are the questions one student wrote on the topic of television talk shows:

Sample Questions

Why do people watch them?
Does it make them feel better to
   see others with problems?
Do viewers get hooked on talk
   shows?
Why aren't they doing more
   important things, like working?
Do the shows help them forget
   their own problems?

How are participants chosen?
Are they paid?
Why do they participate?
What do the participants' families
   think of them?
Why are these shows so popular?
How do they affect those who
   watch?

When to Use Which Technique

Now that you have tried freewriting, brainstorming, branching, and questioning, you are probably wondering when to use each technique. In general, there are no rules to follow. The best advice is to use the technique that you find most comfortable. Try to use each more than twice before deciding which you prefer. You may find that for certain topics, one technique works better than the others. For example, suppose you decided to write an essay about your mother's sense of humor. While it might be difficult to think of questions, freewriting might help you remember important, humorous events in your life together. In a different situation, however, questioning might be the most effective technique. Suppose you are studying religious institutions in your sociology class, and your instructor has assigned a paper that requires you to explain your personal religious beliefs. Asking questions about your beliefs is likely to produce useful ideas that you can include in your paper.

Sorting Usable Ideas

Freewriting, brainstorming, branching, and questioning each produce a wide range of usable ideas, but you shouldn't feel as if you need to write about all of them. You can sort through them to decide which ones you can put together to produce your paper. Sometimes you may find that you would like to narrow your topic and develop just one idea in your paper, as did the student who made the branching diagram on the value of sports.

Organizing Ideas

Once you have used freewriting, brainstorming, branching, or questioning to generate ideas about your topic, the next step is to decide how to organize these ideas. Ideas in an essay should progress logically from one to another. Group or arrange your ideas in a way that makes them clear and understandable. Your essay should follow a logical plan. Turn to Writing Success Strategy #2, "Follow an Organizing Plan for Your Essay," and study it carefully. It shows how to organize your essay and what parts to include.

Suppose you used brainstorming to generate ideas on the topic of television talk shows, as was done on page 11. Then you decided to focus on the narrower topic of reasons why people watch talk shows. From a second brainstorming, you identified the following ideas for possible use in your essay:

shows can be informative	*learn how other people solved their*
forget your own problems	* problems*
can't stop watching	*get "hooked"*
offer a place to belong, feel	*like to watch people be exploited*
* part of something*	* by host*
shows fill empty time	*like to watch audience reactions*
people like to hear about other	
* people*	

In rereading your list, suppose you decide to organize your ideas by arranging them from most to least obvious or well-known. The next step is to rewrite your list, listing your ideas in the order in which you will discuss them in your paper. Then reread your new list and cross off ideas that you don't like, or ideas that are too similar to another idea. For example, "get 'hooked'" is similar to "can't stop watching," so cross it out. Here is a revised list of ideas, arranged from most to least obvious:

1. people like to hear about other people	5. forget your own problems
2. like to watch audience reactions	6. like to watch people be exploited by host
3. learn how other people solved their problems	7. offer a place to belong, feel part of something
4. shows can be informative	8. can't stop watching

Your ideas will not always sort out as neatly as these, but trying to organize your ideas will help you develop a well-structured essay. Sometimes new ideas will grow out of your efforts to rework and rearrange other ideas.

Writing a First Draft

Drafting is a way of trying out ideas to see if and how they work. When drafting, before you settle on what your final essay will say, you can experiment with expressing your ideas one way, then expressing them differently. In your first draft, you might use examples to explain your idea; if that does not work, you might switch to using reasons.

A first draft expresses your ideas in sentence and paragraph form. Review the parts of an essay and a paragraph by studying Writing Success Strategies #2 and #3. Work from your organized list of ideas, focusing on expressing and developing each one more fully. Don't be concerned with grammar, spelling, or punctuation at this stage; instead, concentrate on what you are saying. Use the following suggestions for writing a first draft:

1. After you have thought carefully about the ideas in your list, try to write one sentence that expresses your overall main point. Think of this as a working thesis statement.
2. Concentrate on developing and explaining your working thesis statement.
3. Write down more fully developed ideas from your list in the order in which you organized them.
4. If you are not sure whether you should include an idea from your list, include it. You can always delete it later. Add new ideas as you think of them.
5. Do not get bogged down in finding the best wording for an idea. Just write the idea as you think of it. You will have time to fix it later as you revise.
6. Think of a first draft as a chance to experiment with different ideas and methods of organization. While you are working, if you think

of a better way to organize or express your ideas, make changes or start over.

7. As your draft develops, feel free to change your focus or even your topic. If you decide to change your draft, use freewriting, brainstorming, branching, or questioning to develop new ideas.
8. Be prepared to change things around later. What you write as your last sentence might turn out to be a good beginning.
9. If your draft is not working, don't hesitate to throw it out and start over. Most writers have many false starts before they produce a draft with which they are satisfied.
10. If you think you need more ideas, go back to the generating ideas step. It is always all right to go back and forth among the steps in the writing process.
11. When you finish your first draft, you should feel as if you have the beginnings of an essay you will be happy with.

Here is a sample early draft of an essay on why people watch talk shows.

First Draft

It seems like every time I turn on my television, some kind of talk show is on. A few years ago, they were on mornings or late evenings, but now talk shows are on at all hours of the day. Why do people watch them? They watch them for a number of reasons, some good, some not so good.

The most obvious reason is that people find talk shows relaxing and entertaining. They also like to hear about other people. They like to get involved with other people, their problems, the details of their lives. And certainly talk show participants do tell you everything about their lives. Part of this involvement with other people comes from watching the audience and listening to their reactions and questions. Watching a talk show gives people ideas of how to solve their own problems and to get a sense of where a particular situation is headed if it is not corrected.

Talk shows can be informative. Viewers learn sources of help with personal problems. They may learn something about what to do or not to do to improve a personal relationship.

Talk shows help the viewer forget his or her own problems. By getting involved with someone else's problems, viewers tend to forget their own. Also, the problems on the show are so terrible that the viewer's own problems seem small by comparison.

Talk shows appeal to the instinct that many of us have for enjoying watching other people. We like to watch the participants, but we also like to watch the host exploiting, embarrassing, or taking advantage of the participants.

People like to feel as if they are part of something. Some friends of mine are on a first-name basis with several talk show hosts and talk as if they are personal friends with them.

Finally, some people watch talk shows because they can't help themselves—they're addicted. Before I started back to school I was a talk show addict. I would watch talk shows all morning and a good part of the afternoon. Then I would wonder what happened to my day and why I didn't get anything done. Although talk shows do have benefits, and there are plenty of good reasons people watch them, I feel they are dangerous!

Revising and Rewriting

Revision is a process that involves evaluating a draft and changing it to make it more effective. When you finish a first draft, you are more or less satisfied with it. Then, when you reread it later, you see you have more work to do.

Before you submit a paper, you may need to write two, three, or even four drafts. Revising often involves much more than changing a word or rearranging a few sentences. (See the Revision Checklist on the inside of the front cover.) Revising requires that you *rethink* your ideas. It might mean changing, deleting, or rearranging some of them and adding to them. Revision is not concerned with correcting spelling and punctuation errors, or with making sentences grammatical. Make these changes later when you are satisfied with your ideas. Here is a later draft of the first draft shown on pages 14–15.

Later Draft

It seems as if every time one turns on the television, some kind of talk show is on. A few years ago, they were on mornings or late evenings, but now talk shows are on at all hours of the day. Why do people watch them? They watch them to relax, to watch others, and to feel part of something.

The most obvious reason that people watch talk shows is that they find talk shows relaxing and entertaining. The shows provide a welcome relief from daily hassles. By getting involved with someone else's problems, viewers tend to forget their own. Also, the problems on the show are so terrible that the viewer's own problems seem small by comparison. Who could worry about being able to make a car payment when a man on the show has just discovered that his wife is also married to his brother?

Talk shows are also popular because they appeal to our instinct to enjoy watching other people. This instinct is sometimes called voyeurism. People like to watch and hear about other people. They like to hear about their problems and the details of the lives of others. Certainly talk show participants do tell you everything about their lives. Viewers like to watch the participants, but they also enjoy watching the host exploiting, embarrassing, or taking advantage of them. Viewers enjoy watching the audience react and question the participants.

Finally, people watch talk shows because they like to feel as if they are part of something. Some friends of mine are on a first-name basis with several talk show hosts and talk as if they were personal friends with them. They become personally involved with the participants and act as if they are part of the audience.

There is one last reason why people watch talk shows—because they can't help themselves. They are addicted. Before I started back to school, I was a talk show addict. I would watch talk shows all morning and a good part of the afternoon. Then I would wonder what happened to my day and why I didn't get anything done. Although talk shows do have benefits, and there are plenty of good reasons people watch them, they are dangerous!

In making the above revision, the writer decided that the first draft seemed like a list with many very short paragraphs, and so he decided to group the ideas into three main categories: the need to relax, the need to watch, and the need to feel part of something. Then he reorganized the essay and reworked several paragraphs. The author also removed the idea that talk shows provide information, since it did not seem to fit into any of his new categories.

Use the following suggestions for revising and rewriting:

1. Try to let your first draft sit a while before you begin revising it. If possible, wait until the next day, but even a few hours away from the draft will be helpful.
2. Reread the sentence that expresses your main point. It must be clear, direct, and complete. Experiment with ways to improve it.
3. Reread each of your other sentences. Does each relate directly to your main point? If not, cross it out or rewrite it to clarify its connection to the main point. If all of your sentences relate to a main point that is different from the one you've written, rewrite the sentence that expresses the main point.
4. Make sure your essay has a beginning and an end.
5. Read your draft again to see whether your sentences connect to one another. If necessary, add words or sentences to connect your ideas.
6. Delete or combine sentences that say the same thing.
7. Replace words that are vague or unclear with more descriptive words.
8. If you get stuck at any of these stages and cannot see what changes are needed, ask a friend to read your essay and mark ideas that are unclear or need more explanation.

9. After you have made one set of revisions, wait a few hours and then repeat all of these steps.
10. When you have finished revising, you should feel quite satisfied both with what you have said and with the way you have said it.

Proofreading

Proofreading is checking for errors, a final polishing of your work. Don't be concerned with proofreading until all your rethinking of ideas and other revisions are done. Check for each of these types of errors:

- Run-on sentences
- Sentence fragments
- Spelling
- Punctuation
- Grammar
- Capitalization

When you proofread, keep the following suggestions in mind:

1. Review your essay once for each type of error. First, read it for run-on sentences and sentence fragments. Then read it four more times, each time paying attention to only one thing: grammar, spelling, punctuation, and so forth.
2. To spot spelling errors, read your essay from last sentence to first sentence and from last word to first word. The flow of ideas will not matter, and so you can focus on spotting errors.
3. Read each sentence aloud, slowly and deliberately. This will help you catch missing words, endings you have left off verbs, or missing plurals.
4. Check for errors again as you rewrite or type your essay in final form. Don't do this when you are tired; you might introduce new mistakes. Then proofread your final paper one last time.
5. Use the grammar-and-spell check on your computer. These programs may not catch all your errors, but they may find some you have overlooked.

Chapter 1

Decisions That Shape Our Lives

The Chosen One
Laura Cunningham

Arming Myself with a Gun Is Not the Answer
Bronwyn Jones

Life Is So Good
George Dawson and Richard Glaubman

Saying Good-bye to Eric
Jennifer S. Dickman

Evan's Two Moms
Anna Quindlen

Hello, Goodbye, Hey Maybe I Love You?
Joshua Kurlantzick

The Gift of Sacrifice
Blanca Matute

Each day we make hundreds of decisions. We decide what time to get up, what to wear, where to sit on the bus or train or in a classroom, which assignment to read first, what to eat for dinner, and so forth. Many of these decisions are not very important in the long term. What you choose for dinner tonight will have little impact on your life two years from now, for example.

Other decisions have a more immediate and direct impact on your life. A decision to attend college, to marry, to take a certain job, to have children, to move, or to change careers clearly has long-term effects. Suppose, for instance, that the father of three small children decides to return to school so that he can get a more interesting and better-paying job. Since his family still needs his current income, he attends school at night so that he can keep working during the day. This decision means that he will be able to spend much less time with his family now, but that they will all have a better life a bit later. When we are faced with major decisions, we usually go through a process of weighing our options, looking at the pros and cons, and trying to evaluate the best course of action. The alternative is acting impulsively, which is another kind of decision that shapes people's lives, for better or worse.

The readings in this chapter will give you perspectives on some decisions that other people have made and how their lives have been shaped accordingly. You will read about personal choices involving family, such as a woman who travels to China and must choose which infant to adopt ("The Chosen One"); a woman who must decide whether to leave her fiancé ("Saying Good-bye to Eric"); a man who decides to learn at the age of 98 to read ("Life Is So Good"); and a student's decision to leave her family in Honduras to attend school in the United States ("The Gift of Sacrifice"). You will read about a new quick dating system that allows participants to select other participants they wish to date ("Hello, Goodbye, Hey Maybe I Love You?"). You will also consider two moral or ethical decisions: arming oneself for self-protection ("Arming Myself with a Gun Is Not the Answer") and marriages between partners of the same sex ("Evan's Two Moms").

Brainstorming About Decisions

Class Activity: The following circumstances are situations that require choices. Choose one situation, analyze it, and make a decision. Then write a description of what you think would happen.

>   Situation 1: If you could acquire one new skill or talent by simply asking, what would you ask for?
>   Situation 2: If a drug that made it possible for you to sleep only one night per week became available, would you decide to take it?
>   Situation 3: If you could exchange places for a day with anyone in history, dead or alive, famous or infamous, whom would you choose to be?

The Chosen One

▶ Laura Cunningham

In this reading, the author describes one of the most important decisions in her life—which baby to adopt. This essay originally appeared in the "Hers" column of The New York Times Magazine.

Reading Strategy

This is a personal essay in which the author expresses her feelings, doubts, and fears about adoption. As you read, highlight statements that reveal Cunningham's attitude toward the adoption process and the decision she made.

Vocabulary Preview

articulate (5) put into words
simpatico (6) compatible; holding similar attitudes and
         beliefs
hydraulic (7) forceful
unprecedented (7) unlike anything before
ambiguous (8) unclear, having more than one meaning
emissary (8) an agent representing someone else
paraphernalia (10) equipment; all the objects or items used
         in a place or with an object
staccato (16) abrupt sounds
fetid (19) having an offensive odor
luminous (22) bright

A year ago, I boarded a flight to Shanghai during a gale force wind.   1
The plane shivered and taxied back to the hangar twice before takeoff.
It is testimony to my anxiety about the purpose of my journey that I
felt no fear of flying. I carried with me an empty infant car bed (aptly
named the Dream Ride), a three-week supply of diapers, wipes, pediatric antibiotics, bottles and disposable nipples. I was on my way to
adopt one of the tens of thousands of baby girls abandoned in China
each year.

Today as I write, my 1-year-old daughter sleeps in a crib in the next   2
room. She lies in the position of trust—on her back, her arms widespread, her face tip-tilted as if for the next kiss.

A happy ending, so far, for my darling Chinese daughter, and for   3
me. But the journey to Shanghai has somehow not ended. Many

nights, I wake at 3 A.M.—yanked from my dream, my heart hammering alarms. At that silent, moonlit time, I remember my choice.

I am embarrassed now to recall the doubt that accompanied me to 4
China. The orphanage had sent a fax (yes, in the new China, orphanages send faxes): "We have a baby for you. We would have taken her picture but it was too cold."

My concern, if I can articulate the chill gut slide of panic as a "con- 5
cern," was that somehow I would walk into the orphanage and fail to respond to the baby; that somehow she would not feel like "the right one." I would have to go ahead with the adoption out of momentum, some grim sense of decency, but without the hoped-for love at first sight.

The baby, it seemed from the fax, was already chosen. And while I 6
claimed to love all babies, in my secret, cowering heart I had to admit that I was more drawn to some babies than to others. It wasn't beauty or even intelligence that I required of a baby, but some sign of being, well, simpatico.

I could not see her until the orphanage opened Monday morning. I 7
had arrived in Shanghai on Saturday night. The interval was the high tide of my fear—suspense seemed hydraulic; blood rushed through me at unprecedented speed.

Until Monday I had only the ambiguous answers of Ms. Zhang, the 8
orphanage's emissary who had greeted me at the airport. When I asked: "How old is the baby? How big?" Ms. Zhang answered only with another question: "What size baby clothes have you brought with you?"

Her response raised some possibility of control, or at least influ- 9
ence. Maybe the baby was *not* yet chosen. In my sneaking secret chicken heart, I could still pick the best and the brightest star of abandoned baby girlhood in Shanghai.

Passing the time until I could meet "my baby," I met another 10
baby at the hotel, already adopted by a single man. (China permits adoptions by foreigners, whether married or unmarried. Its adoption policy is unusual in that citizens, as well as foreigners, must be at least 35 years old to adopt.) She struck me, however, as not meant to be my baby. She did seem just right for her new father, an American psychologist, who carried with him a sitcom's supply of baby paraphernalia.

Next I went to the nearest tourist attraction, the Temple of the Jade 11
Buddha, where there was said to be a Buddha to whom mothers pray for a good baby.

The Buddha glowed in the dim temple. It wasn't jet lag that sent me 12
reeling to my knees before the Buddha. Half-Jewish, half-Southern Baptist, all doubt, I knelt in truest prayer. *Let the baby be one I can truly love.*

At 9 sharp the next morning I waited in the orphanage, wearing my 13
winter coat indoors (now I understood the fax). Even in midwinter there was no heat. Vapor rose from the thermoses of hot tea carried by

the female employees. The translator announced that the baby was being carried in from the nursery building.

"You will have a choice," she said.   14

I looked out the window as she pointed across a courtyard filled   15
with dead bamboo and gray laundry. The window itself was grimy, but through it I saw two women in blue smocks, running toward me. Each held a bundle. There were *two* babies.

They were swaddled in comforters, their heads completely draped   16
in towels. The first baby was unveiled. There was a staccato of Chinese, translated as: "Pick this one. She is more beautiful. She is more intelligent." Baby No. 1 was the nurses' favorite, a 2-month-old of unsurpassed good looks and robust health. She smiled.

But I couldn't take my eyes from the second baby, who was   17
revealed almost as an afterthought. She was thin, piteous, a green-complexioned elf, with low-set ears that stuck out. She wheezed. In a pocket of my coat, I held a vial of antibiotics, carried on good advice from a friend.

I had no choice. The second baby was sick. I had medicine impos-   18
sible to obtain here. I accepted the tiny green baby, gasping and oozing, into my arms. I noticed she also had a bald spot, from lying unmoved in her crib.

Shame over my earlier indecision blew from the room like a fetid   19
draft of disease and poverty.

Was it love at first sight? I knew in that instant that we were at the   20
start of our life together.

Love overtakes you at odd moments. I was trying to collect a urine   21
sample, required for a medical test. I held her, her little purple fanny over a rice bowl, in my arms all night. I drew the blankets around us both as a tent to keep away the cold. We waited, silently, all night, until she took a literal "tinkle." Her eyes met mine, on the other side of the world, and I knew Little-Miss-Ears-Stick-Out, With-Tears-in-Her-Eyes was mine, all right.

Within 24 hours, the medicine had taken effect: she turned ivory   22
pink; her eyes cleared. She was beyond my dreams, exquisite, a luminous old soul with contemporary wit. I gazed at her and saw the fatefulness of every mother's choice. It is not the beautiful baby who is chosen, but the chosen baby who becomes beautiful.

To enter a house filled with unwanted babies is to pass through a   23
door that you can never shut. At 3 A.M., I see the others—the aisles of green cribs holding bundled babies. I try to close my eyes to them, but they refuse to disappear. They are lying there. They are cold; they are damp. I see one baby girl especially. She had an odd genetic defect: the skin of her body was coal black, but her face had no color. She looked as if she were wearing the white theatrical mask of tragedy.

Last Christmas, I was able to choose the green, sick baby over the 24
laughing, healthy one. Would I have had the courage to take one of the
others? Would someone? I wake up and see the small faces. They are
lying there waiting, waiting to be chosen.

Examining the Reading

Finding Meaning

1. Why was the author on her way to China?
2. What was the author's greatest concern before she met the baby?
3. Why did she choose one baby over the other?
4. Describe the baby's state of health by the time the author left
   Shanghai.
5. Describe the conditions in the orphanage.

Understanding Technique

1. Cunningham uses sensory details (details that appeal to the senses:
   sight, sound, taste, smell, and touch) in her writing. Underline several places where the sensory details are particularly powerful.
2. Highlight the transitions Cunningham uses to move from one event
   to the next.

Thinking Critically

1. If you were in the author's place and had a choice of two babies to
   adopt, which one would you choose? Why?
2. The Chinese government has a policy that adoptive parents must be at
   least 35 years old. Do you think this is a good policy? Why or why not?
3. Why do you think the orphanage gave the author a choice of two
   babies to adopt?
4. What did the author mean when she said, "It is not the beautiful
   baby who is chosen, but the chosen baby who becomes beautiful"?

Writing About the Reading

A Journal Entry

Write a journal entry explaining how you feel before planned important events, such as job interviews or public presentations.

A Paragraph

1. Write a paragraph describing whether or under what conditions
   you might consider adopting a child.

2. Cunningham seemed to have little difficulty making her decision. She seemed to know intuitively which baby to choose. Write a paragraph describing a similar situation in which you seemed to know the right decision to make.

An Essay

1. The author suggests that all mothers think their own children are beautiful. From your experience as a child, as a parent, or as both, write an essay agreeing or disagreeing that parents see beauty (physical or otherwise) in their children and tend to overlook their children's faults. Support your position with examples from your experience.
2. Cunningham felt doubtful and anxious as she awaited the important moment when she would see her baby. Write an essay describing an event about which you felt anxious or nervous. Explain why you were anxious and how the event turned out.

A Creative Activity

Suppose the author decided to write a letter to the other baby, explaining why she had not chosen her. What do you think she would have said? Write a first draft of the letter.

Arming Myself with a Gun Is Not the Answer

▶ **Bronwyn Jones**

A college professor describes how an experience with a stalker shaped her views on guns, violence, and the mentally ill and helped her decide not to carry a gun for self-protection. This personal account first appeared in Newsweek *magazine in 2001.*

Reading Strategy

As you read, mark the different steps of the author's decision-making process.

Vocabulary Preview

harried (1) busy and hectic to the point of frustration
idyllic (1) peaceful, carefree, charming
incoherent (3) unclear, nonsensical
schizophrenic (4) someone who suffers from a certain mental illness that involves withdrawal from reality, illogical thinking, and delusions, and causes dramatic mood swings
avid (5) enthusiastic
paranoia (8) a feeling of unreasonable suspicion and mistrust toward others
victimization (8) suffering from the effects of a crime or injustice
deterrent (9) a threat intended to discourage unwanted behavior
incarcerated (11) placed in jail

When my father died 15 years ago, my brother and I inherited the old   1
Midwestern farmhouse our grandparents had purchased in the 1930s.
I was the one who decided to give up my harried existence as a teacher
in New York City and make a life in this idyllic village, population 350,
in northern Michigan.

A full-time job in the English department of a nearby college   2
quickly followed. I settled into small-town life, charmed by a commu-

nity where your neighbors are also your friends and no one worries about locking a door. Eventually I forgot about the big-city stress of crowds, noise, and crime.

I felt safe enough to keep my phone number listed so colleagues   3
and students could reach me after hours. I was totally unprepared when I returned home one evening to an answering machine filled with incoherent and horribly threatening messages. I could identify the voice—it belonged to a former student of mine. Shocked and frightened, I called 911, and an officer arrived in time to pick up the phone and hear the man threaten to rape and kill me. The cop recognized the caller as the stalker in a similar incident that had been reported a few years before, and immediately rushed me out of the house. I soon learned that my would-be assailant had been arrested, according to police, drunk, armed with a 19-inch double-edged knife and just minutes from my door.

It was revealed in court testimony that my stalker was a schizo-   4
phrenic who had fallen through the cracks of the mental-health system. In spite of my 10-year personal-protection order, I live with the fear that he will return unsupervised to my community. Time and again, colleagues and friends have urged me to get a gun to protect myself.

And why shouldn't I? This part of rural Michigan is home to an   5
avid gun culture. November 15, the opening day of deer-hunting season, is all but an official holiday. It is not uncommon to see the bumper sticker CHARLTON HESTON[1] IS MY PRESIDENT displayed, along with a gun rack, on the back of local pickup trucks.

A good friend recommended several different handguns. The assis-   6
tant prosecutor on the case told me I'd have no problem getting a concealed-weapons permit. A female deputy offered to teach me how to shoot.

But I haven't gotten a gun, and I'm not going to. When I questioned   7
them, my friends and colleagues had to admit that they've used guns only for recreational purposes, never for self-defense. The assistant prosecutor said that he would never carry a concealed weapon himself. And an ex-cop told me that no matter how much you train, the greatest danger is of hurting yourself.

The truth is when you keep a gun for self-protection, you live with   8
constant paranoia. For me, owning a gun and practicing at a target range would be allowing my sense of victimization to corrupt my deepest values.

---

[1]Well-known actor, gun rights activist, and president of the National Rifle Association (NRA).

Contrary to all the pro-gun arguments, I don't believe guns are   9
innocent objects. If they were, "gunnies"[2] wouldn't display them as
badges of security and freedom. When someone waves a gun around,
he or she is advertising the power to snuff out life. But guns are no deterrent. Like nuclear weapons, they only ensure greater devastation
when conflict breaks out or the inevitable human error occurs.

I never needed a weapon in the years prior to my terrifying experi-   10
ence. And while I learned not to flinch at the sight of men and women
in fluorescent orange carrying rifles into the woods at the start of deer
season, owning a gun for play or protection didn't occur to me. But I've
learned firsthand that even small, close-knit communities are subject
to the kind of social problems—like disintegrating families and sub-
stance abuse—that can propel a troubled person toward violence. So I
now carry pepper spray and my cell phone at all times.

In Michigan—and elsewhere—as federal funding for state mental-   11
health care continues to shrink and state psychiatric hospitals are
forced to close, the numbers of untreated, incarcerated, and homeless
mentally ill are rising. People with serious mental illness and violent
tendencies need 24-hour care. It costs less to house them in group
homes with trained counselors than it does to keep them in prisons or
hospitals. But until states fund more of this kind of care, people like
my stalker will continue to return unsupervised to our communities.

And people like me will be forced to consider getting guns to pro-   12
tect ourselves. I am lucky. I survived, though not unchanged. I know
my fear cannot be managed with a gun. The only reasonable response
is to do what I can to help fix the mental-health system. Awareness, education, and proper funding will save more lives and relieve more fear
than all the guns we can buy.

Examining the Reading

Finding Meaning

1. How did the author come to live in rural Michigan?
2. What happened one evening to change the author's feeling of safety
   to one of fear?
3. How does the author describe the local gun culture?
4. Why doesn't the author believe that guns are "innocent objects"?
5. Why are people like the author's stalker living unsupervised in our
   communities?

---

[2]People who strongly favor gun ownership as a constitutional right.

6. What does the author think would be the best response to her fear of violent people?

Understanding Technique

1. Why does the author include the story of her stalker? How does it contribute to her argument against guns?
2. The author contrasts rural life and urban life. What other contrasts does the author point out in her article?

Thinking Critically

1. Why do you think the author was "unprepared" and "shocked" by the stalker's phone message?
2. Why is the first day of deer-hunting so important in rural Michigan?

Writing About the Reading

A Journal Entry

Write a journal entry that expresses your attitude toward guns. Do guns kill people or do people kill people?

A Paragraph

1. Write a paragraph explaining why women should or should not carry guns.
2. Would you prefer to live in a small town or a big city? Write a paragraph explaining your preference.
3. Write a paragraph about a time when you thought you were safe but found out differently.

An Essay

1. There are many ways to protect yourself against crime and violence. Choose a particular type of crime or violence and describe some of the precautions people can take to protect themselves.
2. Write an essay justifying your position on the issue of gun control.

A Creative Activity

Suppose the author were to meet with a deer hunter or a member of the "avid gun culture" that is part of her community. What would they say to each other?

Life Is So Good

▸ George Dawson and Richard Glaubman

An elderly man tells of his decision to learn to read after a long life of working and raising a family. He wrote a book titled Life Is So Good *with the assistance of Richard Glaubman, who is mentioned in this excerpt from the book.*

Reading Strategy

In a story with dialogue, sometimes it is hard to tell who is speaking. As you read, note each speaker when you come across conversation.

The old man who could not read lives alone in a house that is small 1
and square, in an area that some people call the ghetto. . . . The old man got by until 1996, when a young man knocked on his door and said he was recruiting people for the Adult Basic Education classes at the old high school.

"I've been alone for ten years," the old man told him. "I'm tired of 2
fishing. It's time to learn to read."

—*Seattle Times*, Larry Bingham, February 1, 1998

I always had a dream that I would learn how to read. It was my secret, 3
that I couldn't read. There was nothing I couldn't do and my mind was as good as anyone's. That's just how it was. All my life, I had been just too busy working to go to school. I kept it a secret that I couldn't read.

My mind worked hard. When I traveled somewhere, I could never 4
read a sign. I had to ask people things and had to remember. I could never let my mind forget anything, never let my mind take a vacation.

I listened to the news and had to trust what I heard. I never read it 5
for myself. My wife read the mail and paid our bills. I made sure that each of the children learned to read. When they came home from school, there was milk and cookies on the kitchen table. They would tell me what their classmates did and what the teacher said. I made sure they told me what they had learned that day. I always listened. I always asked if they had worked hard.

The answer was always yes, because they knew I would be waiting 6
to find out. They knew what I expected: hard work. I would tell them, "School is important and there is a lot to learn."

To each of them I would say, "I'm proud of you." 7

I helped them with their homework. 8

"How could you do that," Richard asked, "if you couldn't read?"   9

Just then the screen door banged open and Junior came in. His   10
jacket was dripping with water. "Tell Richard here how I helped you
with your schoolwork. He don't believe me."

Junior laughed and said, "Every night, Daddy made us sit down at   11
the kitchen table and do our homework. We had to show it to him when
we were done. We didn't know he couldn't read. Daddy would say, 'Read
back what you got. You'll learn it better that way,' and that was probably true. I graduated fourth in my class! Daddy, and our mother too,
they didn't want to hear about excuses. It was that simple," Junior said.

"When did you find out that your father couldn't read?"   12

"I was in high school when my father told me."   13

"What did you think?"   14

"He was our father and it didn't change anything, but we kept it a   15
secret for him."

"Why?"   16

"Well, some folks don't understand things like that and we just   17
wanted to protect him."

"So, it became more of a family secret?"   18

"That's a good way to put it."   19

"Back then, did you ever think your father would learn to read?"   20

"I knew he would have liked to. He thought reading was so impor-   21
tant. But back then, there were more people his age that never learned
to read than there is today."

"So it wasn't so uncommon?"   22

"I don't know for sure. It wasn't something people would talk   23
about either."

I listened to the two of them talk, but I know that a lot of people   24
still don't understand. They be thinking I spent my life just waiting to
learn to read. That's not it at all. I didn't think about things I couldn't
do nothing about. Things were just the way they were. And that's that.

People wonder why I didn't go back to school earlier. After I re-   25
tired, I finally had the time. I was proud to get my children through
school and raise them properly. But I understood that school was there
for the children. When I was young, I had missed my turn to go. I had
never heard of these adult education classes. I've never had any extra
money to hire a special teacher. People that been in my house have
seen the sagging ceiling, the cracked window, the broken plaster on the
wall and they know that. So I didn't expect nothing.

One day, out of the blue, a man came to the door. He handed me a   26
piece of paper. Good thing I was home or I would have thrown it out like
most fliers that I couldn't read. But he said there were some classes for
adults. They taught reading. The school, the same one my own children
had gone to, was close enough to walk to. It's maybe six blocks away.

George Dawson

Junior thinks that man might have thought there might be some of Daddy's grandchildren living in the house.   27

No matter. I live by myself now. I shook his hand and told him, "I will be coming to school!"   28

My turn had come. My first day of school was January 4, 1996. I was ninety-eight years old and I'm still going. Except for three funerals, I've gone to school every day for three years. School starts at nine. I can't wait and I'm up by five-thirty to make my lunch, pack my books, and go over my schoolwork. Since I started school, I'm always early. I haven't ever been late.   29

"I was just thinking," Richard said, "how hard it is to learn to read at any age. Not everybody succeeds. Mr. Dawson, were you a little afraid that you wouldn't make it? Didn't you have any doubts?"   30

"Son, I always thought I could drive a *spike*[1] as good as any man   31
and cook as good as any woman. I just figured if everybody else can
learn to read, I could too."

"Was it hard to learn to read?"   32

"Sure, it was. But I been working hard all my life. I'm used to it and   33
it don't scare me none. Mr. Henry, my teacher, he's a good man and he's
a good teacher. Tomorrow, you come to class with me." . . .

I came to school to learn something, but I'm happy to be helping   34
people. Sure, it makes me feel good. You bet I like school! Every morning I get up and I wonder what I might learn that day. You just never
know. I am so grateful to have this chance to go to school.

I have to admit, it's easier for me to do silent reading than it is for   35
me to read out loud. To see how I'm doing, Mr. Henry has me read out
loud to him, but I stumble a lot over words when I read that way. The
day Richard was there, he was sitting at my table. Him being a teacher
too, when I was done I said, "My reading is getting better and better,
but when I read out loud it's harder."

Richard shrugged. "Probably, it's like when you first rode a bicycle.   36
It was hard to keep your balance and then one day it just got easier. Do
you remember how that felt?"

"No. I remember what it felt like the first time I rode a mule."   37

It's like we both speak English, but sometimes we just got to start   38
over so we can understand each other. It's not easy for either of us, but
we keep trying. I showed him the cafeteria where we have lunch. I un-
packed my barbecued beef sandwich, and from a paper sack he took
out a turkey sandwich.

I get hungry at school and besides a sandwich, I bring dessert. Pie   39
is good and if I don't want it I can always trade a slice of pie with someone at my table for some cookies or cupcakes. I do that sometimes.
Richard didn't bring any dessert.

I said, "See, if you don't have any dessert then you don't have noth-   40
ing to trade."

"Next time."   41

Junior stopped by at lunch and he and Richard went over to my   42
house when I went back to class. I followed later. When Richard
comes, he rents these shiny little cars or a van and we drive around
town in those. P.J. [one of Dawson's classmates] gave me a ride. He
usually takes me home. P.J. has got a big old car. But nowadays cars
are all the same to me. Thing is, it's hard to tell a Chevy from a Ford,

---

[1]Work on the railroad; work hard.

plus there's all the other brands that people drive. One thing is they all got radios now. That's not so special like it used to be.

Junior and Richard were already at my house. Junior usually   43
comes by after school anyway. I joined them at the kitchen table. Junior told Richard, "I used to come by almost every day. Now I come by after school. It's nice. It seems that it gives us more to talk about."

"I tell him about my classmates and what the teacher said."   44

Junior said, "He even tells me what they all had for lunch. I always   45
ask, 'Daddy, did you work hard at school?'"

I said, "The answer is always yes."   46

Junior said, "I tell my dad, 'School is important. There is so much   47
to learn. I'm proud of you.'"

Examining the Reading

Finding Meaning

1. What was Mr. Dawson's secret?
2. How did Mr. Dawson cope with daily life without being able to read?
3. What did Mr. Dawson expect from his children?
4. How did Mr. Dawson finally go back to school?
5. How did Mr. Dawson feel about learning to read?
6. Why does Mr. Dawson bring dessert to school?
7. What do Junior and his dad talk about after school?

Understanding Technique

1. The story begins with an excerpt from a *Seattle Times* article. Is this an effective introduction? Why or why not?
2. Mr. Dawson's story is told in the first person (the writer is the speaker in the story). What effect does this style have? Would it be as effective if the story were told by another person?
3. How do Richard and Junior help tell the story?
4. What special details does Mr. Dawson use to add depth to his story? Why are they effective?

Thinking Critically

1. Why did Mr. Dawson and his family keep the fact that he couldn't read a secret?
2. Why did Mr. Dawson tell his children to "read back" their homework to him? How did it help the children?
3. Mr. Dawson writes that he missed only three days of school and has never been late. What makes him so enthusiastic about school?

4. How would you describe Mr. Dawson's attitude toward life?
5. Mr. Dawson was illiterate until he was ninety-eight years old. What other issues do you think he faced as an older person?

Writing About the Reading

A Journal Entry

Write a journal entry about something you have accomplished after a long struggle.

A Paragraph

1. Write a paragraph identifying and discussing one skill other than reading that is needed for academic success. Why is this skill important?
2. Teachers can make a great difference in a student's life. Write a paragraph describing one important quality that a teacher should possess.

An Essay

1. People who cannot read face many challenges. Write an essay describing some of the daily problems an illiterate person may face.
2. Mr. Dawson made the decision to learn to read, although it was a difficult task. Write an essay describing a decision that meant facing a challenging task.
3. If you could be any kind of teacher in any location, what would you choose and why? Where would you teach? Why?

A Creative Activity

Imagine what it would be like to teach someone to read. Create a plan for your first day. Include how you would start the lesson and how you would introduce yourself.

Saying Good-bye to Eric

▸ **Jennifer S. Dickman**

In this essay, published in Nursing *magazine, Jennifer S. Dickman describes how a personal tragedy motivated her to become a nurse.*

Reading Strategy

Eric's accident and what happened afterward certainly took a terrible emotional toll on the author. Review the essay and underline those sections where the author expresses her feelings about the events connected to this tragedy.

Vocabulary Preview

intubated (5) had tubes inserted to assist bodily functions
ventilation (5) breathing
evacuate (5) to remove the contents of
hematoma (5) a blood-filled swelling of the brain
debride (5) surgically remove unhealthy tissue
temporal lobe (5) section of the brain containing the sensory area associated with hearing
frontal lobe (5) section of the brain responsible for higher thought
intraventricular catheter (5) a tube inserted into a ventricle, or small cavity in the brain
intracranial (5) within the skull
neurology (6) dealing with disorders of the brain and nervous system
irony (7) strange twist; joke or a turnaround of events
secretions (8) fluids
weaned (9) gradually removed from

As Eric rode off on his motorcycle that crisp November day, he turned and gave me a smile and a wave. I never dreamed that would be the last expression I'd ever see on my fiancé's face.   1

A few hours later, I was driving to the regional trauma center, my hands trembling on the steering wheel, my eyes blurred with tears. Eric's bike had skidded out of control on wet pavement and he'd been thrown into a field.   2

Please let him be okay, I prayed. *We're in the middle of planning our wedding.*   3

When I arrived at the trauma center, my worst fears were immediately confirmed. He'd suffered a serious brain injury.   4

Caring for Eric

Eric had been intubated in the ED and required assisted ventilation. He was initially admitted to the neurology ICU—later that day he underwent surgery to evacuate a hematoma and to debride damaged parts of his temporal and frontal lobes. During surgery, an intraventricular catheter was inserted to continuously monitor his intracranial pressure.   5

I stumbled through those first few hours—and then days—in a fog of shock and disbelief. I never left the hospital, choosing to sleep in the visitor's lounge. When Eric was finally moved to a private room in the neurology unit, I slept on a cot next to him.   6

Grief prevented me from seeing the irony in my situation. I'd taken a semester off from nursing school because I wasn't sure if I wanted to be a nurse—I didn't know if I was up to it. And now I was devoting all of my time to caring for Eric.   7

I bathed him, turned him, did his catheter care, and learned to give his tube feedings. I read to him, talked to him, and played all of his favorite music. I even convinced his doctors to let me give herbal tea through his feeding tube cause I'd read that certain herbs help decrease lung secretions.   8

After 4 months, Eric's condition improved slightly. He began blinking his eyes, making small hand and foot movements, and trying to breathe on his own. I was thrilled, even though deep down I knew that these weren't signs of recovery. When Eric was finally weaned from the ventilator and began breathing on his own, I felt like shouting for joy. That's when his doctor took me aside.   9

"You'd better get on with your life, Jennifer," he said gently but firmly. "Eric's reached a plateau, and he'll be this way as long as he lives."   10

Confronting Reality

At first, I refused to believe him. But then, with the help of my family and friends, I took an honest look at the situation. For 6 months, I'd given up everything to devote my energy to Eric. I'd lost a lot of weight and was mentally and physically exhausted. I knew the time had come to accept his condition and start living my own life—which, I decided, included returning to nursing school.   11

A few weeks after I'd reached my decision, Eric was transferred to a long-term-care facility. Before he left I said a final good-bye.   12

I still feel the pain of losing Eric—and I'm sure I always will. But I also remember how caring for him helped clear up any confusion over my career choice. Although I couldn't bring Eric back, his tragedy brought me back to nursing.   13

Examining the Reading

Finding Meaning

1. How did Eric's accident occur?
2. Describe the injuries he suffered.
3. How did the author provide care for Eric?
4. What effect did caring for Eric have on Dickman's life and health?
5. What did the author decide to do after six months of caring for Eric?

Understanding Technique

1. What techniques does Dickman use to make her story real and compelling?
2. Why do you think she included in paragraph 5 the technical details of Eric's medical condition?

Thinking Critically

1. How did Eric's accident affect Dickman at first?
2. What did the author mean by "Grief prevented me from seeing the irony in my situation"? What was this irony?
3. Why did the doctor tell the author that she should get on with her life just when Eric seemed to be improving?
4. Was there a chance that Eric might have recovered completely from his accident?
5. Do you think there was a connection between the author's inability to nurse her fiancé back to health and her decision to return to nursing school? Explain.

Writing About the Reading

A Journal Entry

Write a journal entry about a difficult decision that you were forced to make.

A Paragraph

1. Someone might say that if Dickman had truly loved Eric, she would have continued to care for him for the rest of his life. Write a paragraph defending or rejecting this idea.
2. Write a paragraph on what you imagine would be the hardest part of being a nurse and why.

An Essay

1. The author had some difficulty deciding whether or not to become a nurse, but her experiences after Eric's accident helped her make that decision. Write an essay describing an experience in your life that helped you discover your career goals.
2. Sometimes it takes a tragic event to remind us of our blessings or to awaken us to a new, important direction for our lives. Write an essay about how such an experience made you a better person.

A Creative Activity

Imagine that Eric would have survived with only minimal brain damage. How do you imagine this might have changed the ending for the author? Rewrite the ending as though this were the case.

Evan's Two Moms

▸ Anna Quindlen

Anna Quindlen, a Pulitzer Prize–winning syndicated columnist for The New York Times *and many other newspapers, presents her position on same-sex marriages in the following essay. It was taken from her 1993 book:* Thinking Out Loud: On the Personal, the Political, the Public, and the Private.

Reading Strategy

The author of this essay has a definite opinion on the idea of same-sex marriages, which is expressed in various parts of the essay. After you have read the essay, review it and underline those phrases or sentences that most clearly express the author's position on same-sex marriages.

Vocabulary Preview

bulwark (1) strong support or protection; defense
quadriplegic (2) a person who is paralyzed in both arms and both legs
rads (5) radicals: those who wanted to bring about sweeping changes in society
linchpin (5) most important part; unifying feature
tenets (7) beliefs; convictions
ironically (7) by a strange twist; just the opposite
secular (7) nonreligious
amorphous (9) unclear or vague; open to many meanings
thwart (10) block; prevent
guise (10) form; way; manner

*E*van has two moms. This is no big thing. Evan has always had two   1
moms—in his school file, on his emergency forms, with his friends.
"Ooooh, Evan, you're lucky," they sometimes say. "You have two

---

moms." It sounds like a sitcom, but until last week it was emotional truth without legal bulwark. That was when a judge in New York approved the adoption of a six-year-old boy by his biological mother's lesbian partner. Evan. Evan's mom. Evan's other mom. A kid, a psychologist, a pediatrician. A family.

The matter of Evan's two moms is one in a series of [recent] 2 events . . . that led to certain conclusions. A Minnesota appeals court granted guardianship of a woman left a quadriplegic in a car accident to her lesbian lover, the culmination of a seven-year battle in which the injured woman's parents did everything possible to negate the partnership between the two. A lawyer in Georgia had her job offer withdrawn after the state attorney general found out that she and her lesbian lover were planning a marriage ceremony; she's brought suit. The computer company Lotus announced that the gay partners of employees would be eligible for the same benefits as spouses.

Add to these public events the private struggles, the couples who 3 go from lawyer to lawyer to approximate legal protections their straight counterparts take for granted, the AIDS survivors who find themselves shut out of their partners' dying days by biological family members and shut out of their apartments by leases with a single name on the dotted line, and one solution is obvious.

Gay marriage is a radical notion for straight people and a conser- 4 vative notion for gay ones. After years of being sledgehammered by society, some gay men and lesbian women are deeply suspicious of participating in an institution that seems to have "straight world" written all over it.

But the rads of twenty years ago, straight and gay alike, have other 5 things on their minds today. Family is one, and the linchpin of family has commonly been a loving commitment between two adults. When same-sex couples set out to make that commitment, they discover that they are at a disadvantage: No joint tax returns. No health insurance coverage for an uninsured partner. No survivor's benefits from Social Security. None of the automatic rights, privileges, and responsibilities society attaches to a marriage contract. In Madison, Wisconsin, a couple who applied at the Y with their kids for a family membership were turned down because both were women. It's one of those small things that can make you feel small.

Some took marriage statutes that refer to "two persons" at their 6 word and applied for a license. The results were court decisions that quoted the Bible and embraced circular argument: marriage is by definition the union of a man and a woman because that is how we've defined it.

No religion should be forced to marry anyone in violation of its 7 tenets, although ironically it is now only in religious ceremonies that gay people can marry, performed by clergy who find the blessing of two who love each other no sin. But there is no secular reason that we should take a patchwork approach of corporate, governmental, and legal steps to guarantee what can be done simply, economically, conclusively, and inclusively with the words "I do."

"Fran and I chose to get married for the same reasons that any two 8 people do," said the lawyer who was fired in Georgia. "We fell in love; we wanted to spend our lives together." Pretty simple.

Consider the case of *Loving* v. *Virgina*, aptly named. At the time, 9 sixteen states had laws that barred interracial marriage, relying on natural law, that amorphous grab bag for justifying prejudice. Sounding a little like God throwing Adam and Eve out of paradise, the trial judge suspended the one-year sentence of Richard Loving, who was white, and his wife, Mildred, who was black, provided they got out of the State of Virginia.

In 1967 the Supreme Court found such laws to be unconstitu- 10 tional. Only twenty-five years ago and it was a crime for a black woman to marry a white man. Perhaps twenty-five years from now we will find it just as incredible that two people of the same sex were not entitled to legally commit themselves to each other. Love and commitment are rare enough; it seems absurd to thwart them in any guise.

Examining the Reading

Finding Meaning

1. What legal and economic disadvantages are faced by gay couples?
2. Why does Quindlen conclude that same-sex marriage would be a solution to many of these problems?
3. Why does the author think some gay people are suspicious of marriage?
4. Why did some court decisions reject same-sex marriages?
5. How does the author think that the controversy over same-sex marriages will be resolved?

Understanding Technique

1. What is Quindlen's thesis?
2. What type of evidence does she offer to support it?

Thinking Critically

1. What does Quindlen believe is the most important reason for gay couples to marry legally?

2. What is a "circular argument," as described in paragraph 6?
3. Why does the author think it is ironic that gay couples can be married only in religious ceremonies?
4. Why do you think the *Loving* v. *Virginia* case was included in this essay?

Writing About the Reading

A Journal Entry

The author describes the experience of a lesbian couple being turned down for family membership by the Y as, "one of those small things that can make you feel small." Write a journal entry about an incident in your life that might seem small to others but had a tremendous impact on the way you felt about yourself.

A Paragraph

Write a paragraph giving your definition of what makes up a family.

An Essay

1. Do you think same-sex couples should be allowed to marry? Write an essay explaining and supporting your viewpoint.
2. Think of another social isue that was considered controversial in the past but is acceptable today. Write an essay explaining how public opinion has changed and what you think these changes tell us about society.

A Creative Activity

Describe a law or a school or family rule that you think is unfair. How should it be changed and what can you do to change it?

Hello, Goodbye, Hey Maybe I Love You?

▶ Joshua Kurlantzick

Many single people have difficulty finding dates and deciding whom to date. The new fast-dating industry may help millions connect with that special someone. This article, which originally appeared in U.S. News and World Report, *describes this new approach to dating.*

Reading Strategy

Create a two-column list. In the first column, write the advantages of fast-dating. In the second, list its disadvantages, either as stated in the article or as you think of them as you read.

Vocabulary Preview

arbitrage (1) to purchase something now to make a profit on it later
spawning (2) giving rise to; producing
avid (3) enthusiastic
banalities (4) bland and common remarks
outfits (7) businesses or associations

Dot coms come and go, the economy lurches along, but love is al-   1
ways a thriving market—if not the most efficient one. But wait, there's hope. At a suburban Virginia coffeehouse one night last week, attractive young singles paid $25 to arbitrage a month's worth of dates in a single evening.

The event was run by SpeedDating, a thriving organization that   2
sets up turbocharged encounters—in this case, seven face-to-face conversations lasting seven minutes each. SpeedDating, which is a non-profit serving Jewish singles, was the orginial fast-date service, but its success is spawning a host of companies that are in it for the cash. The for-profit 8minute-Dating, which started in Boston this year, charges $28 to $33 per event and is selling out its functions. Justin Rudd, founder of Gay Sprint Dating, a service in Long Beach, Calif., arranges events where gay men meet 20 potential partners for three minutes each and is unable to keep pace with demand. "The market is growing

so fast . . . I originally anticipated getting 50 men per event, but around 160 guys have been showing up," Rudd says.

Yet few people attending dating events are focusing on matchmaking's business potential. So avid were some daters at the Virginia date-a-thon that they drove for 90 minutes to participate, despite tornado warnings in the area.

Keeping It Moving

SpeedDating's formula is simple. At the cafe, an organizer matched men and women, ensured that they rotated among tables, and rang a bell to end each short-lived "date." As the dates started, a babble of conversation enveloped the room, and men and women tossed out awkward standard opening lines about the weather. Perhaps because of the enforced time limits, however, the banalities soon gave way to comparisons of evil bosses, questions about most-romantic evenings, and furious debates over the correct use of herbal medicine. At the bell, several seven-minute couples gazed into each other's eyes, seemingly unaware that, at least for now, their time was up.

Turbo dating has an appeal. Many psychologists believe face-to-face services are more successful than online matchmakers, since the Internet cannot convey body language. Just as important, as *U.S. News* found out after a seven-minute date with a woman who disagreed with nearly every statement our reporter made, a bad match is quickly forgotten. "Since the interactions are short, we avoid the awkwardness of a horrible blind date," says 8minute-Dating CEO Tom Jaffee. One pair observed by *U.S. News* apparently didn't hit it off: The man and woman spent their seven minutes making the residents of Gracie Mansion[1] look cordial by comparison. But when the bell sounded, the daters never have to see each other again.

The format also guards against stalking. At SpeedDating, participants are prohibited from exchanging phone numbers and are identified, Kafka-like,[2] by their first names. The daters use scorecards to check off people whom they'd like to see again. The organizer collects the cards and contacts participants only if someone they checked marked their name as well.

---

[1]Refers to former New York City Mayor Rudolph Giuliani and his wife, who were going through a highly publicized and messy divorce. Gracie Mansion is the official residence of the mayor of New York City.

[2]Bizarre, anxiety-ridden. Franz Kafka was an author who lived from 1883–1924. He wrote in German about the anxiety felt by common people being oppressed in modern society.

Most outfits boast high rates of success. SpeedDating says that over 50 percent of its participants meet someone with whom there is mutual interest in another date. Rudd claims that 70 percent of his guys get at least one match. "You don't even need three minutes—you know in the first seconds whether you like someone, and if you do, that three minutes is just a tease for better things," he says. 7

Turbo dating isn't for everyone; a number of psychologists express concerns that fast-date functions put more time pressure on already stressed Americans. Still, the fast-date industry is only getting started. SpeedDating now hosts events in over 30 cities, including Paris and Kiev. According to Jaffee, 8minute-Dating is considering franchising nationwide. Rivals such as Nanodate, InstadateNY, 10-Minute Match, and Brief Encounters are snapping at the leaders' heels. 8

But with roughly 85 million singles in the United States, there seems to be room for everyone. Already, online dating services like Matchmaker.com enroll more than 150,000 new users per month. Demonstrating Matchmaker's value, the site was purchased last year by Web giant Terra Lycos for $44 million. 9

Fast-date outfits also enjoy several advantages over traditional dating services. According to Jaffee, once initial capital investments are completed, fast-date services enjoy low overheads and sizable profit margins, yet cost less than traditional firms. "Friends of mine have paid $1,600 for a dating service, but I only charge around $15," Rudd says. "Who could turn down that offer?" 10

Examining the Reading

Finding Meaning

1. How does a SpeedDating event work?
2. What group does the SpeedDating organization serve?
3. Why are speed-dating events more successful than Internet dating services?
4. How does SpeedDating protect participants from stalkers?
5. How can the market support so many dating organizations and services?
6. Name four fast-dating businesses mentioned in the article.

Understanding Technique

1. How does the author support his thesis that speed-dating is a fast-growing and successful industry?
2. Because this article refers to business, the writer focuses on finances and statistics. Cite some examples, and explain their effectiveness.

3. How does the author's use of quotations enhance the article?
4. The author mentions that a *U.S. News and World Report* reporter participated in a fast-dating session. How does this experience add to the article?

Thinking Critically

1. Why do groups such as Jewish singles and gay men look to specialized services for dating help?
2. Why would some daters travel long distances in bad weather to attend a speed-dating event?
3. Why does speed-dating have such wide appeal?
4. What kind of people would not like speed-dating? Why?
5. How is fast-dating more effective than online matchmaking and traditional dating services?
6. Why has SpeedDating expanded internationally?

Writing About the Reading

A Journal Entry

Write a journal entry explaining why you would or would not want to participate in a fast-dating session.

A Paragraph

1. Write a paragraph describing the types of questions you would ask each person you were to meet in a speed-dating session.
2. Write a paragraph about a blind date that you had.
3. Describe a "perfect date."

An Essay

1. Relationships take a great deal of effort. Write an essay explaining and illustrating several important elements of a good relationship.
2. Write an essay explaining the pros and cons of being single.

A Creative Activity

Create a seven-minute conversation between two fast-daters. Another suggestion for this activity is to imagine that you can go out on a date with anyone famous from the past or present. Who would this person be and why would you choose him or her?

The Gift of Sacrifice

▸ **Blanca Matute**
Student Essay

*In this essay, a young woman describes a childhood decision to
leave her parents and move to the United States. Matute wrote
this essay while she was a student at college.*

When we make decisions, we have to live with the consequences.   1
Hopefully, we like the decisions and are grateful that we made them,
but in some cases, we regret the decision. Unfortunately, we cannot go
back in time and change our original choice, even though the decision
we made put us in a difficult or challenging position. Eight years ago,
I learned that when a person makes a decision, he or she must stick
with the choice and persevere.

   When I was ten years old, I made a decision that greatly affected   2
my life. I had to decide whether to move to the United States to continue my education or stay in Honduras with my family. The idea of
studying in the United States sounded like a wonderful opportunity,
but it meant growing up without my mother's constant presence and
guidance. I decided to leave my mother in Honduras with the rest of
my family to journey to New York to pursue a better education. My
family supported this decision because they knew it was a good opportunity for me. They were also sad because I would be away for
many years.

   I came to the United States because I believed it was going to make   3
a difference in my life. At first I found it difficult to understand how my
family expected me to get a good education without my mother's support. In the beginning, I regretted my decision to come to this country.
Adjusting to the different languages, the diverse cultures, and the
crowded surroundings was an enormous challenge. With the help of
the family I lived with, my sisters and their mother, I worked hard to
adjust to my new life. I still, however, missed my mother.

   As time passed, I was often sad because I had not seen my mother   4
for many years. I doubted my decision and questioned my mother's
motives for encouraging me to come to the United States. At times, I
felt as if my life was over because I thought that she had just wanted to
get rid of me. Eventually, I learned that I had made the right decision
and that my mother had supported it because she loved me. I realized

that our separation had been just as difficult for her as it had been for me. Because of her love for me, she was willing to let me go so that I could have better opportunities in life. Ultimately, she taught me an important lesson in life, the gift of sacrifice.

As I became accustomed to my new life, many wonderful things began to happen; I learned a new language; I made new friends; I started to do well in school. Because of my academic achievement, I represented my junior high school at various assemblies in New York State. For example, I traveled to upstate New York as a school representative to receive an award for my school's having the best bilingual program in the public schools' twelfth district. 5

In 1990, I was awarded a scholarship to Aquinas High School for high achievement in junior high school, and I was selected to participate in the Student/Sponsor Partnership Program. This program sponsors academically gifted students through high school. At Aquinas I met teachers who really cared about their students' education. A new world opened up to me. I joined the Spanish Club, the Math Club, the String Ensemble, where I learned to play the viola, and the Concert Band, where I played the clarinet. I became class president in my senior year. 6

Each time I wrote my mother to tell her how well I was doing, she wrote back expressing her pride in me and my accomplishments. Even in my second year at Aquinas, when my grades were not as good as they could have been, my mother was still proud of me. With the help of a special teacher at Aquinas and hard work, I was able to bring my grades back up again. Now, I look back on all I have learned and what I have accomplished since I left Honduras and my mother eight years ago. It seems impossible that I ever regretted my decision to come to the United States. 7

I have learned that making a decision can sometimes lead to happiness and sometimes to sadness; in my case it led to both. At first I regretted coming to this country, but now I see that I made the right decision. It gave me not only a chance for a good education, but also a good opportunity to succeed in life. Even though I still miss my mother, I know that she is happy and proud to know of my college plans. I look to the future with awe and excitement. 8

Examining the Essay

1. How did Matute organize her ideas?
2. In which paragraph(s) do you think more detail is needed?
3. Evaluate the author's use of descriptive language—words that help you visualize and imagine people, places, or objects.

Writing an Essay

1. In "The Gift of Sacrifice," Matute describes the sacrifice that her mother made for her. Write an essay evaluating a sacrifice you made or one that was made for you. Was it worth it?
2. In leaving Honduras, Matute faced numerous challenges and difficult situations, including learning a new language, meeting new friends, and so forth. Write an essay discussing a difficult situation you faced and how you handled it.

Making Connections

1. Both Matute in "The Gift of Sacrifice" and Dickman in "Saying Good-bye to Eric" make a decision and experience its consequences. Write an essay comparing the type of decisions they made and the importance and possible outcomes of these decisions.

2. Some decisions take longer than others to make. Examine the role that time plays in the decision-making process described in Dawson's "Life Is So Good" and Kurlantzick's "Hello, Goodbye, Maybe I Love You?"

3. Cunningham in "The Chosen One," Dickman in "Saying Good-bye to Eric," and Matute in "The Gift of Sacrifice" face difficult decisions. Compare how each author made her decision. Was it primarily rational or emotional? Was it well thought out or impulsive, and is one approach better than the other? Why or why not?

Internet Connections

1. Examine the "25 Facts About Organ Donation and Transplantation" at the National Kidney Foundation's web site **http://www.kidney.org/general/news/25facts.cfm**. Write a paragraph evaluating the effectiveness of this list. Which facts lead to the most compelling reasons for organ donation?

2. On the web site of the National Adoption Information Clearinghouse (**http://www.calib.com/naic/parents/crisis.htm**) there is a fact sheet about "adopting children from areas of crisis or disaster." Evaluate the recommendations made

there. Are the reasons for not adopting these children convincing? Why or why not?

3. Visit this site, which lists the steps to making decisions:
   **http://www.shpm.com/articles/growth/decisionmaking.
   html**. Write an essay evaluating your own decision-making
   process. Do you have a system? How well does it work for
   you? Do you use any of the steps outlined at the web site
   you just visited? What is the most important decision you
   have had to make?

   (If any of these web sites are unavailable, use a search
   engine to locate another appropriate site.)

Chapter 2

Events That Shape Our Lives

The Scholarship Jacket
Marta Salinas

Ragtime, My Time
Alton Fitzgerald White

A Letter to My Daughter
Siu Wai Anderson

To Mr. Winslow
Ian Frazier

Breaking Glass
Jonathan Rosen

Blind to Faith
Karl Taro Greenfeld

Desert Storm and Shield
Scott Stopa

Many daily events—conversations, meals, classes, purchases, interactions with friends—seem important at the time but are not particularly memorable in the long term. Occasionally, however, a single event will make a difference and leave a lasting impression. It may be a landmark event, such as meeting your future spouse, getting a job, playing in a big game, celebrating a big birthday in a notable way, or receiving an important prize or award. Or perhaps something happened to your health that led you to make a change in your habits or behavior.

Other times, it may be a much smaller, more ordinary, and seemingly less significant event that has a dramatic or meaningful effect on the direction of your life or contributes to making you who you are. For example, the first time you picked up a guitar or heard a piano, you

51

may have realized that you wanted to be a musician. One friend's frank comment might have caused you to reexamine your priorities and decide to pursue a more practical way to make a living. But another friend might have encouraged you to work hard at your music, and you could go on to have a successful recording career. Watching children play on a playground might help you realize that having a child must be an important part of your future plans.

The selections in this chapter describe how events, both large and small, both chance and planned, can have a shaping effect on people's lives. Each reading will help give you a perspective on the importance of events in the human experience. You will read about encounters with birth ("A Letter to My Daughter") and death, both in war ("Desert Storm and Shield") and in a neighborhood park ("To Mr. Winslow"). You'll also read about how an academic award shaped a young girl's attitude toward the world ("The Scholarship Jacket") and how a date chosen for a marriage ceremony connects the bridegroom to his past ("Breaking Glass"). In addition, you'll read about an important event in a blind man's life ("Blind to Faith") and a young black man's experience with an incident of racial profiling ("Ragtime, My Time").

Brainstorming About Events

Class Activities:

1. Working in groups of three or four, list events that are *supposed* to be memorable (graduations, birthdays, etc.).
2. Prepare a second list, including only events that made a difference in your life.
3. Compare the two lists. How frequently does the same event appear on both lists?
4. Discuss conclusions that can be drawn.

The Scholarship Jacket

▸ Marta Salinas

This fictional story describes a young girl's experience in which she struggles to receive an award she has earned. The essay was reprinted from Cuentos Chicanos: A Short Story Anthology.

Reading Strategy

When reading short stories such as this one, try to identify the following elements:

- Setting—Where and when does the story take place?
- Characters—Who are the important people involved in the story?
- Point of view—Through whose eyes is the story being told?
- Plot—What major events occur?
- Theme—What is the meaning of the story? What is its message?

Vocabulary Preview

agile (2) coordinated
eavesdrop (4) listen in
rooted (4) held uncontrollably
filtered (7) passed through
fidgeted (8) moved about nervously
muster (12) gather
mesquite (15) a sugary plant with bean pods
gaunt (25) extremely thin
vile (29) foul; repulsive
adrenaline (31) a chemical secreted by the body, causing a
                 great surge of energy

*T*he small Texas school that I attended carried out a tradition every 1
year during the eighth grade graduation; a beautiful gold and green
jacket, the school colors, was awarded to the class valedictorian, the
student who had maintained the highest grades for eight years. The
scholarship jacket had a big gold S on the left front side and the winner's name was written in gold letters on the pocket.

My oldest sister Rosie had won the jacket a few years back and I 2
fully expected to win also. I was fourteen and in the eighth grade. I had
been a straight A student since the first grade, and the last year I had

looked forward to owning that jacket. My father was a farm laborer who couldn't earn enough money to feed eight children, so when I was six I was given to my grandparents to raise. We couldn't participate in sports at school because there were registration fees, uniform costs, and trips out of town; so even though we were quite agile and athletic, there would never be a sports school jacket for us. This one, the scholarship jacket, was our only chance.

In May, close to graduation, spring fever struck, and no one paid   3
any attention in class; instead we stared out the windows and at each other, wanting to speed up the last few weeks of school. I despaired every time I looked in the mirror. Pencil thin, not a curve anywhere, I was called "Beanpole" and "String Bean" and I knew that's what I looked like. A flat chest, no hips, and a brain, that's what I had. That really isn't much for a fourteen-year-old to work with, I thought, as I absentmindedly wandered from my history class to the gym. Another hour of sweating in basketball and displaying my toothpick legs was coming up. Then I remembered my P.E. shorts were still in a bag under my desk where I'd forgotten them. I had to walk all the way back and get them. Coach Thompson was a real bear if anyone wasn't dressed for P.E. She had said I was a good forward and once she even tried to talk Grandma into letting me join the team. Grandma, of course, said no.

I was almost back at my classroom's door when I heard angry   4
voices and arguing. I stopped. I didn't mean to eavesdrop; I just hesitated, not knowing what to do. I needed those shorts and I was going to be late, but I didn't want to interrupt an argument between my teachers. I recognized the voices: Mr. Schmidt, my history teacher, and Mr. Boone, my math teacher. They seemed to be arguing about me. I couldn't believe it. I still remember the shock that rooted me flat against the wall as if I were trying to blend in with the graffiti written there.

"I refuse to do it! I don't care who her father is, her grades don't   5
even begin to compare to Marta's. I won't lie or falsify records. Marta has a straight A plus average and you know it." That was Mr. Schmidt and he sounded very angry. Mr. Boone's voice sounded calm and quiet.

"Look, Joann's father is not only on the Board, he owns the only   6
store in town; we could say it was a close tie and—"

The pounding in my ears drowned out the rest of the words, only a   7
word here and there filtered through. ". . . Marta is Mexican. . . . resign. . . . won't do it. . . ." Mr. Schmidt came rushing out, and luckily for me went down the opposite way toward the auditorium, so he didn't see me. Shaking, I waited a few minutes and then went in and grabbed my bag and fled from the room. Mr. Boone looked up when I came in but didn't say anything. To this day I don't remember if I got in trouble in P.E. for being late or how I made it through the rest of the

afternoon. I went home very sad and cried into my pillow that night so Grandmother wouldn't hear me. It seemed a cruel coincidence that I had overheard that conversation.

The next day when the principal called me into his office, I knew what it would be about. He looked uncomfortable and unhappy. I decided I wasn't going to make it any easier for him so I looked him straight in the eye. He looked away and fidgeted with the papers on his desk.   8

"Marta," he said, "there's been a change in policy this year regarding the scholarship jacket. As you know, it has always been free." He cleared his throat and continued. "This year the Board decided to charge fifteen dollars—which still won't cover the complete cost of the jacket."   9

I stared at him in shock and a small sound of dismay escaped my throat. I hadn't expected this. He still avoided looking in my eyes.   10

"So if you are unable to pay the fifteen dollars for the jacket, it will be given to the next one in line."   11

Standing with all the dignity I could muster, I said, "I'll speak to my grandfather about it, sir, and let you know tomorrow." I cried on the walk home from the bus stop. The dirt road was a quarter of a mile from the highway, so by the time I got home, my eyes were red and puffy.   12

"Where's Grandpa?" I asked Grandma, looking down at the floor so she wouldn't ask me why I'd been crying. She was sewing on a quilt and didn't look up.   13

"I think he's out back working in the bean field."   14

I went outside and looked out at the fields. There he was. I could see him walking between the rows, his body bent over the little plants, hoe in hand. I walked slowly out to him, trying to think how I could best ask him for the money. There was a cool breeze blowing and a sweet smell of mesquite in the air, but I didn't appreciate it. I kicked at a dirt clod. I wanted that jacket so much. It was more than just being a valedictorian and giving a little thank you speech for the jacket on graduation night. It represented eight years of hard work and expectation. I knew I had to be honest with Grandpa; it was my only chance. He saw me and looked up.   15

He waited for me to speak. I cleared my throat nervously and clasped my hands behind my back so he wouldn't see them shaking. "Grandpa, I have a big favor to ask you," I said in Spanish, the only language he knew. He still waited silently. I tried again. "Grandpa, this year the principal said the scholarship jacket is not going to be free. It's going to cost fifteen dollars and I have to take the money in tomorrow, otherwise it'll be given to someone else." The last words came out in an eager rush. Grandpa straightened up tiredly and leaned his chin on the hoe handle. He looked out over the field that was filled with the tiny green bean plants. I waited, desperately hoping he'd say I could have the money.   16

He turned to me and asked quietly, "What does a scholarship   17
jacket mean?"

I answered quickly; maybe there was a chance. "It means you've   18
earned it by having the highest grades for eight years and that's why
they're giving it to you." Too late I realized the significance of my
words. Grandpa knew that I understood it was not a matter of money.
It wasn't that. He went back to hoeing the weeds that sprang up between the delicate little bean plants. It was a time consuming job;
sometimes the small shoots were right next to each other. Finally he
spoke again.

"Then if you pay for it, Marta, it's not a scholarship jacket, is it? Tell   19
your principal I will not pay the fifteen dollars."

I walked back to the house and locked myself in the bathroom for   20
a long time. I was angry with Grandfather even though I knew he was
right, and I was angry with the Board, whoever they were. Why did they
have to change the rules just when it was my turn to win the jacket?

It was a very sad and withdrawn girl who dragged into the princi-   21
pal's office the next day. This time he did look me in the eyes.

"What did your grandfather say?"   22

I sat very straight in my chair.   23

"He said to tell you he won't pay the fifteen dollars."   24

The principal muttered something I couldn't understand under his   25
breath, and walked over to the window. He stood looking out at something outside. He looked bigger than usual when he stood up; he was a
tall gaunt man with gray hair, and I watched the back of his head while
I waited for him to speak.

"Why?" he finally asked. "Your grandfather has the money. Doesn't   26
he own a small bean farm?"

I looked at him, forcing my eyes to stay dry. "He said if I had to pay   27
for it, then it wouldn't be a scholarship jacket," I said and stood up to
leave. "I guess you'll just have to give it to Joann." I hadn't meant to
say that; it had just slipped out. I was almost to the door when he
stopped me.

"Marta —wait."   28

I turned and looked at him, waiting. What did he want now? I   29
could feel my heart pounding. Something bitter and vile tasting was
coming up in my mouth; I was afraid I was going to be sick. I didn't
need any sympathy speeches. He sighed loudly and went back to his
big desk. He looked at me, biting his lip, as if thinking.

"Okay, damn it. We'll make an exception in your case. I'll tell the   30
Board, you'll get your jacket."

I could hardly believe it. I spoke in a trembling rush. "Oh, thank   31
you, sir!" Suddenly I felt great. I didn't know about adrenaline in those
days, but I knew something was pumping through me, making me feel

as tall as the sky. I wanted to yell, jump, run the mile, do something. I ran out so I could cry in the hall where there was no one to see me. At the end of the day, Mr. Schmidt winked at me and said, "I hear you're getting a scholarship jacket this year."

His face looked as happy and innocent as a baby's, but I knew better. Without answering I gave him a quick hug and ran to the bus. I cried on the walk home again, but this time because I was so happy. I couldn't wait to tell Grandpa and ran straight to the field. I joined him in the row where he was working and without saying anything I crouched down and started pulling up the weeds with my hands. Grandpa worked alongside me for a few minutes, but he didn't ask what had happened. After I had a little pile of weeds between the rows, I stood up and faced him. 32

"The principal said he's making an exception for me, Grandpa, and I'm getting the jacket after all. That's after I told him what you said." 33

Grandpa didn't say anything, he just gave me a pat on the shoulder and a smile. He pulled out the crumpled red handkerchief that he always carried in his back pocket and wiped the sweat off his forehead. 34

"Better go see if your grandmother needs any help with supper." 35

I gave him a big grin. He didn't fool me. I skipped and ran back to the house whistling some silly tune. 36

Examining the Reading

Finding Meaning

1. Why didn't the author participate in school sports, although she was athletic?
2. What were Marta's two teachers arguing about?
3. Why did Marta's grandfather refuse to give her the money for the scholarship jacket?
4. What kind of a person was Marta's grandfather?
5. Why did Marta's math teacher, Mr. Boone, want the scholarship jacket to go to another student?

Understanding Technique

1. Discuss Salinas's use of dialogue. What purpose does it serve in the story?
2. What is the theme of the story?

Thinking Critically

1. Why do you think the Board decided to charge for the scholarship jacket?

2. Why do you think the principal changed his mind about charging Marta for the jacket?
3. Discuss the character differences between Marta's teachers.
4. After Marta told her grandfather she was getting the scholarship jacket, what did she mean when she said his reaction "didn't fool me"?

Writing About the Reading

A Journal Entry

Write a journal entry exploring your attitudes about winning games, prizes, or awards. Is this important to you? Why or why not?

A Paragraph

1. The author implied that Mr. Schmidt, her history teacher, was willing to quit his job if Marta did not receive the scholarship jacket that was rightfully hers. Suppose you were Mr. Schmidt: would you have been willing to quit your job over the issue of fairness? Write a paragraph stating and defending your decision.
2. Suppose you were in a position to win a game or contest and then realized that someone else was about to win it unfairly. Write a paragraph describing how you would handle the situation.

An Essay

1. The author became so anxious while talking to her principal that she was afraid she was going to become sick. Write an essay describing a situation in your life that caused you the same level of anxiety and explain how you resolved it.
2. The awarding of the scholarship jacket is a memorable event illustrating a choice between right and wrong that the author recalls from her childhood. Write an essay recalling such an event from your childhood, and explain how it affected you and whether it ended happily or not.

A Creative Activity

Suppose the principal had decided not to make an exception for Marta. How might she have felt? What, if anything, might she say to Joann? What might her grandfather say? Rewrite the ending of the story, answering the above questions.

Ragtime, My Time

▸ Alton Fitzgerald White

A young African-American actor living in Harlem describes being unfairly arrested by police. This article first appeared in The Nation *in 1999.*

Reading Strategy

The author tells his story chronologically. As you read, create a time line of his experiences.

Vocabulary Preview

naïvely (2) innocently; simply
ovation (3) thunderous applause
portraying (3) representing in a play; playing the part of
overt (4) plain to see; not hidden
charismatic (4) having a special charm
splurged (5) treated to something special
vestibule (5) entranceway, hallway
acknowledging (7) recognizing someone's existence
ailing (8) sick; needing care
residue (9) remainder; trace amount
ordeal (10) difficult experience
pseudo (15) fake; false

As the youngest of five girls and two boys growing up in Cincinnati, I   1
was raised to believe that if I worked hard, was a good person, and always told the truth, the world would be my oyster.[1] I was raised to be a gentleman and learned that these qualities would bring me respect.

While one has to earn respect, consideration is something owed to   2
every human being. On Friday, June 16, 1999, when I was wrongfully arrested at my Harlem apartment building, my perception of everything I had learned as a young man was forever changed—not only because I wasn't given even a second to use the manners my parents

---

[1]A place where great opportunities open up.

taught me, but mostly because the police, whom I'd always naïvely thought were supposed to serve and protect me, were actually hunting me.

I had planned a pleasant day. The night before was payday, plus I had received a standing ovation after portraying the starring role of Coalhouse Walker Jr. in the Broadway musical *Ragtime*. It is a role that requires not only talent but also an honest emotional investment of the morals and lessons I learned as a child.

Coalhouse Walker Jr. is a victim (an often misused word, but in this case true) of overt racism. His story is every black man's nightmare. He is hard-working, successful, talented, charismatic, friendly, and polite. Perfect prey for someone with authority and not even a fraction of those qualities. On that Friday afternoon, I became a real-life Coalhouse Walker. Nothing could have prepared me for it. Not even stories told to me by other black men who had suffered similar injustices.

Friday for me usually means a trip to the bank, errands, the gym, dinner, and then off to the theater. On this particular day, I decided to break my pattern of getting up and running right out of the house. Instead, I took my time, slowed my pace, and splurged by making strawberry pancakes. Before I knew it, it was 2:45; my bank closes at 3:30, leaving me less than 45 minutes to get to midtown Manhattan on the train. I was pressed for time but in a relaxed, blessed state of mind. When I walked through the lobby of my building, I noticed two light-skinned Hispanic men I'd never seen before. Not thinking much of it, I continued on to the vestibule, which is separated from the lobby by a locked door.

As I approached the exit, I saw people in uniforms rushing toward the door. I sped up to open it for them. I thought they might be paramedics, since many of the building's occupants are elderly. It wasn't until I had opened the door and greeted them that I recognized that they were police officers. Within seconds, I was told to "hold it"; they had received a call about young Hispanics with guns. I was told to get against the wall. I was searched, stripped of my backpack, put on my knees, handcuffed, and told to be quiet when I tried to ask questions.

With me were three other innocent black men who had been on their way to their U-Haul. They were moving into the apartment beneath mine, and I had just bragged to them about how safe the building was. One of these gentlemen got off his knees, still handcuffed, and unlocked the door for the officers to get into the lobby where the two strangers were standing. Instead of thanking or even acknowledging us, they led us out the door past our neighbors, who were all but begging the police in our defense.

The four of us were put into cars with the two strangers and taken to   8
the precinct station at 165th and Amsterdam. The police automatically
linked us, with no questions and no regard for our character or our lives.
No consideration was given to where we were going or why. Suppose an
ailing relative was waiting upstairs, while I ran out for her medication?
Or young children, who'd been told that Daddy was running to the corner store for milk and would be right back? My new neighbors weren't
even allowed to lock their apartment or check on the U-Haul.

After we were lined up in the station, the younger of the two His-   9
panic men was identified as an experienced criminal, and drug residue
was found in a pocket of the other. I now realize how naïve I was to
think that the police would then uncuff me, apologize for their mistake, and let me go. Instead, they continued to search my backpack,
questioned me, and put me in jail with the criminals.

The rest of the nearly five-hour ordeal was like a horrible dream. I   10
was handcuffed, strip-searched, taken in and out for questioning. The
officers told me that they knew exactly who I was, knew I was in *Ragtime,* and that in fact they already had the men they wanted.

How then could they keep me there, or have brought me there in   11
the first place? I was told it was standard procedure. As if the average
law-abiding citizen knows what that is and can dispute it. From what
I now know, "standard procedure" is something that every citizen,
black and white, needs to learn, and fast.

I felt completely powerless. Why, do you think? Here I was, young,   12
pleasant, and successful, in good physical shape, dressed in clean athletic attire. I was carrying a backpack containing a substantial pay-
check and a deposit slip, on my way to the bank. Yet after hours and
hours I was sitting at a desk with two officers who not only couldn't tell
me why I was there but seemed determined to find something on me,
to the point of making me miss my performance.

It was because I am a black man!   13

I sat in that cell crying silent tears of disappointment and injustice   14
with the realization of how many innocent black men are convicted for
no reason. When I was handcuffed, my first instinct had been to pull
away out of pure insult and violation as a human being. Thank God I
was calm enough to do what they said. When I was thrown in jail with
the criminals and strip-searched, I somehow knew to put my pride
aside, be quiet, and do exactly what I was told, hating it but coming to
terms with the fact that in this situation I was a victim. They had guns!

Before I was finally let go, exhausted, humiliated, embarrassed,   15
and still in shock, I was led to a room and given a pseudo-apology. I
was told that I was at the wrong place at the wrong time. My reply? "I
was where I live."

Everything I learned growing up in Cincinnati has been shattered.   16
Life will never be the same.

Examining the Reading

Finding Meaning

1. According to White, how does one earn respect?
2. Why did White think paramedics were coming to his building?
3. Who was finally identified as a criminal that day?
4. What reason did the police give for bringing White to the police station?
5. What was White's reaction to being handcuffed? How did he instinctively want to react?
6. How did White feel about the apology that the police finally gave him?

Understanding Technique

1. Describe how this essay is organized.
2. The author uses many descriptive details in this personal account. Highlight some that are particularly revealing and explain what they add to the story.
3. White compares himself with Coalhouse Walker, Jr. How does this comparison contribute to the story?
4. The author uses many short descriptive sentences. How effective is this style?

Thinking Critically

1. Predict what would have happened if White had been Caucasian and in the same place at the same time.
2. Why didn't White's manners help him the day he was arrested?
3. The author writes that *victim* is an "often misused word." What does he mean?
4. What does the author mean when he describes Coalhouse Walker, Jr. as "perfect prey for someone with authority"?
5. Why didn't the police show White any consideration? What factors should the police have taken into account?
6. Why did White feel powerless?
7. Why will life never be the same for the author?

Writing About the Reading

A Journal Entry

Create a list of words describing how racism or racial profiling makes you feel.

A Paragraph

1. Write a paragraph describing a time when your actions were misunderstood or you were wrongly accused.
2. The incident shattered the lessons that White learned during his childhood. Write a paragraph describing a childhood belief that you have discovered is no longer true.
3. Write a paragraph describing a situation in which you had to put your pride aside and accept an unpleasant situation.

An Essay

1. Write an essay exploring the issue of racial profiling. First, define the issue, and then outline the points on which police, minorities, and other citizens agree and those on which they disagree.
2. White's concept of earning respect and receiving fair treatment was changed dramatically by this incident. Write an essay describing a situation that changed your attitudes or perceptions.
3. Power can corrupt. Write an essay discussing what actions might be taken to prevent police from abusing their power.
4. Write an essay describing a situation in which you felt completely powerless or in which you felt victimized.

A Creative Activity

Imagine you are in jail, falsely accused of a crime. Describe your cellmate.

A Letter to My Daughter

▶ **Siu Wai Anderson**

*This letter, written by a mother to her infant daughter, discusses
issues of cross-cultural adoptions. It was first published in an
anthology of writings by women of color:* Making Face,
Making Soul.

Reading Strategy

Anderson uses a personal letter to describe her ancestry and
express her feelings toward her daughter. As you read, think
about why Anderson uses the letter format. What advantages
does it give her as a writer?

Vocabulary Preview

auspicious (1) favorable
travail (1) painful work; childbirth
demographical (3) conforming to the average of the
                                        population
proverbial (3) as in a popular saying or proverb
legacy (3) inheritance
agonizing (4) extremely painful
ancestral (5) having to do with forebears
hail (7) welcome
deprivation (7) doing without necessities
lavishing (10) giving abundantly

August 1989, Boston

Dear Maya Shao-ming,

You were born at Mt. Auburn Hospital in Cambridge on June 6, 1989,   1
an auspicious date, and for me, the end of a long, long travail. Because
you insisted on being breech, with your head always close to my heart,
you came into the world by C-section into a chilly O.R. at the opposite
end of the labor and delivery suite where, exhausted yet exuberant, I
pushed out your brother in a birthing room nearly four years ago.

I couldn't believe my ears when your father exclaimed, "A girl!" All   2
I could do was cry the tears of a long-awaited dream come true. You

are so beautiful, with your big dark eyes and silky black hair. Your skin is more creamy than golden, reflecting your particular "happa haole" blend. But your long elegant fingers are those of a Chinese scholar, prized for high intelligence and sensitivity.

You are more than just a second child, more than just a girl to match our boy, to fit the demographical nuclear family with the proverbial 2.5 children. No, ten years ago I wrote a song for an unborn dream: a dark-haired, dark-eyed child who would be my flesh-and-blood link to humanity. I had no other until your brother came. He was my first Unborn Song. But you, little daughter, are the link to our female line, the legacy of another woman's pain and sacrifice thirty-one years ago.

Let me tell you about your Chinese grandmother. Somewhere in Hong Kong, in the late fifties, a young waitress found herself pregnant by a cook, probably a co-worker at her restaurant. She carried the baby to term, suffered to give it birth, and kept the little girl for the first three months of her life. I like to think that my mother—your grandmother—loved me and fought to raise me on her own, but that the daily struggle was too hard. Worn down by the demands of the new baby and perhaps the constant threat of starvation, she made the agonizing decision to give away her girl so that both of us might have a chance for a better life.

More likely, I was dumped at the orphanage steps or forcibly removed from a home of abuse and neglect by a social welfare worker. I will probably never know the truth. Having a baby in her unmarried state would have brought shame on the family in China, so she probably kept my existence a secret. Once I was out of her life, it was as if I had never been born. And so you and your brother and I are the missing leaves on an ancestral tree.

Do they ever wonder if we exist?

I was brought to the U.S. before I was two, and adopted by the Anglo parents who hail you as their latest beautiful grandchild. Raised by a minister's family in postwar American prosperity and nourished on three square meals a day, I grew like a wild weed and soaked up all the opportunities they had to offer—books, music, education, church life and community activities. Amidst a family of blue-eyed blonds, though, I stood out like a sore thumb. Whether from jealousy or fear of someone who looked so different, my older brothers sometimes tormented me with racist name-calling, teased me about my poor eyesight and unsightly skin, or made fun of my clumsy walk. Moody and impatient, gifted and temperamental, burdened by fears and nightmares that none of us realized stemmed from my early years of deprivation, I was not an easy child to love. My adoptive mother and I clashed countless times over the years, but gradually came to see one another as real human beings with faults and talents, and as women of strength in our own right. Now we love each other very much, though the scars and memories of our early battles will never quite fade. Lacking a mirror image in the mother who raised me, I had to seek my identity as a woman on my own. The Asian American community has helped me reclaim my dual identity and enlightened my view of the struggles we face as minorities in a white-dominated culture. They have applauded my music and praised my writings.

But part of me will always be missing: my beginnings, my personal   8
history, all the subtle details that give a person her origin. I don't know how I was born, whether it was vaginally or by Cesarean. I don't know when, or where exactly, how much I weighed, or whose ears heard my first cry of life. Was I put to my mother's breast and tenderly rocked, or was I simply weighed, cleaned, swaddled and carted off to a sterile nursery, noted in the hospital records as "newborn female"?

Someone took the time to give me a lucky name, and write the ap-   9
propriate characters in neat brush strokes in the Hong Kong city register. "Siu" means "little." My kind of "wai" means "clever" or "wise." Therefore, my baby name was "Clever little one." Who chose those words? Who cared enough to note my arrival in the world?

I lost my Chinese name for eighteen years. It was Americanized for   10
convenience to "Sue." But like an ill-fitting coat, it made me twitch and fret and squirm. I hated the name. But even more, I hated being Chinese. It took many years to become proud of my Asian heritage and work up the courage to take back my birthname. That plus a smattering of classroom Cantonese, are all the Chinese culture I have to offer you, little one. Not white, certainly, but not really Asian, I straddle the two worlds and try to blaze your trails for you. Your name, "Shao-ming," is very much like mine—"Shao" is the Mandarin form of "Siu," meaning "little." And "ming" is "bright," as in a shining sun or moon. Whose lives will you brighten, little Maya? Your past is more complete than mine, and each day I cradle you in your babyhood, lavishing upon you the tender care I lacked for my first two years. When I console you, I comfort the lost baby inside me who still cries out for her mother. No wonder so many adoptees desperately long to have children of their own.

Sweet Maya, it doesn't matter what you "become" later on. You   11
have already fulfilled my wildest dreams.

I love you,

Mommy

Examining the Reading

Finding Meaning

1. What does the author know about her biological mother?
2. Why did the author's brothers tease her and call her names?
3. Explain Siu Wai's reaction to being called Sue.
4. How does the author feel about her Asian identity?
5. What did the author most want to tell her daughter?

Understanding Technique

1. What type of details does Anderson include to make her essay lively and interesting?
2. Although she describes events, Anderson does not follow a strict chronological sequence. Why doesn't she and what effect does this have?

Thinking Critically

1. As a Chinese female raised by American parents and not knowing her biological mother, the author faces numerous problems in growing up. What kinds of problems do you think these were?
2. It seems to be especially important to the author that she be an excellent mother to her infant daughter. Why do you think this is?
3. What does the author mean at the end of the story when she writes to her daughter, "It doesn't matter what you 'become' later on. You have already fulfilled my wildest dreams"?
4. Suppose the author had given birth to a second son instead of a daughter. Do you think she would have written a letter? If so, how would it differ from the letter to Maya?

Writing About the Reading

A Journal Entry

Write a journal entry discussing your reactions to this letter. How did it make you feel? What questions did it raise?

A Paragraph

1. If you could see a videotape of one day of your childhood, what day would you choose? Write a paragraph explaining your choice.

2. If you could communicate briefly with only one deceased relative or friend, whom would you choose? Write a paragraph explaining your choice and what you would want to say.

An Essay

1. Write a letter to someone close to you explaining a difficult part of your childhood.
2. Suppose you have just learned that the parents who raised you were not your biological parents. Next week you will meet your biological parents. Write an essay identifying the three most important questions you want to ask them. Explain why each is important. If you are adopted, explain whether you know or want to know your birth parents.

A Creative Activity

Suppose Maya is now 15 years old and has decided to write a letter to her biological grandmother (Siu Wai's biological mother). What do you think she will say? Write the opening paragraph of the letter.

To Mr. Winslow

▶ **Ian Frazier**

The death of Mr. Winslow was a tragic event that affected the lives of many. This essay, first published in The New Yorker *magazine, describes how community members memorialized his death.*

Reading Strategy

This essay is a good example of the use of descriptive language. Frazier conveys his ideas by presenting numerous details that show you the scene of Mr. Winslow's death and help you to understand the community's response to it. As you read, highlight particularly striking and descriptive words and phrases that help capture the author's meaning.

Vocabulary Preview

cobbled (1) paved with rounded stones
discarded (2) thrown away
carafe (2) bottle
avenge (2) punish; take revenge for
accumulation (3) gathering of items
sprigs (3) twigs; small branches
converge (6) come together; meet

*O*n June 1st, in the afternoon, four teen-agers approached a forty-two-   1
year-old drama teacher named Allyn Winslow on Quaker Hill, in Brooklyn's Prospect Park, and tried to steal his new mountain bike. When he resisted and rode away, they shot him four times with a .22-calibre pistol. He rode down the hill to the cobbled path leading to the Picnic House, fell off his bike, and died. The TV news that evening showed the bike on the grass, and his body, covered by a sheet, next to it. I recognized the spot where he lay. I take my daughter to the pond nearby to throw bread to the ducks. She and I had sat there, or near there.

I walked by the spot the next day. It was marked by a wad of dis-   2
carded surgical tape and an inside-out surgical glove. The day after, when I went by there I saw a Timberland shoebox with a bouquet of flowers in it, and a glass wine carafe with more flowers. In the shoebox was a piece of lined paper on which someone had written in blue ink:

"To the biker Mr. Winslow, May you be in a better place with angels on a cloud." These words echoed in the media as reporters quoted and misquoted them. Men and women were carrying microphones and TV cameras in the vicinity, and if you weren't careful they would interview you. About a week later, an American flag had been stuck into the ground next to the shoebox. There was a bunch of papers in a clear-plastic envelope, and the one on top said, "AVENGE THIS ACT OF COWARDICE." In and around the shoebox were notes addressed to Mr. Winslow and his wife and their two children; a blue-and-white striped ribbon; a ceramic pipe; a bike rider's reflector badge in the image of a peace sign; a red-and-white bandanna; a flyer from the Guardian Angels organization; and an announcement of an upcoming service to be held in his memory.

The following week, the accumulation around the shoebox had   3
grown. The flowers in it and in the wine carafe were fresh—roses, peonies, yellow freesias. Someone had arranged many pinecones and sprigs of oak leaves in a circle on the perimeter. In the ground by the flag was a cross made of wood, bound with red ribbon and draped with a string of purple glass beads, and, near the cross, a photocopy of a newspaper photograph of Allyn Winslow. A Dover edition of Shakespeare's "Complete Sonnets" rested on a pedestal made of a cross-section of a branch from a London Plane tree. There were also several anti-N.R.A. stickers, a blue candle in a plastic cup, and a five of spades from a pack of Bicycle playing cards. Chunks of paving stones held down a poster showing the number of people killed in 1990 by handguns in various countries: thirteen in Sweden, ninety-one in Switzerland, eighty-seven in Japan, sixty-eight in Canada, ten thousand five hundred and sixty-seven in the United States. A girl visiting the park on a class picnic asked another girl, "Is he buried here?"

A week or two later, many of the items had vanished. Someone had   4
burned the flag, but the charred flagpole remained. The cross, broken off at the base, lay on the ground. The plastic cup with the candle was cracked. The grass around the spot was worn down in a circle and littered with dried flower stems. The carafe had a big chip out of the top. The shoebox had begun to sag. The papers were gone, except for a rain-stained sign saying, "To Honor, To Mourn Allyn Winslow," and a pamphlet, "Verses of Comfort, Assurance and Salvation."

By mid-July, the shoebox was in pieces. There were a few rocks,   5
two small forked branches stuck in the ground, the ashes of a small fire, and a "You gotta have Park!" button. By mid-August, the tramped-down grass had begun to grow back. I noticed a piece of red-and-white string and a scrap from the shoebox. By September, so little of the memorial remained that the spot was hard to find. A closer look revealed the burned patch, some red and white string now faded to pink,

and flower stems so scattered and broken you'd have to know what they were to recognize them.

Just now—a bright, chilly fall day—I went by the place again. Color in the park's trees had reached its peak. In a grove of buckskin-brown oaks, yellow shot up the fountain of a ginkgo tree. A flock of pigeons rose all at once and glided to a new part of the Long Meadow, circling once before landing, like a dog before it lies down. A police car slipped around the corner of the Picnic House, a one-man police scooter rode down the path, a police helicopter flew by just above the trees. At first, I could find no trace of the memorial at all: grass and clover have reclaimed the bared dirt. I got down on one knee, muddying my pants. Finally, I found a wooden stake broken off about half an inch above the ground; the base of the memorial cross, probably—the only sign of the unmeasured sorrows that converge here. 6

Examining the Reading

Finding Meaning

1. Why was the memorial site located in a park?
2. Give some examples of how other people who used the park expressed their feelings about Mr. Winslow's death.
3. Why did people choose items such as Shakespeare's "Complete Sonnets" and anti-N.R.A. stickers for the memorial?
4. How did the media handle the tragedy of Mr. Winslow's death?

Understanding Technique

1. Describe the essay's organization.
2. Evaluate the essay's title. What is Frazier's thesis? Is it stated or implied (suggested)?

Thinking Critically

1. What impact did this event seem to have on the community and on the author?
2. What is the main message that the author is trying to get across to the reader?
3. Judging from his tone, how do you think the author felt about the media? Why?
4. One of the papers in the clear-plastic envelope said, "Avenge this act of cowardice." What do you think the writer was suggesting?
5. Do you think Mr. Winslow's family was comforted by the memorial in the park? Why?

6. What conclusion(s) can you draw from the number of handgun deaths in the United States compared to the number in other countries? Why do we have so many handgun deaths?

Writing About the Reading

A Journal Entry

Write a journal entry about how you would like to be remembered after you die.

A Paragraph

1. Write a paragraph on how this type of event alters the lives of everyone involved.
2. Write a paragraph about how this tragedy might have been prevented.

An Essay

1. Imagine that you were one of Mr. Winslow's students. Write an essay discussing what you might say to his family to comfort them in their tragedy.
2. If someone you knew well died the way Mr. Winslow did, what would you do to honor him or her?

A Creative Activity

Suppose you were the person who wrote the message, "Avenge this act of cowardice" that was placed at Winslow's memorial. Continue this story by telling what you would do to avenge this killing and what would result from your actions.

Breaking Glass

▶ Jonathan Rosen

This essay, which was originally published in The New York Times Magazine *in 1996, explains what a Jewish wedding custom came to mean to the author. He also describes how his wedding anniversary has become linked with his father's past.*

Reading Strategy

The writer of this essay switches back and forth in time. After you read the essay, construct a time line, a list, or diagram of the events in the order in which they occurred.

Vocabulary Preview

pulverizing (2) crushing
symbolic (2) standing for or representing something else
euphoniously euphemistic (3) more pleasant sounding than
the truth
ran amok (3) savagely attacked everyone in their path
eerie (5) weird; strange
perverse (5) odd; offbeat
pogrom (6) organized violence against an identified group
obliterating (6) wiping out
commemoration (6) act of honoring the memory of an event
grandiose (8) extremely ambitious and impressive
naïve (8) simple-minded

*T*he morning of my wedding, my father gave me a piece of unexpected   1
advice. "When you step on the glass," he said, "why don't you imagine
that all the doubts and fears of childhood are inside and that you're
smashing them too?"

He was referring to one of the more mysterious customs at a Jew-   2
ish wedding, in which the bridegroom stamps on a glass, marking the
end of the ceremony. I liked my father's suggestion, though I was so
afraid that the wineglass, wrapped in a white handkerchief, would
shoot out unbroken (as I had once seen happen) that I forgot everything in my pulverizing zeal. But I was touched by his words, particularly because breaking the glass had already assumed a symbolic place

in my mind—though one connected not to my own childhood but to his.

I was married on November 10, the anniversary of Kristallnacht. 3 The German name, which means "the night of broken glass," is too euphoniously euphemistic to describe accurately what really happened in 1938, beginning on the night of November 9 and running into the next day. Mobs, urged on by the Nazi Government, ran amok throughout Germany and Austria, murdering, looting, smashing Jewish shop windows and burning synagogues. Thirty thousand Jews were arrested—including my grandfather, my father's father.

My father was 14, and Kristallnacht shattered his world. One 4 month later he left Vienna on a children's transport, finding refuge first in Scotland and later in the United States. He never saw his parents again. Strange then, that I chose the anniversary of this terrible day for my wedding five years ago.

I cannot claim this was strictly by design. I'd wanted to get married 5 in winter and my wife-to-be had inched the date forward until we settled on November 10. It was my father who pointed out the eerie accident. He did not ask me to change the date, but we easily could have. We had planned a small wedding in my parents' house. But after initial discomfort the coincidence had a distinct, if perverse, appeal.

More than 50 years had passed since the pogrom of 1938. The 6 world could not be counted on to remember forever—hadn't I myself forgotten the date? Here was a way to graft my father's story onto my own. Soon the year 2000, with its obliterating zeros, would roll the terrible events of the twentieth century deeper into the past. My wedding would at least guarantee a kind of private commemoration. I would lash a piece of history to my back and carry it with me into the future.

But by mingling Kristallnacht with my own wedding, was I pre- 7 serving it or erasing it further? Perhaps I did not wish to mark the date so much as unmark it—a typical childhood fantasy. I wanted to make whole my father's broken past, to offer up my own wedding as the joyful answer to tragic times.

Both impulses, of course, are equally grandiose and impossibly 8 naïve. My own life can never contain or summarize the suffering of earlier generations, any more than it can answer or redeem those losses. My father understood this when he spoke to me on the morning of my wedding. For all he knew of the world, he could still have for me a father's wish—that I would banish the fears of childhood, even though the fears of *his* childhood were fully founded in real events. Every generation is born innocent, and if that is bad for history, it is nevertheless necessary for life.

And yet how can I stop trying to connect myself in some way to the 9 past? Which brings me back to my wedding and the ritual of the broken glass, which forms the final moment of the traditional Jewish ceremony. There are several explanations for this practice. The one I like is that it is a reminder of the destruction of the temple in Jerusalem—an event that happened some 1,900 years ago—and in a larger sense, a reminder that the world itself is broken and imperfect. Smashing the glass recalls this fact and introduces a fleeting note of sadness into an otherwise festive occasion.

It is in this spirit that I celebrate my wedding anniversary today. I think about my grandparents who were murdered and their son—my father—who escaped to America and married my mother. I think about my own lucky American life and joyful marriage and how little, and how much, separates the past from the present, sorrow from celebration. I hear my father's kind advice, the cheerful cries of friends and family and the distant echo of breaking glass.

Examining the Reading

Finding Meaning

1. What happened in Germany and Austria, on November 9–10, 1938?
2. What happened to Jonathan Rosen's father and grandparents after Kristallnacht?
3. Why does the bridegroom break a glass at traditional Jewish weddings?
4. What did the author's father want him to think about when he broke the glass?
5. Why didn't the author change his wedding date?

Understanding Technique

1. Discuss the effect of using dialogue to open this essay.
2. Evaluate how Rosen's use of questions helps to develop the essay.

Thinking Critically

1. Why did the author want to remember such a sad event at a happy occasion?
2. What are the different meanings of "breaking glass" in this essay?
3. What does the author think will happen to memories of twentieth-century events, after the year 2000, "with its obliterating zeros"?
4. What does the author mean by "every generation is born innocent, and if that is bad for history, it is nevertheless necessary for life"?

Writing About the Reading

A Journal Entry

Write a journal entry about an event in your life or your family's history that you would like people to remember.

A Paragraph

1. If you were the author, would you have chosen a different wedding date? Why or why not?
2. Why is it important for people to remember what happened during the Holocaust?

An Essay

1. Write an essay about how your childhood was different from your parents'. In what ways do you think yours was better; in what ways was theirs better?
2. Write an essay about some of your family's traditions and what they mean to you.

A Creative Activity

What do you think the author will tell his children about their grandparents' and great-grandparents' experiences?

Blind to Faith

▶ Karl Taro Greenfeld

Erik Weihenmayer, blind since age thirteen, climbed to the summit of Mount Everest—a feat most sighted people can't ever hope to undertake. His amazing story first appeared in Time *magazine in 2001.*

Reading Strategy

As you read, highlight the many dangers faced by the climbers.

Vocabulary Preview

misgivings (1) doubts; feelings of uncertainty
crevasse (1) deep crack in the ice
hereditary (3) passed down genetically
banal (3) commonplace
deprivation (3) not having enough; being denied something
diabolically (6) devilishly; with evil
treacherously (6) dangerously
seracs (6) large chunks of ice broken off from a glacier
nubbins (8) small pieces
insurmountable (9) impossible to conquer or overcome
rapport (9) relationship
preserve (14) something restricted to one group
slog (16) an exhausting hike
shale (17) fine, crumbly rock
contemporary (21) modern day
jubilant (22) very happy

When he saw Erik Weihenmayer arrive that afternoon, Pasquale 1
Scaturrro began to have misgivings about the expedition he was leading. Here they were on the first floor of Mount Everest, and Erik—the reason for the whole trip—was stumbling into Camp 1 bloody, sick and dehydrated. "He was literally green," says fellow climber and teammate Michael O'Donnell. "He looked like George Foreman had beat the crap out of him for two hours." The beating had actually been administered by Erik's climbing partner, Luis Benitez. Erik had slipped into a crevasse, and as Benitez reached down to catch him, his climbing pole raked Erik across the nose and chin. Wounds heal slowly at that altitude because of the thin air.

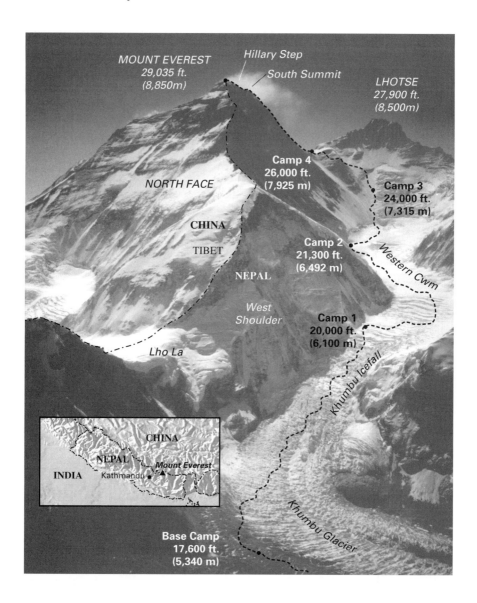

MOUNT EVEREST
29,035 ft.
(8,850m)

Hillary Step

South Summit

LHOTSE
27,900 ft.
(8,500m)

Camp 4
26,000 ft.
(7,925 m)

NORTH FACE

Camp 3
24,000 ft.
(7,315 m)

CHINA

TIBET

Camp 2
21,300 ft.
(6,492 m)

NEPAL

Western Cwm

West Shoulder

Camp 1
20,000 ft.
(6,100 m)

Lho La

Khumbu Icefall

CHINA

NEPAL

Mount Everest

INDIA Kathmandu

Base Camp
17,600 ft.
(5,340 m)

Khumbu Glacier

As Erik passed out in his tent, the rest of the team gathered in a   2
worried huddle. "I was thinking maybe this is not a good idea," says
Scaturro. "Two years of planning, a documentary movie, and this blind
guy barely makes it to Camp 1?"

This blind guy. Erik Weihenmayer, 33, wasn't just another yuppie   3
trekker who'd lost a few rounds to the mountain. Blind since he was
13, the victim of a rare hereditary disease of the retina, he began attacking mountains in his early 20s. But he had been having the same

doubts as the rest of the team. On that arduous climb to camp through the Khumbu Icefall, Erik wondered for the first time if his attempt to become the first sightless person to summit Mount Everest was a colossal mistake, an act of Daedalian hubris[1] for which he would be punished. There are so many ways to die on that mountain, spanning the spectacular (fall through an ice shelf into a crevasse, get waylaid by an avalanche, develop cerebral edema from lack of oxygen and have your brain literally swell out of your skull) and the banal (become disoriented because of oxygen deprivation and decide you'll take a little nap, right here, in the snow, which becomes a forever nap).

Erik, as he stumbled through the icefall, was so far out of his comfort zone that he began to speculate on which of those fates might await him. For a moment he flashed on all those clichés about what blind people are supposed to do—become piano tuners or pencil salesmen— and thought maybe they were stereotypes for good reason. Blind people certainly shouldn't be out here, wandering through an ever changing ice field, measuring the distance over a 1,000-ft.-deep crevasse with climbing poles and then leaping, literally, over and into the unknown.   4

The blind thrive on patterns: stairs are all the same height, city blocks roughly the same length, curbs approximately the same depth. They learn to identify the patterns in their environment much more than the sighted population do, and to rely on them to plot their way through the world.   5

But in the Khumbu Icefall, the trail through the Himalayan glacier is patternless, a diabolically cruel obstacle course for a blind person. It changes every year as the river of ice shifts, but it's always made up of treacherously crumbly stretches of ice, ladders roped together over wide crevasses, slightly narrower crevasses that must be jumped, huge seracs, avalanches and—most frustrating for a blind person, who naturally seeks to identify patterns in his terrain—a totally random icescape.   6

In the icefall there is no system, no repetition, no rhyme or reason to the lay of the frozen land. On the other hand, "it is so specific in terms of where you can step," Erik recalls. "Sometimes you're walking along and then boom, a crevasse is right there, and three more steps and another one, and then a snow bridge. And vertical up, then a ladder and then a jumbly section." It took Erik 13 hrs. to make it from Base Camp through the icefall to Camp 1, at 20,000 ft. Scaturro had allotted seven. . . .   7

Watching Erik scramble up a rock face is a little like watching a spider make its way up a wall. His hands are like antennae, gathering information as they flick outward, surveying the rock for cracks, grooves, bowls, nubbins, knobs, edges, and ledges, converting all of it into a road map etched into his mind. "It's like instead of wrestling   8

---

[1]Excessive pride. Daedalus was the father of Icarus, in Greek mythology. Icarus made wings but flew too close to the sun, fell into the sea, and drowned.

*One False Step . . . Weihenmayer moves
across a ladder bridge over one of the
mountain's many crevasses.*

with a person, I am moving and working with a rock," he explains. "It's
a beautiful process of solving a puzzle." He is an accomplished rock
climber, rated 5.10 (5.14 being the highest), and has led teams up sections of Yosemite's notorious El Capitan. On ice, where one wrong
strike with an ice ax can bring down an avalanche, Erik has learned to
listen to the ice as he pings it gently with his ax. If it clinks, he avoids
it. If it makes a thunk like a spoon hitting butter, he knows it's solid ice.

Despite being an accomplished mountaineer—summiting Denali,[2]   9
Kilimanjaro in Africa and Aconcagua in Argentina, among other
peaks, and, in the words of his friends, "running up 14ers" (14,000-
ft.—peaks)—Erik viewed Everest as insurmountable until he ran into
Scaturro at a sportswear trade show in Salt Lake City, Utah. Scaturro,
who had already summited Everest, had heard of the blind climber,
and when they met the two struck an easy rapport. A geophysicist who
often put together energy-company expeditions to remote areas in

---

[2]Native American name for Mount McKinley in Alaska.

search of petroleum, Scaturro began wondering if he could put together a team that could help Erik get to the summit of Everest.

"Dude," Scaturro asked, "have you ever climbed Everest?"   10

"No."   11

"Dude, you wanna?"   12

Climbing with Erik isn't that different from climbing with a   13
sighted mountaineer. You wear a bell on your pack, and he follows the
sound, scuttling along using his custom-made climbing poles to feel
his way along the trail. His climbing partners shout out helpful descriptions: "Death fall 2 ft. to your right!" "Emergency helicopter-evacuation
pad to your left!" He is fast, often running up the back of less experienced climbers. His partners all have scars from being jabbed by Erik's
climbing poles when they slowed down.

For the Everest climb, Scaturro and Erik assembled a team that   14
combined veteran Everest climbers and trusted friends of Erik's.
Scaturro wrote up a Braille proposal for the Everest attempt and sub-
mitted it to Marc Maurer, president of the National Federation of the
Blind [N.F.B.]. Maurer immediately pledged $250,000 to sponsor the
climb. (Aventis Pharmaceuticals agreed to sponsor a documentary on
the climb to promote Allegra, its allergy medication; Erik suffers from
seasonal allergies.) For Erik, who already had numerous gear and
clothing sponsors, this was the greatest challenge of his life. If he
failed, he would be letting down not just himself but all the blind, con-
firming that certain activities remained the preserve of the sighted. . . .

When Erik and the team began the final ascent from Camp 4—the   15
camp he describes as Dante's Inferno[3] with ice and wind—they had
been on the mountain for two months, climbing up and down and then
up from Base Camp to Camps 1, 2, and 3, getting used to the altitude
and socking away enough equipment—especially oxygen canisters—to
make a summit push. They had tried for the summit once but had
turned back because of weather. At 29,000 ft., the Everest peak is in the
jet stream,[4] which means that winds can exceed 100 m.p.h. and that
what looks from sea level like a cottony wisp of cloud is actually a killer
storm at the summit. Bad weather played a fatal role in the 1966
climbing season documented in *Into Thin Air*.[5]

On May 24, with only seven days left in the climbing season, most of   16
the N.F.B. expedition members knew this was their last shot at the peak.
That's why when Erik and Chris Morris reached the Balcony, the beginning of the Southeast Ridge, at 27,500 ft., after a hard slog up the South
Face, they were terribly disappointed when the sky lit up with lightning,

---

[3]Hell.

[4]High-speed wind high up in the atmosphere.

[5]An account of a disastrous climb up Mount Everest in May 1996 that resulted in
five deaths.

driving snow, and fierce winds. "We thought we were done," Erik says. "We would have been spanked if we made a push in those conditions." A few teammates gambled and went for it, and Jeff Evans and Brad Bull heroically pulled out fixed guidelines that had been frozen in the ice. By the time Base Camp radioed that the storm was passing, Erik and the entire team were coated in 2 in. of snow. Inspired by the possibility of a break in the weather, the team pushed on up the exposed Southeast Ridge, an additional 1,200 vertical feet to the South Summit. At that point the climbers looked like astronauts walking on some kind of Arctic moon. They moved slowly because of fatigue from their huge, puffy down suits, backpacks with oxygen canisters and regulators and goggles.

With a 10,000-ft. vertical fall into Tibet on one side and a 7,000-ft.   17
fall into Nepal on the other, the South Summit, at 28,750 ft., is where many climbers finally turn back. The 656-ft.-long knife-edge ridge leading to the Hillary Step consists of ice, snow, and fragmented shale, and the only way to cross it is to take baby steps and anchor your way with an ice ax. "You can feel the rock chip off," says Erik. "And you can hear it falling down into the void."

The weather was finally clearing as they reached the Hillary Step,   18
the 39-ft. rock face that is the last major obstacle before the true summit. Erik clambered up the cliff, belly flopping over the top. "I celebrated with the dry heaves," he jokes. And then it was 45 minutes of walking up a sharply angled snow slope to the summit.

"Look around, dude," Evans told the blind man when they were   19
standing on top of the world. "Just take a second and look around."

It could be called the most successful Everest expedition ever, and   20
not just because of Erik's participation. A record 19 climbers from the N.F.B. team summited, including the oldest man ever to climb Everest—64-year-old Sherman Bull—and the second father-and-son team ever to do so—Bull and his son Brad.

What Erik achieved is hard for a sighted person to comprehend.   21
What do we compare it with? How do we relate to it? Do we put on a blindfold and go hiking? That's silly, Erik maintains, because when a sighted person loses his vision, he is terrified and disoriented. And Erik is clearly neither of those things. Perhaps the point is really that there is no way to put what Erik has done in perspective because no one has ever done anything like it. It is a unique achievement, one that in the truest sense pushes the limits of what man is capable of. Maurer of the N.F.B. compares Erik to Helen Keller.[6] "Erik can be a contemporary symbol for blindness," he explains. "Helen Keller lived 100 years ago. She should not be our most potent symbol for blindness today."

---

[6]Helen Keller, blind and deaf since infancy, learned to read and write. She became an advocate for sightless people.

Erik, sitting in the Kathmandu international airport, waiting for the   22
flight out of Nepal that will eventually return him to Golden, Colo., is sur-
rounded by his teammates and the expedition's 75 pieces of luggage. Success has made the group jubilant. This airport lounge has become the
mountaineering equivalent of a winning Super Bowl locker room. As
they sit amid their luggage, holding Carlsberg beers, they frequently raise
a toast. *"Shez! Shez!"* shouts a climber. That's Nepali for drink! drink! "No
epics," a climber chimes in, citing what really matters: no one died.

In between posing for photos and signing other passengers' board-   23
ing passes, Erik talks about how eager he is to get back home. He says
summiting Everest was great, probably the greatest experience of his
life. But then he thinks about a moment a few months ago, before
Everest, when he was walking down the street in Colorado with daughter Emma in a front pack. They were on their way to buy some banana
bread for his wife, and Emma was pulling on his hand, her little fingers
curled around his index finger. That was a summit too, he says. There
are summits everywhere. You just have to know where to look.

Examining the Reading

Finding Meaning

1. Why did Scaturro have misgivings at the beginning of the expedition?
2. How did Erik lose his sight?
3. Name some ways climbers are injured or die on Mount Everest.
4. What problems did Erik encounter in the Khumbu Icefall?
5. What special gear does Erik use when climbing?
6. How did Scaturro and Erik raise the money for the climb?
7. What kinds of weather may prevent climbers from reaching the
   summit?
8. Why do some climbers turn back after they reach the South Summit?

Understanding Technique

1. The opening paragraphs do not paint a positive picture of Erik.
   Why does the author begin the article this way?
2. The author is writing about a remarkable event. How does he convey the greatness of Erik Weihenmayer's climb?
3. Examine the last paragraph. What is its purpose?

Thinking Critically

1. Who are the "yuppie trekkers" mentioned by the author?
2. Why would blind people be thought of as piano tuners and pencil
   salesmen?
3. Why is Erik like a spider when he climbs?

4. Erik thought of Everest as insurmountable. What changed his mind?
5. Do you agree that Erik would have let down all the blind if he had failed to reach the summit? Explain your answer.
6. What did Evans mean when he told the blind climber to look around at the summit?
7. Why can't we comprehend Erik's accomplishment?
8. Why does the blind community need a symbol other than Helen Keller? Can Erik be that symbol?
9. Explain the phrase, "there are summits everywhere."

Writing About the Reading

A Journal Entry

Write a journal entry about a time when you achieved a difficult or challenging goal.

A Paragraph

1. Write a definition of a hero. Then write a paragraph evaluating whether Erik fits your definition of a hero.
2. Mountain climbing is a challenging activity. Write a paragraph about a difficult pursuit or challenging activity you have undertaken.
3. The climbers worked together as a team. Write a paragraph describing the most important aspect of teamwork.

An Essay

1. Erik and his team succeeded in their climb, but many climbers do not, often at great risk and expense to their rescuers. Write an essay exploring the issue of whether limitations, qualifications, restrictions, or bans are appropriate in high-risk sports.
2. At the end of the article, the author states, "There are summits everywhere. You just have to know where to look." Write an essay defining *summits* and discuss where you personally look for them.
3. Write an essay giving reasons why people engage in high-risk sports.

A Creative Activity

Imagine that you lost your sight. How would you have to change your daily routine? Another suggestion for this activity is to pick a sport at which you would like to excel. What sport would you pick and why?

Desert Storm and Shield

▶ **Scott Stopa**
Student Essay

Scott Stopa, a college student, wrote this essay explaining how a phone call from his platoon sergeant changed his life. His essay describes how his experiences in the Persian Gulf became a turning point in his life.

*T*here are many events that have been major turning points in my life. Some of these are my marriage, the birth of my children, my divorce, going back to school, and joining the Marine Corps. The biggest turning point in my life, however, was going off to war in the Persian Gulf (Operations Desert Shield and Desert Storm). It was November 1990 when the 8th Tank Battalion, of which I was a part, was activated. I was 20 years old and just out of boot camp. I had only been home for two weeks when we were sent overseas.

When Iraq invaded Kuwait, there was a lot of talk of the United States going to war, but of course I never thought in a million years that I would be sent off to war. I thought, no, I'd never be sent. After all, I'm only in the reserves. Boy, was I wrong. The news came by phone. I was living at my parents' house at the time. My mother answered the phone. It was my platoon sergeant. When my mother handed me the phone, I could see the tears in her eyes. Then he gave me the news. My heart dropped. I was speechless when I got off the phone. All I could do when I looked at my mother was tell her I'm sorry.

I remember that night like it was yesterday. I got in my car and drove, with nowhere special in mind. I ended up down by the falls, where I walked around and did a lot of thinking. What would we be in for, and how would I react if certain situations arose? At that point I made up my mind that no matter what, I was coming home. I was scared, and if anybody says they weren't, they're lying. This was going to be life as I never knew it, and it was.

Other than the ground war, the first month was probably the most difficult. A lot of thinking about home and being there for Christmas didn't make matters any better. After a while I got used to it. A situation like that makes you grow up quickly and appreciate the basic things in life, like running water, hot showers, hot meals, a bed—just things like that. You don't realize how much you take these things for granted until you're forced to be without them. I can remember countless nights of walking guard duty in the pouring rain, being soaked all day, going to sleep wet and freezing, and being totally miserable because of these discomforts. But now I realize that it has made me a very strong person.

The night before the ground war started, our company was briefed   5
on what was expected and what exactly our mission was after we breached the minefield and got into Kuwait. During the briefing, they told us we were expected to take at least 70 percent casualties. You could have heard a pin drop. We knew it wasn't going to be easy because we were a tank battalion and we'd be right on the front line with the tanks. If ever at one instant I felt like I "grew up overnight," that was it, definitely.

The morning came, and we went in. We took incoming fire going   6
through the minefield. Fortunately, we made it through. The ground war only lasted three days, but it was the most intense three days of my life. Explosions, blown-up tanks and vehicles everywhere, fires, lots of smoke, planes and helicopters flying overhead—it was like a movie. But it was reality, definitely reality, and when I encountered sights of death, more and more I realized this is war. I guess you could say reality set in. Seeing things like that really makes you cherish your life a little more. Unfortunately, I lost a very good friend over there, but his memory will never be forgotten—Thomas Scholand, from Semper, Florida.

Although these experiences may all seem bad, nothing can ever   7
take away the feeling of pride, rolling through Kuwait City and seeing people lining the streets waving and calling out in appreciation of the fact that we had just liberated their country. Seeing the faces of the men, women, and especially the children was a feeling that no words can explain.

In summary, of all the events that unfolded for me as well as for   8
others who served in Operations Desert Shield and Desert Storm, this was a major turning point in my life. I learned a lot about myself and life in general. I now look at things in a positive perspective. I've grown up a lot overseas, and now I take nothing for granted anymore. Life's short; appreciate all it has to offer, and live it to the fullest. I will!

Examining the Essay

1. Evaluate Stopa's thesis statement.
2. Stopa uses details to make his experiences seem real and vivid. In which parts of the essay was his use of detail particularly effective?

Writing an Essay

1. Write an essay describing your response to receiving surprising or important news. Describe how you reacted and how the news affected you.
2. Stopa says he felt as if he grew up overnight. Write an essay discussing a situation in which you were forced to grow up or accept responsibility. Explain how the situation affected you.
3. Stopa's experiences made him value his life and appreciate basic things in life. Write an essay recounting an experience that helped you see life in a new or different way.

Making Connections ───────────

1. Salinas's "The Scholarship Jacket" and White's "Ragtime, My Time" both deal with racism. Compare the experiences, reactions, and lasting effects described in these readings.

2. Compare the once-in-a-lifetime experiences from Greenfeld's "Blind to Faith" and Stopa's "Desert Storm and Shield."

Internet Connections ───────────

1. The American Civil Liberties Union has launched a campaign to end racial profiling. Read about highlights of this campaign at **http://www.aclu.org/profiling/highlight.html**. Write a summary of their activities. Do you think their actions will be effective? Why or why not?

2. Speeches at ceremonies often mark important events in our lives. Visit the following sites, which give advice about and examples of speeches for special occasions:

   http://www.foreverwed.com/speeches/examples.htm

   http://www.toastmasters.org/tips.htm

   http://www.uiowa.edu/~c100298/anxiety.html

   Write a paragraph discussing whether the quality of a speech can affect your attitude toward and perception of an event. Use examples from the web sites you just visited and from your own experience.

3. Every year around December 31, we look back at the major events of that year. When the calendar moved from

1999 to 2000, we looked back on a whole millennium. Go to **http://www.infoplease.com/millennium1.html#century** and examine the information there. Try a quiz or look over a few of the lists. Write an essay examining the ways in which one of the events listed at this web site affected your life.

(If any of these web sites are unavailable, use a search engine to locate another appropriate site.)

Chapter 3

Work That Shapes Our Lives

Mr. Mom's World
David Case

Working Students Need to Look
for Career Experience
Sabra Chartrand

The Family Farm
David Mas Masumoto

Disney's Head Trips
Jane Keunz

Mojado Like Me
Joseph Tovares

What Are They Probing For?
Barbara Ehrenreich

A Seafood Survey
Robert Wood

Work is a complex, important part of our lives. Jobs, of course, provide needed income to purchase life's necessities. Some jobs offer an outlet for creative expression or help develop skills such as problem-solving. Other jobs can simply be repetitive and dull. Even those jobs, however, can be a source of personal satisfaction, a means of demonstrating that we are competent, self-sufficient individuals. By contrast, work can also make leisure time valuable and meaningful. Work can open new doors, as well as lead to new friends, new experiences, and new realizations.

The readings in this chapter provide several different perspectives on work and the workplace. You will read about a new trend among families with young children—stay-at-home fathers ("Mr. Mom's World"). You will also discover how to use part-time jobs to prepare yourself for your career ("Working Students Need to Look for Career Experience"). Two readings demonstrate the meaning of work experiences and how they affected the lives of the authors ("The Family Farm" and "*Mojado* Like Me"). The issue of pre-employment drug and personality testing is addressed by a well-known journalist who posed as an applicant for low-paying jobs ("What Are They Probing For?"). A student offers a humorous perspective on his part-time job at a fish market ("A Seafood Survey").

Brainstorming About Work

Class Activity: Working in groups of three or four students, discuss and attempt to define the ideal or perfect job. Identify its characteristics and try to think of examples. Also try to take into account individual differences. Why may a job be ideal for one person and unappealing to another?

Mr. Mom's World

▶ David Case

More and more fathers are staying home to raise their children while mothers work. This article, which first appeared in an online magazine called Salon **(www.salon.com),** *profiles several of these families.*

Reading Strategy

Many details, including names, ages, and occupations, of several different families are included in this article. As you read, focus on the issues and trends these families illustrate.

Vocabulary Preview

scenario (1) string of events
progressive (1) forward thinking; broad-minded; interested in new ideas
conjure (2) call to mind
regime (2) system or pattern
vulnerability (4) exposure; open to attack
transpired (5) happen; occur
progeny (8) children
deft (12) skilled at; clever at
stigma (12) shame
pundits (14) teachers; authorities
vociferous (14) loud and noisy
oratory (14) speech; public speaking
parity (16) equality
kudos (16) praise

When we imagine what it takes to raise a happy, healthy child, most   1
of us picture fresh air, a green yard with a blow-up wading pool, and maybe even a golden retriever standing guard. Most important, we imagine a nurturing, attentive caregiver willing to dedicate endless days to encouragement, discipline, and guidance. In this perfect parenting scenario, most of us probably visualize ideal moms like Carol Brady or June Cleaver, no matter how progressive we may be.

Most of us probably wouldn't conjure up someone like my old   2
friend Tal Birdsey. Here's a guy who, when we met during college, could

go for months without washing his hair, a guy who bragged about laundering his sheets only once a semester. The closest he came to taking care of another human was nurturing his gut, a jiggly beast widely known as Joe, which he kept healthy on a strict regime of barley and hops. And now he's molding in his image not one, but two tiny lives? Simultaneously? With no help?

"It's like this," he says. "When I was first taking care of the kids, my   3
wife Blair had to come home every three hours to breast-feed the baby. One day she's real late. The baby starts wailing hysterically—I worry he's gonna drop. So I fix him a bottle, which he's never had before. I'm trying to convince him the plastic nipple works just as well as his mom's, then nature calls—urgently. I don't know, maybe the stress loosened my bowels.

"Next thing, I'm sitting on the loo, cradling the baby, balancing his   4
bottle under my chin. After a few moments repose, 'brrrrrrnng, brrrrrrnng.' It must be Blair calling from a pay phone. I've got to get it before the voice mail picks up. So with my trousers around my ankles, the baby in my arms, I scurry, bent at the waist, across the living room. I pick it up—a man's voice. The bank calling about our mortgage application. From behind, the 3-year-old senses my momentary vulnerability, and attacks. Giggling like a madman, he starts spanking me. Funniest thing he's ever seen—his daddy bare-assed in the living room cradling the baby and talking on the phone."

This certainly isn't a scene that could have transpired under my   5
mother's roost. But a growing number of men in their 30s find themselves at home full time, changing diapers, hunting down lost socks, playing daddy rides the hay wagon. . . .

"When I was a child," remembers Tom Funk, 33, who shares the   6
parenting and income-generating more or less equally with his wife, Liz, "I remember a neighbor's father, during a rare bout with solo parenting, being confronted with a dangerously dirty diaper. He packed the crying child in the back of the car and drove 45 minutes to find a woman who could change it for him. That doesn't cut it anymore."

Well, men, we've got something to thump our chests about. More   7
and more of us are pulling our weight at home. In the late '90s, men in dual-earner couples take on 60 percent more child care than did our fathers. And we do an impressive 2.5 times more housework, according to Scott Coltrane, a professor of sociology at the University of California at Riverside and author of the book *Family Man: Brotherhood, Housework and Gender Equity.* Sadly, that brings us to a mere 28 percent of the housework and 33 percent of child care. The emerging class of stay-at-home dads, or SAHDs, are no doubt helping our stats.

So who are these domesticated dads, and what are they thinking?   8
Some are the disillusioned progeny of workaholic fathers—stockbro-

kers, lawyers, and executives—sons who seek a closer bond with their kin. For others, office politics out-repulse even the most colicky child. "This is a lot better than most of the jobs I could get," points out Yale Lewis, a journalist and, for now, stay-at-home dad. Many, like Lewis and Birdsey, have advanced degrees, though these days they're more apt to cite "Mike Mulligan and the Steam Shovel" than Milton. Along with their wives, SAHDs feel strongly that even the best day care can't replace an attentive parent. When both Birdseys were working, Tal says, "The only time I ever felt comfortable, the only time I stopped thinking about the baby was when he was napping. Then I knew he was all right."

The SAHDs may be the first significant group of men with little lin- 9
gering notion of male superiority. While they may remain haunted by societal biases, some readily admit that their wives are more clever, more energetic, and better able to cope in society—or at least that they had played their cards more effectively.

Andrew Stockwood has great admiration for his partner, Shirley 10
Netten, a lawyer and political advisor. "Shirley has the education, ex- perience, and talent to make lots of money," says Stockwood, who re- cently passed up a job as a roving photojournalist in the South Pacific. Having relished two years with his first child, he prefers to stay home in anticipation of "oogling" his soon-to-arrive second. "I love the fact that this lets us live an alternative lifestyle and still be very comfort- able. Her skills are extremely valuable and sought after. Succeeding as a professional still feels like a triumph for women," Stockwood muses. "I was always expected to be a successful professional, so that route seemed boring and constraining to me. And given the choice, I would rather bake the bread than buy the flour." . . .

For the time being, some SAHDs say they feel isolated. Away from 11
the workaday adult world, they're often alone in their convictions, and are outcasts among the generally more traditional moms they see dur- ing the day. "Yesterday at the playground there was a little boy who got along so well with Emily," says Andy Murray, referring to his 2-year-old, an adorable firecracker with an Einsteinian flop of white hair. "I wanted the kids to get together again, but there's this whole thing about me, a man alone with a child, giving out my phone number to a woman."

The flip side is the sandbox-as-pickup joint, a throwback to the 12
parents' own schoolyard days. Some moms admit to going gooey at the site of a man with a stroller, a male counterpart deft at caring for a child in a way that perhaps their spouses aren't. The dads, however, contend that they're family types, and are not apt to notice this femi- nine yearning. Instead, they're preoccupied with the "Mr. Mom" stigma—the hairy eyeball from older relatives and neighbors who still believe that it takes three men to handle a baby.

"You should see the stares I get at the playground," says Walter   13
Garschagen, a photographer whose wife is an actress. "It's like, Why
isn't he working, and why does he make his wife toil 80 hours a week
to support him? I love taking care of Emma (another 2-year-old), but
I'd feel better about myself if I were out moving rocks. At least I'd be
sweating." . . .

While relatively little research has been done on the impact of   14
father-reared families, so far the pundits say that generally, everyone
wins. When men participate in routine child care, women enjoy a higher
public status and share political authority with men, says UC-Riverside
professor Coltrane. "Men who do more parenting report they are more
in touch with their emotions, are more compassionate, and can relate
better to their wives. [They] are unlikely to celebrate their manhood
through combative contests, vociferous oratory, and violent rituals."

And growing up with dad around benefits kids in unique ways.   15
"Compared to mothers, men spend more of their child-care time in
games or rough-and-tumble play. We know the children learn important skills in this kind of interaction, such as how to regulate their
emotions," says Coltrane. Joseph Pleck of the University of Illinois
adds, "Children with involved fathers tend to do better socially and
academically, they generally have better self-control, confidence, and
self-esteem and they avoid gender stereotyping." . . .

But don't let all this mushy man-speak fool you into believing that   16
America is finally achieving domestic parity. Women, it seems, are still
routinely overburdened. While the SAHDs deserve kudos for their efforts, even they tend to kick back when mom gets home. Whether it's
guilt or higher standards that drive them, even some women who are
the sole wage earners put in an extra effort at home. As Birdsey's wife,
Blair, an ad copywriter, puts it, "Tal is a typical guy. He's never cleaned
the toilet, he doesn't even notice the hair balls gathering dust on the
staircase, or the musty towels in a ball on the bathroom floor. I still
have to do all the housework and cook." But, she adds, "I guess it's fair,
because I like to do it."

Funk admits late one evening while his wife washes the dishes, "I'd   17
like to think that we do half and half, but in reality it's probably more
like 30–70." Men, he says, justify this by comparing themselves to
other men who do even less. Like most guys, Funk finds child care
much harder than office work. "On the days when I have the baby,
we're more apt to just get a pizza for dinner."

Women, he concedes, are just more capable of working long hours.   18

Examining the Reading

Finding Meaning

1. Summarize the ideal parenting situation that the author describes in paragraph 1.
2. What was the author's old friend, Tal Birdsey, like in college? What is he like now?
3. Why did the author include the funny experience Birdsey had one day while watching his children?
4. According to Scott Coltrane's figures, what percentage of men are helping with housework and child care? How much higher is this percentage compared to that of their fathers' generation?
5. List some of the reasons men become stay-at-home dads.
6. Why do some SAHDs feel isolated?
7. Who makes the SAHDs feel like outcasts?
8. What are the benefits of a father-reared family?
9. How do many SAHDs act when their wives come home from work?

Understanding Technique

1. The author profiles several different families. How do these personal accounts add to Case's article? Would the article be effective if he had interviewed only one family in depth?
2. How does Case use humor in this story? What does humor contribute to the article?
3. How does the author show the positive and negative aspects of an SAHD's life?

Thinking Critically

1. Why is it not progressive to think of television moms as ideal parents?
2. Why didn't the author think that Tal Birdsey could be a good parent?
3. Tom Funk's neighbor drove a long way to get his child's diaper changed. Why doesn't this "cut it anymore"? What has changed?
4. Why would the son of a workaholic father feel the need to stay at home with his own children?
5. Why does Andrew Stockton consider his family to be living an "alternative lifestyle"?
6. Why does Andy Murray feel he cannot give his phone number to women at the playground?
7. Why does Walter Garschagen say that he would feel better about himself if he were "out moving rocks"?

8. Why do you think children whose fathers spend more time with them do better in school?

Writing About the Reading

A Journal Entry

Write a journal entry about a funny experience you had as a child, as a parent, or as a caregiver.

A Paragraph

1. Write a paragraph about the most important quality a mother or father should possess.
2. Write a paragraph describing a time when you took on someone else's responsibilities. What were the outcomes?
3. Housework never ends. Write a paragraph about how you either accomplish or avoid household chores.

An Essay

1. Write an essay describing the ways in which men and women are still not equal in the workplace.
2. Mothers and fathers often differ in their approaches to raising children. Write an essay comparing and contrasting male and female childrearing practices that you have observed or experienced.
3. Not all families have mothers and fathers. Write an essay about a nontraditional family that you have observed or experienced and describe its effect on the children.

A Creative Activity

If you could reverse roles with someone for a day, who would it be and why?

Working Students Need to Look for Career Experience

▸ **Sabra Chartrand**

The following article examines the benefits of a part-time job for college students and offers suggestions on how to find one. It appeared in a weekly column titled "Careers" found on the Job Market *page of* The New York Times *web site.*

Reading Strategy

Before you read, divide your paper in two columns. Label one "Benefits of Part-Time Jobs"; label the other "How to Find Part-Time Jobs." Fill in both columns during or after reading.

Vocabulary Preview

internships (3) temporary jobs that can provide career experience, money, and college credit
stipend (3) salary; regular pay
dominate (3) take over; control
mentors (4) experienced professionals who offer advice and guidance
complement (9) help; improve

*M*illions of young people are heading to university and college campuses [soon], but they won't just be students for the next few years. Many also have jobs—for some, work they began over the summer, for others, jobs they will find through a campus bulletin board or placement center. For a vast majority, work is a financial necessity to help pay for tuition, supplies, and campus living. But a part-time job during college should be more than just a way to pay the bills and earn pocket money—it should also serve as a career planning tool. 1

The Bureau of Labor Statistics says that in 1996, over half of full-time college students also worked, and 86 percent of part-time college students held jobs. 2

Not all of those are jobs worked for money. Some students accept internships in order to gain work experience with a company or in a chosen field. In return for that kind of experience, many people agree to an internship that doesn't pay or provides only a minor 3 stipend. Students who need to earn money often take whatever job is available. But since a part-time job can consume free time from school and dominate a student's priorities, a way should be found to make it part of the education experience. Internships are generally seen as a career tool. Students should approach the part-time job search the same way.

Part-time work can offer students the best of both worlds—a flexi-   4
ble schedule with the ability to earn money, find mentors, gain experience and references. Students have a chance to practice skills learned in the classroom, acquire real-world professional skills, keep up-to-date on workplace technology, and test the waters of specific careers and companies.

A part-time job can have unexpected results, too—experience on the   5
job or advice from a mentor can help a student choose college courses and electives tailored for a future job. Some careers require specific technical skills, for example, and a student can improve his chances of eventually landing that job by getting the technical training in college.

With demand high for computer scientists, engineers, and soft-   6
ware developers, some recruiters are approaching college students through internships, part-time employers, and even during their junior or early senior years through college placement centers.

Students have particular needs, like the ability to arrange their   7
work hours around class schedules, to work flexible shifts with full days reserved for weekends, and to have the option of working full-time during holidays, between semesters, and in the summer. So they should look for job openings, employers, and recruiters that take those conditions into account.

One way of finding a part-time job is through a temporary staffing   8
agency. Olsten Corporation (**www.olsten.com**), one of the largest of those firms, says it will find jobs for thousands of college students. . . . Temping may be a good way for a student to get experience at several companies in one year without having to commit to any of them. Many of Olsten's openings are in office, technical, and clerical jobs.

Other companies recruit students to fill traditional part-time jobs.   9
Recruiting sites like **www.collegexpress.com** encourage students to sign up early in college so they can plan their school-and-work schedules to complement each other. Others, like the College Connection page at **www.careermosaic.com**, offer links that jump to some of the more prominent sites with information about internships. At **www.occ.com**, the On Campus page links to a list of college placement centers, corporate recruiters, and job search services.

Many colleges have work-study programs like the one posted on   10
www.stanford.edu that lists job openings for students receiving financial aid.

Other online job sites have part-time openings buried in their list- 11
ings of thousands of jobs. Use **www.espan.com** to plug in key words
like *part-time,* a city, and profession to find out whether there are any
openings beyond those listed on the college pages. And then there's always the direct approach—choose a specific company and go straight
to its web page. The Boeing Company (**www.boeing.com**), for example, allows interested students to do a key word search for jobs or to
browse all Boeing openings from its home page.

Elsewhere on the web, **www.jobtrack.com** boasts connections to 12
600 colleges and universities, MBA programs, and alumni associations. Its site allows students to plug in their school's name and get
back listings of part-time jobs and internships in their area.

These programs offer no guarantee of a job after graduation. It is 13
difficult for many 18- and 19-year-olds to plan strategies for the working world when that need seems a few years down the road. But it's a
fact that most college students have to hold down a part-time job. So
they might as well make it work for them.

Examining the Reading

Finding Meaning

1. In addition to earning money, how can part-time employment be
   useful to college students?
2. According to the author, what are some "unexpected results" of a
   part-time job?
3. According to this article, what career fields currently have the most
   job openings?
4. What are the advantages of working for a temp agency?
5. Name three sources of job information mentioned in this article.

Understanding Technique

1. This reading appeared on an Internet site. Discuss how the reading
   differs from essays that appear in print sources.
2. Evaluate the author's use of transitions. Where are they used effectively? Where could transitions be added?

Thinking Critically

1. Why do you think it is important for college students to get work experience in their career fields?
2. Under what circumstances do you think an internship would be a
   better choice than a part-time job?

3. The author identifies finding a mentor as one of the benefits of working part-time. How do you think a mentor could help advance your career?
4. Where at your school can you find the career and job information described in this article?
5. Do you think internships should be required for college students? Why or why not?

Writing About the Reading

A Journal Entry

Write a journal entry describing one of your job-search experiences.

A Paragraph

1. Write a paragraph describing some of the ways college students can find part-time jobs, other than those described in the reading.
2. Write a paragraph describing a part-time job that helped you learn something you did not expect to learn from it.

An Essay

1. Think of a part-time job in your field of study for which you could apply. Write a cover letter to submit with your résumé. Describe your career goals, academic and work experiences, and personal characteristics that qualify you for the job.
2. Write an essay describing the ideal part-time job for you while attending college. Be sure to include a discussion of why this job would be the best option.

A Creative Activity

Imagine that you are required to participate in an internship for five hours a week each week during the semester. Where would you choose to do your internship and why?

The Family Farm

▶ **David Mas Masumoto**

For most people, there is a clear separation between home and the workplace. In this essay, the author, who lives and works on the family farm, describes what it is like when home and work are joined. This reading was taken from his book, Epitaph for a Peach: Four Seasons on My Family Farm.

Reading Strategy

As you read, highlight words and phrases that reveal Masumoto's attitudes toward his family farm. Using a different color, highlight the attitudes of others toward the farm.

Vocabulary Preview

cringed (1) backed off in fear; winced
ventured (3) went; took a chance
alienated (4) turned off; distanced emotionally
disdain (5) lack of respect and deep dislike
condescension (5) looking down upon another; snobbishness
ritual (9) usual habit; regular activity
reluctance (11) unwillingness; resistance

I grew up knowing my father's work. He was a peach and grape 1
farmer, and I saw him at work daily, sometimes working alongside him. As a young child I knew some of the crises he faced. I cringed at the sight of worms attacking ripe fruit. I too could feel the searing heat of the summer sun as it blistered exposed fruit.

Now I farm the California land that my father and mother farmed, 2
the land where my grandparents labored as farm workers. My children will know the work of their father, too. But where my father rarely showed emotion, I show it all. My daughter has seen me yell at the sky

as September rain clouds approach my raisins or curse about lousy fruit prices when no one wants my peaches. It is a family farm—my parents, wife and children spend time in the fields—and our family is bound to the land. Our farm survives as both a home and a workplace.

When I was in college, I asked friends about their parents' work. I thought my questions would be a safe way of getting to know someone. But most of my friends never ventured beyond one-line answers: "My dad is an engineer" or "He works for a bank" or "He handles sheet metal for an air-conditioning company." 3

I would respond, "What kind of engineer?" or "Why'd he choose banking?" or "How's the sheet-metal business?" Such questions alienated some of my friends: family seemed to be a painful subject. After I told them my dad was a farmer, rarely did they ask a second question. I stopped interpreting their initial response, "Oh, really?" as one of positive surprise. 4

Returning home after college, I felt uncomfortable telling others, "I farm." I translated blank looks as disdain mixed with condescension. I could see images flashing through their minds of Old MacDonald and hayseeds who spend weekends watching corn grow. As my peers were securing their corporate jobs and advancing as professionals in law or medicine, I spent long hours talking with my dad, getting to know fifty acres of vines and twenty acres of peach trees, preparing to take over the farm. 5

I'd listened for hours before I noticed that Dad's stories of growing up on the farm seemed to revolve around the pronoun *they.* "They" meant my grandparents and the entire family of four sons and two daughters. I had to adjust my thinking. My image of work was singular in nature, one man in one job, not a family's combined effort to make a living. I learned the significance of work that is inseparable from home, when work is also the place you live and play and sleep. 6

Dad tells the story of hot, summer nights when he was a boy and the wooden platform that *Jiichan* (grandfather) built. Fresno's one-hundred-degree heat would beat down on the place where they lived, a shack with a tin roof that required hours to cool after sunset. They didn't have a cooler or fan (out in the country there was no electricity), but it didn't matter. 7

Jiichan made a low wooden platform from old barn wood. It rose about two feet off the ground with a flat area big enough for the whole family. In the evenings everyone would lie on the platform, side by side, almost touching. 8

After a long day together in the fields, and following a simple dinner and refreshing *ofuro* (Japanese bath), the family would gather and begin an evening ritual of talking, resting, and gazing upward at the night sky, waiting until their shack home had cooled down. The dirt 9 yard was beneath them, the closest vineyards a few feet away. If a little breeze came they could hear the grape leaves shifting and rustling, creating an illusion of coolness. It seemed to make everyone feel better.

Years later, my brother and I passed hot summer nights together, sometimes camping out in the fields. During a break between the summer fruits and the family packing-shed work, we pitched a tent made from an old bed sheet and tree rope. You would think after working all day with the peaches and grapes, we'd be weary of them. But we wanted to sleep "in the wilderness" and drew no lines between our fields of play and the fields of work. This wasn't just a farm, it was our home.   10

When I tell these stories to friends, their eyes widen and they smile. They tell me how fine it must be to raise children on a farm. I now realize that my college friends' reluctance to talk about family arose from a youthful notion that one could get away from them. We hoped to journey beyond that horizon; what we didn't know was that some of us were actually seeking what was right in front of us.   11

It's been a struggle to keep the farm, but I know now that I am not just competing with nature—I am creating, as my father did, something called home.   12

Examining the Reading

Finding Meaning

1. How did Masumoto's college friends react to his questions about their parents' jobs?
2. Why did the author decide to become a farmer after graduating from college?
3. The author states that "stories of growing up on the farm seemed to revolve around the pronoun *they.*" Who are "they"?
4. How did the author's friends react to his decision to become a farmer?
5. What do his friends today think about his life as a farmer?

Understanding Technique

1. How does Masumoto demonstrate his close connections to the family farm?
2. Why does Masumoto include the story of his grandfather? What does it contribute to the essay?

Thinking Critically

1. Why didn't Masumoto's college friends want to talk about their families?

2. Why did the platform the author's grandfather built mean so much to his family?
3. Why do you think Masumoto's friends now think differently about his occupation?
4. What does the author mean when he says "our family is bound to the land"?
5. Do you think the writer likes having no separation between work and home life? Why?

Writing About the Reading

A Journal Entry

Write a journal entry describing a family member's job. Explain why you would or wouldn't want to follow in this person's footsteps.

A Paragraph

1. Write a paragraph describing a situation in which you were treated with disdain or condescension.
2. Write a paragraph comparing your view of work with that of an older family member.

An Essay

1. The author's attitudes toward being a farmer changed as he grew older. Write an essay describing how your own attitudes or opinions about something changed as you matured.
2. Write an essay about an incident in your life when you discovered that what you were seeking was right in front of you.

A Creative Activity

If the author owned a restaurant, do you think each member of the family would be as involved in this business as they are in the farm? Why or why not? If yes, in what ways?

Disney's Head Trips

> **Jane Keunz**

Do you think it would be fun to work as a character at Disney World? This selection describes some difficulties faced by people who hold this kind of job. It was published as an article in South Atlantic Quarterly. *Jane Keunz is the author of* Inside the Mouse: Work and Play at Disney World.

Reading Strategy

As you read, highlight details that are particularly effective in creating an impression of Disney World.

Vocabulary Preview

realm (1) territory; world; place
perception (1) idea; way of thinking
cardinal (2) main; most important
illusion (2) fantasy; make-believe
dicey (4) risky; dangerous
regurgitation (5) vomit
exhibition (7) showing; display

*W*hen employees of Florida's Disney World arrive at the park each day for work, they enter a realm with its own rules and its own language, one that borrows phrases from both the language of real estate and the language of theater. When they are within the boundaries of the park, they are "on property." This is not the same thing as "on-stage," which implies being in public view and being in contact with guests as an employee and representative of the Walt Disney Company. For Disney's employees, however, this is only a rough distinction; their perception is that anyplace they might go "on property" is always a workplace, a stage, whether or not they are actually at work. This is a place where workers, workplace, and labor are referred to as cast,

1

theater, and performance; a place where the entire staff shows up each day not in "uniform" but in "costume."

For the workers who walk around the park dressed as Mickey, Min-   2
nie, and the rest of the Disney "cast," the cardinal rule is never to be seen out of costume and particularly out of the head; in other words, never to let the costume be seen as a costume. Such a display would destroy the park's magic, the illusion that the characters are real. One Disney spokesperson I talked to refused for an hour to acknowledge even that there are actual human beings inside the character cos- tumes: "That's one of the things I really can't talk about. Not because I work there but because it keeps it kind of sacred."

Inside the huge heads, the heat of a Florida afternoon builds. Some   3
say it gets as high as 130 degrees. Characters are supposed to appear for no longer than twenty or twenty-five minutes at a time, but, even then, it is not unusual for characters to pass out onstage.

It's unclear exactly how many of the Disney characters faint on a   4
given summer day, although everyone is sure that some do pass out. One man reports that during the summer a large part of his job is de- voted to driving around retrieving characters where they fall. One day he picked up three at one stop: Donald, Mickey, and Goofy. "All of them had passed out within five minutes of each other. They were just lined up on the sidewalk." This took place in Epcot, which, unlike the Magic Kingdom with its system of underground tunnels, has a backstage area behind the various attractions to which the characters can escape if they have to. If they are in the Magic Kingdom, however, or on a pa- rade float, they must simply ride it out or wait until they're recovered enough to walk unassisted, in costume, to a tunnel entrance. This can get a bit dicey, since passing out is sometimes preceded by throwing up inside the head, which cannot be removed until the character is out of public view.

> You're never to be seen in a costume without your head, ever. It was auto-   5
> matic dismissal. It's frightening because you can die on your own regurgi- tation when you can't keep [away from] it. I'll never forget Dumbo—it was coming out of the mouth during the parade. You have a little screen over the mouth. It was horrible. And I made $4.55 an hour.
>
> During the parades, I've seen many characters in ninety-degree heat   6
> vomit in their costumes and faint on the floats and were never taken off the float. There's so much going on during a parade that people are not go- ing to notice if Dopey is doing this [*slumps*] and he's not waving. . . . I've never seen them take a character off a float.

In one instance described to me, Chip of Chip 'n Dale fame passed   7
out while mounted to the top of a float by a post that ran up one leg of the costume and into the head. Although this was intended as a pre-

caution to keep him from falling off when the float jerked or hit a bump, the visual effect was crucifixion: Chip held up by a post for public exhibition, head hanging to one side, out cold.

Examining the Reading

Finding Meaning

1. Explain the difference between being "on property" and being "onstage" in Disney World.
2. What is the "cardinal rule" at Disney World?
3. What happens at Disney World if a character is seen in costume but without the head on?
4. What are these employees expected to do if they feel ill while in costume?
5. Why do so many of the characters faint during a parade?

Understanding Technique

1. Identify and evaluate the essay's thesis. How well is it supported?
2. Describe the tone of the essay's introduction and final paragraph. Are they similar or different? Why?

Thinking Critically

1. What does the author mean by "this is a place where workers, workplace, and labor are referred to as cast, theater, and performance"?
2. Why do you think the Disney spokesperson refused to talk to the author about the people inside the character costumes?
3. From reading this article, what image do you think Disney World is trying to present to its visitors?
4. Do you think that the rules at Disney World are fair or unfair? Explain.
5. Considering the working conditions, why do you think people want to work at Disney World?

Writing About the Reading

A Journal Entry

Imagine you are working as Mickey Mouse at Disney World. Write a journal entry about your day's experiences.

A Paragraph

1. Write a paragraph describing one of your jobs. Include your duties, the working conditions, and how the management treated you.

2. Would you like to work at Disney World? Write a paragraph explaining why or why not.

An Essay

1. Write an essay about the differences between the public's image of Disney World and the experiences of its employees.
2. Write a letter to the president of the Disney World Corporation about the working conditions and what you think should be done about them.

A Creative Activity

Imagine that, on a hot summer day at Disney World, Donald Duck felt sick. He removed his head in a public area and sat down to rest. Write about this scene and the reactions of the Disney World visitors, coworkers, and the Disney executives.

Mojado Like Me

▸ Joseph Tovares

For people born in America, it is often easy to forget about the roots of their ethnic heritage. This reading, first published in His-panic *magazine, defines one man's cultural roots and describes how he got in touch with his past.*

Reading Strategy

While or after you read, highlight words and phrases that de-scribe Tovares's life as a television producer. Use a different color to highlight descriptions of Mexican farm laborers.

Vocabulary Preview

permeates (3) spreads throughout
infiltrate (5) to enter into gradually
albeit (6) although
pejorative (7) negative; meant to belittle
condescending (8) snobby; superior; uppity
exacerbated (11) made worse; intensified
menial (11) low status; unskilled; tedious
odyssey (18) travels; quest
segued (18) proceeded without pause from one scene or
            musical number to another
cathartic (19) providing relief of feelings that had been
            hidden

*T*he Mambo Kings. That's what we jokingly called ourselves as we   1
drove across California shooting an undercover story for ABC's *Prime-Time Live*. We were three college-educated, U.S.-born Latinos, but for this story we dressed as farm workers, spoke Spanish and broken Eng-lish, and tried hard to look poor. There was Steve Blanco, a half Cuban American, half Puerto Rican from Miami and an ace freelance sound recordist; Gerardo Rueda, a first-generation Mexican American as well as a first-rate shooter and sound recordist; and me, a documentary producer, a Tejano/Chicano with roots in Texas stretching back to pre-Alamo days who just happens to be Jewish. As we traveled across the state in our beat-up Ford pickup, drawing nervous stares from shop

owners and accusatory glances from policemen, I learned something about who I am and remembered much about who I used to be.

Back home in San Antonio and Miami, we led the good life. We worked for the networks, made good money, dressed well, and drove nice cars. We were living out our parents' dreams—the dreams of immigrants who longed for a better future for their children. . . .

But over the years, like most television veterans, I had picked up some bad habits. There is an "us and them" attitude that permeates our business. We're on the inside and everyone else is on the outside. Objectivity often forces journalists to put up walls, and Latino journalists are no different. A wall had developed between myself and almost everyone else, including other Chicanos. I somehow saw myself as different. After all, I was a freelance professional and I worked steadily. No one guaranteed me work; I worked because I was good and because I had paid my dues.

After much hard work, I had achieved a measure of success that I felt I had earned. I had been through what most professionals of color go through in this country. As a student I had put up with all the nonsense from white teachers, from first grade through graduate school. I had put up with all the snide remarks from coworkers who had never worked with a "Mexican." All that was behind me now. I didn't have to put up with anybody. In my mind I was a success. I had accomplished much more than I was supposed to. But with that success came the wall that divided me from my people and from my past.

I got the call from *PrimeTime Live* on a Sunday, and a few days later the job was set. Gerardo and I set out from San Antonio and Steve Blanco flew in from Miami a few days later. Susan Barnett, the producer, and Claudia Swift, the associate producer, had done their homework. Our job was to infiltrate work groups made up of Mexican workers, then determine their legal status and whether or not they were being exploited. Unconfirmed sources indicated that the workers were being illegally charged for transportation and tools. It was the old "company store" routine. In the end, the workers owed the boss money. If that wasn't bad enough, many workers were often forced to live in subhuman conditions deep inside our national forests. We suspected all of this was occurring under the watchful eye of the U.S. Forest Service, which awarded the contracts for reforestation. The scenario had the two most essential elements for a good story: clearly identifiable victims and bad guys.

We began our new, albeit temporary, life in old faded work pants, well worn flannel shirts, and dusty work boots. Susan and Claudia provided us with the proper vehicle—a 1979 Ford truck that had been in so many accidents it was now composed mostly of Bondo.

At first the job reminded me of *Black Like Me,* a sixties book by John Howard Griffin in which a white man foolishly thinks he can understand what it's like to be a black man in America by temporarily changing his skin color. A friend would later kid me about my adventure, referring to it as "*Mojado* Like Me." *Mojado* is a pejorative term, the Spanish equivalent of "wetback." But I didn't need to change my skin color; nor was I venturing into completely new territory.

We entered the town of Lindsay, California, anxiously looking for work. We walked the streets, chatting with everyone we could. On street corners, in restaurants, and in bars, we searched out employment in the *sierra,* the mountains. We only spoke Spanish—not the Spanish we learned in school but the language of the *campesinos*. By the end of the first day we knew we were "passing." We knew by the help we received from real farm workers and others we approached for information on jobs. Waitresses, barkeeps, and people on the streets would all refer us to contractors. But we also knew we were "passing" by the stares we received. Cops, shopkeepers, businesspeople would look at us with suspicion and speak to us in condescending tones. I had forgotten what that felt like, and it took me back to Michigan, to 1969. . . .

It had been almost 25 years since that summer in Michigan. That was the last time I worked the fields. . . .

A lot had changed in 25 years. I had gone from *campesino*[1] child to East Coast–educated, hip (or so I thought) Latino. But like a lot of Latino professionals, there had developed a great distance between who I had once been and who I had become. I never forgot where I came from, but the memory had become fuzzier with time.

I had forgotten how much baggage poverty carries. Being without money is only part of the story. There is a side to poverty, exacerbated by race, that is much more difficult to understand. It is subtle yet oppressive. It is communicated by stares, gestures, and tone. Unless you've been there, you can't possibly understand. I had tried very hard to leave those feelings of inferiority far behind. I had graduated from high school, won a scholarship to college, and obtained a fellowship at graduate school. I thought I had come a long way. Yet, as I walked the streets looking for menial work, I realized that after all these years I had been only one change of clothes away from my past. A past I had tried to bury long ago.

The competition for jobs was stiff. There was a surplus of labor

---

[1]Field worker; peasant.

around, and it was hard to pin down the *contratistas*[2] as to when they would get their contracts. We dogged one guy for days, hanging around his storefront office until he finally agreed to add us to his work crew. The entire time we were wired for video and sound, wondering if our mannerisms and movements would give us away and wondering what would happen if we were found out. . . . Landing the job was a cause for some celebration—not only did we get work, we got it on tape. But the scope of the accomplishment was diminished by the severe reality of the work we were going to have to perform.

The work in the California mountains was more than hard—it was brutal. We left camp at six in the morning and returned around seven at night. The official term for the job is "manual release" but the other workers, all of whom were from Mexico and undocumented, simply called it *"limpieza,"* or "cleaning." In "manual release," workers move along in a line, and with hoes, shears, and brute force, clear thick brush from around recently planted pine trees. Those little seedlings had value; in many ways they were much more valuable than we were. Lots of money went into planting those little trees, and we were there to protect them. The thick brush we were taking out had been robbing the pine trees of valuable nutrients and had to be removed. But it was no easy matter. Some bushes were bigger than we were and virtually impossible to completely take out. I hadn't worked that hard in a long time. There I was, my hands cut and scratched, my body completely covered in dirt, trying to chip away at thicket after thicket. We had no idea how much we would wind up being paid or when; no idea when we would eat lunch, no idea if we would get a break. Under the watchful eye of our *patron*, a fellow Chicano, we worked. At his request, several men sang old Mexican songs. The National Forest had been transformed into a hacienda. 13

The plan was for us to complete fourteen acres that first day of work, but we only finished six. Midway through the afternoon the boss gave us a pep talk. "The quicker we finish, the more money you make," he said. But the work was too much. The Mambo Kings were the first to quit. We got the pictures we needed and left. 14

Over the course of several days, we wandered among various work camps, taking more pictures and gathering information. Living in tents and working twelve hours a day proved too much of a strain for many of the laborers. Fresh workers were brought in to replace those who left. We were told that during a period of seven weeks more than 100 men had come and gone from the crew. . . . 15

---

[2]Contractors who hire workers.

All day we would crawl to reach the trunks of the large and thorny   16
bushes—constantly on the lookout for dangerous snakes. We were allowed fifteen minutes for lunch and given a ten-minute break in the
late afternoon. . . .

Our job with ABC News lasted three weeks, but the memory will be   17
with me forever. I can still remember the pain of the distrustful stares,
the agony of watching men being treated like animals, and the anger of
seeing Chicano contractors exploit Mexican workers. The lessons from
those three weeks were startling. It didn't matter how different I thought
I was from these men who hail from places like Oaxaca and Michoa-
can. To virtually all the people I met, I was one of them. The walls that
I had built turned out to be made of paper, and they quickly crumbled.

Barely a month after the odyssey began, I was back home attend-   18
ing my twentieth high school reunion. There were doctors, lawyers,
accountants, and businessmen—a dozen Hispanic success stories.
Drinking and dancing at the San Antonio country club, we represented
the new Chicano middle class. Part of me felt very much at home there,
and the feeling troubled me. As I tried to make sense of my conflict, I
glanced down and touched a small scar on my left hand. The scar had
been left there by a careless boy trying to work as a man 25 years ago
in Michigan. Daydreaming and machetes don't mix. Effortlessly the
band segued from a rock tune to a Mexican polka, and the Chicanos
shifted into barrio gear and slid across the dance floor with ease. As my
wife and I danced, I realized that it is impossible to leave one life behind and simply begin another. Our lives are built on a series of experiences and, like it or not, even the difficult ones count.

So what started out as a good job with lots of overtime potential   19
turned into a cathartic event that changed my life. I had tried for years
to bury unpleasant memories, to deny they even existed. My career had
made it easy to do. But during those weeks in California I was forced
into a deep reexamination of myself. The experience made me confront ugly realities about how this society treats a hidden underclass.
Most important, it made me realize how easy it is for many of us who
have escaped to simply forget.

Examining the Reading

Finding Meaning

1. What was Joseph Tovares's assignment for *PrimeTime Live*?
2. Before starting on this assignment, what was the author's attitude
   toward his ethnic background?
3. Why was this article entitled *"Mojado* Like Me"?
4. How did the television crew know that they were successfully passing as Mexican farm workers?

5. What experiences during the three-week undercover assignment had the longest lasting effect on the author?

Understanding Technique

1. Analyze the meaning and effectiveness of the title.
2. In the introduction, the author summarizes the adventure his entire essay describes. Evaluate this technique. In what other ways might Tovares have begun the essay?

Thinking Critically

1. How did the author's career as a journalist affect his interactions with other people?
2. What did the author mean when he said, "I realized that after all these years I had been only one change of clothes away from my past."
3. Why do you think Tovares said that the tree seedlings "in many ways . . . were much more valuable than we were"?
4. Why do you think the Chicano contractors treated the Mexican workers so badly?
5. Why was the author troubled that he felt at home among the other middle class Chicanos at his high school reunion?

Writing About the Reading

A Journal Entry

Write a journal entry describing your family's ethnic, racial, or national background and what it means to you.

A Paragraph

1. Write a paragraph about some of the ways you think the author's life may have changed after this assignment.
2. Write a paragraph describing the most difficult or most challenging job you ever had or task you ever completed.

An Essay

1. Have you ever had an experience that significantly changed your self-image? Write an essay describing this experience and how it affected you.
2. There is an old saying that, to understand someone from a different background accurately, it is necessary to "walk a mile in their

shoes," that is, to live the same way they do, for a time. Write an essay explaining why you agree or disagree with this statement.

A Creative Activity

Imagine that Joseph Tovares wrote a letter to one of his former teachers or to the Mexican workers described in this article. What do you think the letter would say?

What Are They Probing For?

▸ Barbara Ehrenreich

Barbara Ehrenreich, a well-known journalist, analyzes the drug and personality tests given by companies to potential employees. Her essay first appeared in Time *magazine in 2001.*

Reading Strategy

As you read, highlight statements that reveal the author's attitude toward pre-employment testing.

Vocabulary Preview

simulation (1) imitation; copy
proclivities (1) tendencies
trumped (2) outdone; surpassed
discernible (4) recognizable
vagrant (5) drifter; roamer; homeless person
propositions (6) statements; suggestions
blatantly (6) obviously
innocuous (7) harmless; unlikely to offend

One of the great things about a job, as opposed to a position as a serf   1
or slave, is that a job is supposed to have definite boundaries. You show up in the morning, do your level best or some reasonable simulation thereof for eight to 10 hours, then you're free to go home and indulge your neurotic proclivities: gorging on Doritos, tormenting small animals, practicing Satanism, whatever. At least that's how things worked before the invention of pre-employment testing.

Now that the boss has the tools to get at them, he wants your week-   2
ends, your secret self-doubts and—to the extent that you still possess one after trying to fake your way through the tests—your soul. First there's the pre-employment drug test, now routine at more than 80% of large companies—and not just for the person who will be piloting the executive jet or loading plutonium rods into the reactor. Winn-Dixie tests the people who stack Triscuit boxes; Wal-Mart tests its people greeters. What a preference for weed over Bud as a Saturday-night relaxation aid says about your work habits has never been established,

but this in no way dulls management's eagerness to pry into your personal recreational choices. You may have a brillant résumé and a unique set of skills, but all these can be trumped by your pee.

And now, arising in just the past decade or so, there's the pre- 3 employment "personality test." This practice is at an all-time high, according to *The New York Times,* with 2,500 tests on the market supplied by the $400 million-a-year "personality-assessment" industry. In the past three years, I have taken five of these tests in the course of applying for a series of jobs: as a cleaning person, a supermarket clerk, and as an "associate" at various big-box stores. No, I hadn't given up on writing; I was doing research for a book on the low-wage life. I was expecting to toil and sweat, even wear unflattering uniforms. But I wasn't expecting to have to share my innermost thoughts.

Some of the standard questions on these personality tests are, I 4 suppose, justifiable. Management probably has a right to ask, for example, what you would do if you caught a fellow worker stealing, or whether you have ever gone postal[1] on the job. But other questions bore no discernible relevance to the task at hand: Do you consider yourself a loner? Do you often think other people are talking about you behind your back? And my personal favorite, this from a test for a housecleaning job paying $6.63 an hour: Do you suffer from "moods of self-pity"?

Fortunately, the tests are easy to ace. Take the common question 5 "In the past year, I have stolen (check dollar amount below) from my employers." If you can't guess that the answer is zero, proceed directly to the nearest park bench and begin your career as a vagrant. Or: "I tend to get into fistfights more than other people?" (Not!) and "It's easier to work when you're a little bit high." (Not, again!)

True, some of the test propositions are confusingly worded, like 6 "Marijuana is the same as a drink." (The same? How?) But the only way I ever screwed up was by being too clever. My strategy had been to give the "right" answers, but not so blatantly right that it would look as if I was faking out the test. Then, at a Wal-Mart in Minnesota, the personnel manager informed me I had got a couple of answers "wrong," apparently forgetting that she had introduced the test by telling me there were "no right or wrong answers, just whatever you think." In one case, I had agreed that "rules have to be followed to the letter at all times" only "strongly" rather than "totally," in the hope of not appearing to be too much of a suck-up. But no, she told me, the

---

[1]The term *postal* alludes to recent violence committed by frustrated post-office employees.

correct answer was "totally." You can never be too much of a suck-up in low-wage America.

The mystery is why employers are so addicted to these pre-employment tests. Drug tests seldom detect anything but the most innocuous of illegal drugs, usually marijuana; and personality tests only measure some combination of literacy and hypocrisy, not your ability to get the job done. Maybe the real function of the tests is not to convey information to the employer but to the potential employee, and the information being conveyed is, You will have no secrets from us. We don't just want your time and your effort, we want your entire self.   7

Examining the Reading

Finding Meaning

1. According to the author, what do today's bosses want from their employees?
2. For whom are drug tests now routine?
3. Why has the author been applying for so many jobs in recent years?
4. What personality test question is Ehrenreich's "personal favorite"?
5. How did the author "screw up" on one of the personality tests?
6. What does Ehrenreich feel is the true purpose of pre-employment testing?

Understanding Technique

1. What is the author's thesis? How does she support it?
2. How does the author's inclusion of her personal experiences contribute to the story?
3. Tone is the author's attitude toward his or her subject. Describe the tone of this article.

Thinking Critically

1. What does Ehrenreich mean when she says that we do a "reasonable simulation" of our best at work?
2. Why are companies so eager to test their employees?
3. Why are some of the questions on the personality tests "justifiable"?
4. Why would the author be asked about "moods of self-pity" for a housecleaning job?
5. Do you think the author would be "faking out the test" by giving all the right answers?
6. What effect do you think pre-employment tests have on potential employees?

7. Why do you think employers continue to ask questions to which the "right" answer is very obvious?

Writing About the Reading

A Journal Entry

Write a journal entry describing your experiences with testing, either in the workplace or in the classroom.

A Paragraph

1. Employers often have difficulty finding and keeping quality workers. Write a paragraph about the most important characteristics a good employee should have.
2. Write a paragraph about a job interview that you have had. Describe what questions you were asked, and explain whether or not you feel your privacy was violated.
3. Many people are worried about their personal privacy. Based on the article and your own experiences, write a paragraph explaining whether you feel pre-employment testing violates peoples' right to privacy.
4. Write a paragraph identifying jobs or positions for which you feel drug and personality tests are necessary.

An Essay

1. Write an essay describing a low-wage job you have held and how you were treated. Did your employer want "your entire self"?
2. Write an essay giving reasons why you think pre-employment testing is or is not appropriate.

A Creative Activity

Imagine that you are the boss of a company of your choice. What questions would you ask potential employees before hiring them?

A Seafood Survey

▶ **Robert Wood**
Student Essay

*Robert Wood, a student at Niagara County Community College,
humorously describes his work experiences at the fish department of a local supermarket. You will be surprised by the questions his customers ask him and how he responds.*

*O*verall, I would have to say I have a very unique part-time job. I   1
work in the seafood department at Wegmans supermarket, and since I
deal with customers all day long, I get a wide range of questions and
requests from people of all ages. Sometimes the questions come so fast
that it feels like I am responding to a seafood survey!

When I first started at Wegmans I really didn't know very much   2
about seafood, only what I had tried in the past. At first I was kind of
nervous when customers would ask me question after question about
seafood and I didn't have the answers. Now, after two years on the job,
I think I know a great deal about seafood, and more than I want to
know about customers and how to handle them.

Most of the time, customers' questions are just the routine ones.   3
They might want to know how long the fish should be cooked or what
recipes are best for a particular type of fish. Routine, polite answers are
all that are required. But once in a great while I get some really out of the
ordinary questions or requests and they require diplomatic handling.

Once a customer asked me for a lobster. We have those live in a big   4
tank, so you have to go in with these special tongs and get them out.
But they had just brought in a lot of lobsters that day, and they were all
packed on top of each other. So, the lady picked out the one she wanted
which, of course, was on the bottom of the pile. The tongs kept slip-
ping, and each time I would go to grab the lobster she wanted, he'd get
away. Finally, I got a good hold on him and dragged him up to the top,
and he was struggling. I didn't think anything of it because they always
do that, but the lady was watching him the whole time and I guess she
felt sorry for him or something because she told me to put him back!
Naturally, I asked her why, and she said that after seeing him fight for
his life, she couldn't take him home and cook him. It was as if she
thought he would be on her conscience. She went over to the meat department instead and bought a steak.

Another thing about lobsters is that once people see them crawling   5
around alive in that tank, they think all the other fish on the ice is
frozen and maybe not really fish. One customer asked me once, "How
fresh are those fish—really?" He stressed the word *really* like he didn't
believe they were all that fresh. I told him they were, and he tried to tell
me that to be really fresh, they should be swimming around in a tank
of their own! I explained to him, politely of course, that if Wegmans
had a tank for each fish, there wouldn't be room for anything else. He
said he thought he'd rather go down to the river and catch his own.
That way he'd know it was fresh.

One of the weirdest requests I ever had was made when we han-   6
dled "whole fish" at my store, and we would scale, clean, and fillet each
fish to order. One day, an old lady wanted to purchase some whole yellow pike. She selected her fish and I weighed it up and asked what she
would like done to it. She said that she would like it scaled, gutted, and
the head and fins removed—so far a normal order. But then she said
she wanted me to dig out the eyes for her and wrap them separately. I
thought to myself, "What does she want with a yellow pike's eyes?" I
finished processing the fish and marked the package with the eyes in it
so she could find it when she got home. After I handed her order to her,
I had to ask her why she needed the eyes. She replied that she used the
eyes in a recipe for a delicious soup! I didn't ask her what it tastes like.

Every once in awhile you get those questions or customers that   7
make your day. There was a young boy who came to the seafood department every Saturday when I would be working, to look at the fish
on display. He was about eight years old, was very bright, and was interested in fish. He always asked questions about where particular fish
came from and what they ate. One time, he asked me if he could have
a clam for his aquarium at home. Of course I gave him one to take
home. The next Saturday, he came back and asked me what clams eat
for food because he thought his clam was hungry. I was surprised that
the clam was still alive. When I told him this, he said he thought it was
still alive, but it never moved or opened up. He said he had taken good
care of it. He had even cleaned it up and removed some meat that was
stuck in its shell. I tried not to laugh as I explained to him that the meat
part was the clam's body and that was why it wasn't moving. He
replied, "Well, it tasted pretty good, anyway."

One of the funniest things that ever happened, though, was when a   8
girl about my age came up to me with a shopping cart that had about
10 cans of tuna fish in it. She told me she wanted to impress her new
boyfriend by cooking outdoors for him, and he didn't eat meat. She
asked me what was the easiest way to grill tuna. I thought she was
pulling my leg, so I told her she could open all those cans and empty
them onto the barbecue or she could just buy one big one. That's how
I said it, "one big one." And she looked at me like I was crazy! Then she

looked at all the cans of tuna fish in her cart and said, "You mean I can buy, like, one really, really big can of tuna fish?" Then I realized she didn't have a clue, so I pointed to the whole tuna lying there on the ice next to the flounder, and she got really wide-eyed and said, "Oh, you mean there's an actual fish called a tuna? I thought they only came in a can." I couldn't help laughing. Fortunately, she laughed too, or I could've lost my job.

During the time I worked at Wegmans, I have learned many im-   9
portant skills. In addition to the skills required for processing and sell-ing seafood, this job has taught me important "people" skills. I have learned that if you keep an open mind and maintain your sense of hu-mor, you can succeed not only at the seafood market but also at any-thing in your life.

Examining the Essay

1. Evaluate the essay's title.
2. Wood relates stories about customers to support his thesis. What other types of details might he have used?
3. Evaluate Wood's use of transitions to connect his ideas.

Writing an Essay

1. Write an essay describing strange or peculiar people you have met, tasks that you have been asked to perform, or questions or requests that you have encountered on the job.
2. Wood asserts that he has learned a great deal about customers and how to handle them. Write an essay discussing what you have learned from a job that you hold now or have held.

Making Connections

1. Both "The Family Farm" and *"Mojado* Like Me" are concerned, in part, with family or cultural roots. Write an essay comparing Masumoto's attitudes toward his family with those of Tovares toward his Tejano/Chicano roots.

2. "Disney's Head Trips" and "A Seafood Survey" discuss employment issues. Write an essay comparing Wood's working conditions with that of the Disney employees.

3. Write an essay explaining what Sabra Chartrand ("Working Students Need to Look for Career Experience") would think of Robert Wood's part-time job ("A Seafood Survey").

Internet Connections

1. Every year The Great Place to Work Institute produces the "100 Best Companies to Work for in America." This list is published in *Fortune* magazine and appears on the web site **http://www.greatplacetowork.com/best_companies/ us_2001.html**. Look over this list. Examine the nomination process (**http://www.greatplacetowork.com/best_ companies/nomination_process.html**). Write a summary and evaluation of the steps followed in creating this list.

2. Visit several of the career planning sites listed below. Then write an essay explaining what you learned about the career planning process.

   http://www.careerweb.com/inventory/

   http://www.mois.org/moistest.html

   http://www.careerexplorer.net/features/ career_assessment.asp

3. The U.S. government publishes a guide to careers called the *Occupational Outlook Handbook*. Browse some of the job types listed in the online version at **http://stats.bls. gov/oco/ocoiab.htm**. Write a paragraph contrasting two of the jobs listed at the site—one you would like to have and one you would not like to have.

   (If any of these web sites are unavailable, use a search engine to locate another appropriate site.)

Chapter 4

Cultures That Shape Our Lives

Primary Colors
  Kim McLarin

Black *and* Latino
  Roberto Santiago

Fifth Chinese Daughter
  Jade Snow Wong

Through Tewa Eyes
  Alfonso Ortiz

Dumpster Diving
  Lars Eighner

Silenced Voices: Deaf Cultures
and "Hearing" Families
  Richard Appelbaum and William J. Chambliss

Cultural Education in America
  Jonathan Wong

People in the United States represent a wide variety of cultural backgrounds. Culture refers to the values and ways of doing things that a group of people share. Except for the Native Americans, our ancestors all came from somewhere else—Africa, China, Eastern or Western Europe, South America, Vietnam, and so on. Although Americans are an ethnically diverse bunch, they share some common concerns, goals, and values. Regardless of our cultural heritage, we all value our families; we value our friendships; we seek self-worth and self-esteem; we seek freedom, opportunity, and knowledge.

Subcultures exist within a culture. They are groups that share some common identity. From the shared identity, shared customs and behaviors develop. A good example is the college student subculture. All members of this group attend college (their shared identity), and many act and dress in similar ways (many carry backpacks, wear jeans, etc.). Other subcultures include religious sects, sports players, and musicians.

Learning about others' cultures and subcultures can give life and meaning to our shared concerns and values. As we discover how different cultures celebrate a holiday, for example, the significance of our own celebrations becomes more important and more clear. Or as we study birth and death rituals of various groups, our own traditions become more meaningful, and feelings toward those experiences surface, making us richer, more self-aware people. Cultural awareness shapes our lives by expanding our self-awareness.

The readings in this chapter are about subcultures, ethnic and otherwise, and how they define who we are. For example, you will read a description of the birth and burial rituals of the Tewa tribe ("Through Tewa Eyes"). But many times, these cultural "definitions" are limiting and lead to divisions between cultures. This is the topic of "Fifth Chinese Daughter," in which a young woman attempts to break away from cultural traditions; "Cultural Education in America," in which a college student experiences differences between his American college friends and the cultural tradition of his native Hong Kong; "Primary Colors," which describes how an interracial child fits in society; and "Black *and* Latino," which relates a young man's experience of being both black and Puerto Rican. Subcultures do not always have to be racial or ethnic divisions, as you will see in a homeless man's account of how he searches for food ("Dumpster Diving") and how some deaf people wish to maintain a separate subculture ("Silenced Voices: Deaf Cultures and 'Hearing' Families").

Brainstorming About Culture

Class Activity: Each group of students should brainstorm to create lists of all the cultures and subcultures of which any group member has any inside knowledge or experience.

Primary Colors

▶ **Kim McLarin**

In this essay from The New York Times Magazine, *a mother writes about how society has trouble seeing the connection between her and her lighter-skinned daughter.*

Reading Strategy

As you read, highlight words and phrases that reveal the author's attitude toward her daughter.

Vocabulary Preview

retrospect (5) looking back
eccentricities (6) oddities; exceptions
umber (6) brownish
abduction (9) kidnapping
disconcerting (10) unsettling; upsetting
condemnation (13) strong criticism or disapproval
allegiances (13) loyalties
denounce (13) condemn; criticize openly
align (14) identify; join

A few weeks after my daughter was born, I took her to a new pedia-   1
trician for an exam. The doctor took one look at Samantha and exclaimed: "Wow! She's so light!" I explained that my husband is white,
but it didn't seem to help. The doctor commented on Sam's skin color
so often that I finally asked what was on her mind.

"I'm thinking albino," she said.   2

The doctor, who is white, claimed she had seen the offspring of   3
many interracial couples, but never a child this fair. "They're usually a
darker, coffee-with-cream color. Some of them are this light at birth,
but by 72 hours you can tell they have a black parent."

To prove her point, she held her arm next to Samantha's stomach.   4
"I mean, this could be my child!"

It's funny now, in retrospect. But at the time, with my hormones   5
still raging from childbirth, the incident sent me into a panic. Any fool
could see that Samantha wasn't an albino—she had black hair and
dark blue eyes. It must be a trick. The doctor, who had left the room,
probably suspected me of kidnapping this "white" child and was outside calling the police. By the time she returned I was ready to fight.

Fortunately, her partner dismissed the albino theory, and we es-   6
caped and found a new pediatrician, one who knows a little more
about genetic eccentricities. But the incident stayed with me because,
in the months since, other white people have assumed Samantha is not
my child. This is curious to me, this inability to connect across skin
tones, especially since Samantha has my full lips and broad nose. I'll
admit that I myself didn't expect Sam to be quite so pale, so much
closer to her father's Nordic coloring than my own umber tones. My
husband is a blue-eyed strawberry blond; I figured that my genes
would take his genes in the first round.

Wrong.   7

Needless to say, I love Sam just as she is. She is amazingly, heart-   8
breakingly beautiful to me in the way that babies are to their parents.
She sweeps me away with her mischievous grin and her belly laugh,
with the coy way she tilts her head after flinging the cup from her high
chair. When we are alone and I look at Samantha, I see Samantha, not
the color of her skin.

And yet, I admit that I wouldn't mind if she were darker, dark   9
enough so that white people would know she was mine and black
people wouldn't give her a hard time. I know a black guy who, while
crossing into Canada, was suspected of having kidnapped his fair-
skinned son. So far no one has accused me of child abduction, but I
have been mistaken for Samantha's nanny. It has happened so often
that I've considered going into business as a nanny spy. I could sit in
the park and take notes on your child-care worker. Better than hiding
a video camera in the living room.

In a way it's disconcerting, my being mistaken for a nanny. Be-   10
cause, to be blunt, I don't like seeing black women caring for white
children. It may be because I grew up in the South, where black
women once had no choice but to leave their own children and suckle
the offspring of others. The weight of that past, the whiff of a power
imbalance, still stains such pairings for me. That's unfair, I know, to the
professional, hard-working (mostly Caribbean) black nannies of New
York. But there you are.

On the flip side, I think being darker wouldn't hurt Samantha with   11
black people, either. A few weeks ago, in my beauty shop, I overheard
a woman trashing a friend for "slathering" his light-skinned children
with sunscreen during the summer.

"Maybe he doesn't want them getting skin cancer," suggested the   12
listener. But my girl was having none of that.

"He doesn't want them getting black!" she said, as full of righteous   13
condemnation as only a black woman in a beauty shop can be. Now,
maybe the woman was right about her friend's motivation. Or maybe
she was 100 percent wrong. Maybe because she herself is the color of
butterscotch she felt she had to declare her allegiances loudly, had to

place herself prominently high on the unofficial black scale and denounce anyone caught not doing the same. Either way, I know it
means grief for Sam.

I think that as time goes on my daughter will probably align with   14
black people anyway, regardless of the relative fairness of her skin. My
husband is fine with that, as long as it doesn't mean denying him or his
family.

The bottom line is that society has a deep need to categorize   15
people, to classify and, yes, to stereotype. Race is still the easiest, most
convenient way of doing so. That race tells you, in the end, little or
nothing about a person is beside the point. We still feel safer believing
that we can sum up one another at a glance.

Examining the Reading

Finding Meaning

1. When McLarin took Samantha to her pediatrician, how did the
   doctor respond?
2. Why did this incident cause the author to "panic"?
3. Why did McLarin find a new pediatrician?
4. What does the author's husband look like?
5. How does the author feel about black women caring for white children who are not their own?

Understanding Technique

1. Identify McLarin's thesis and evaluate its placement.
2. How does McLarin reveal the attitude of various groups within our
   society toward her daughter?

Thinking Critically

1. What does the author mean by an "inability to connect across skin
   tones" (paragraph 6)?
2. Describe the tone of this essay.
3. What do you think was the author's purpose in writing this essay?
4. Why does the author say, "I think being darker wouldn't hurt
   Samantha."
5. What does the author most worry about for her daughter?

Writing About the Reading

A Journal Entry

Write a journal entry about an event or situation in which you felt that you stood out from other people around you.

A Paragraph

1. Write a paragraph explaining what you notice first when you meet a person for the first time.
2. Write a paragraph about how it feels to be different in any sense of the word.

An Essay

1. Do you agree with the author that society needs to categorize, classify, and stereotype people? Write an essay defending or rejecting this idea.
2. Write an essay explaining how your first impression of another person proved to be incorrect.

A Creative Activity

Imagine yourself in the author's situation. If you were part of an interracial couple, what concerns might you have for your child? What could you do to protect your child?

Black *and* Latino

▶ **Roberto Santiago**

Am I black or am I Latino? This is the question that troubled Santiago throughout his childhood as a member of two ethnic groups. Read this essay, first published in Essence *magazine, to discover how he resolved this issue.*

Reading Strategy

To strengthen your comprehension of this essay, highlight statements by Santiago that reveal his attitude toward his biracial heritage.

Vocabulary Preview

perplexes (1) confuses
heritages (1) inherited backgrounds
parody (4) ridiculous imitation
eons (6) long periods of time
conquests (6) subjugations; forced colonizations
predominant (6) most important
determinant (6) deciding
slur (8) disrespectful remark
solace (9) comfort
pegged (11) marked; identified
iconoclast (11) someone who overthrows a traditional idea
                        or image

*"T*here is no way that you can be black and Puerto Rican at the same   1
time." What? Despite the many times I've heard this over the years, that statement still perplexes me. I *am* both and always have been. My color is a blend of my mother's rich, dark skin tone and my father's white complexion. As they were both Puerto Rican, I spoke Spanish before English, but I am totally bilingual. My life has been shaped by my black and Latino heritages, and despite other people's confusion, I don't feel I have to choose one or the other. To do so would be to deny a part of myself.

There has not been a moment in my life when I did not know that   2
I looked black—and I never thought that others did not see it, too. But growing up in East Harlem, I was also aware that I did not "act black," according to the African-American boys on the block.

My lighter-skinned Puerto Rican friends were less of a help in this   3
department. "You're not black," they would whine, shaking their
heads. "You're a *boriqua* [slang for Puerto Rican], you ain't no *moreno*
[black]." If that was true, why did my mirror defy the rules of logic?
And most of all, why did I feel that there was some serious unknown
force trying to make me choose sides?

Acting black. Looking black. Being a real black. This debate among   4
us is almost a parody. The fact is that I am black, so why do I need to
prove it?

The island of Puerto Rico is only a stone's throw away from Haiti,   5
and, no fooling, if you climb a palm tree, you can see Jamaica bobbing
on the Atlantic. The slave trade ran through the Caribbean basin, and
virtually all Puerto Rican citizens have some African blood in their
veins. My grandparents on my mother's side were the classic *negro
como carbón* (black as carbon) people, but despite the fact that they
were as dark as can be, they are officially not considered black.

There is an explanation for this, but not one that makes much   6
sense, or difference, to a working-class kid from Harlem. Puerto Ricans identify themselves as Hispanics—part of a worldwide race that
originated from eons of white Spanish conquests—a mixture of white,
African, and *Indio* blood, which, categorically, is apart from black. In
other words, the culture is the predominant and determinant factor.
But there are frustrations in being caught in a duo-culture, where your
skin color does not necessarily dictate what you are. When I read Piri
Thomas's searing autobiography, *Down These Mean Streets,* in my early
teens, I saw that he couldn't figure out other people's attitudes toward
his blackness, either.

My first encounter with this attitude about the race thing rode on   7
horseback. I had just turned six years old and ran toward the bridle
path in Central Park as I saw two horses about to trot past. "Yea! Hor-
sie! Yea!" I yelled. Then I noticed one figure on horseback. She was
white, and she shouted, "Shut up, you f—g nigger! Shut up!" She
pulled back on the reins and twisted the horse in my direction. I can
still feel the spray of gravel that the horse kicked at my chest. And suddenly she was gone. I looked back, and, in the distance, saw my parents playing Whiffle Ball with my sister. They seemed miles away.

They still don't know about this incident. But I told my Aunt Aure-   8
lia almost immediately. She explained what the words meant and why
they were said. Ever since then I have been able to express my anger
appropriately through words or action in similar situations. Self-
preservation, ego, and pride forbid men from ever ignoring, much less
forgetting, a slur.

Aunt Aurelia became, unintentionally, my source for answers I   9
needed about color and race. I never sought her out. She just seemed

to appear at my home during the points in my childhood when I most needed her for solace. "Puerto Ricans are different from American blacks," she told me once. "There is no racism between what you call white and black. Nobody even considers the marriages interracial." She then pointed out the difference in color between my father and mother. "You never noticed that," she said, "because you were not raised with that hang-up."

Aunt Aurelia passed away before I could follow up on her observation. But she had made an important point. It's why I never liked the attitude that says I should be exclusive to one race.   10

My behavior toward this race thing pegged me as an iconoclast of sorts. Children from mixed marriages, from my experience, also share this attitude. If I have to bear the label of iconoclast because the world wants people to be in set categories and I don't want to, then I will.   11

A month before Aunt Aurelia died, she saw I was a little down about the whole race thing, and she said, "Roberto, don't worry. Even if—no matter what you do—black people in this country don't, you can always depend on white people to treat you like a black."   12

Examining the Reading

Finding Meaning

1. What problems did Santiago face during childhood?
2. According to the author, what other race (besides white and African) do all Puerto Rican citizens have in their blood?
3. What explanation does the author give for his maternal grandparents being "black as carbon" and yet being "officially not considered black"?
4. Describe the author's first encounter with prejudice.
5. According to his aunt, why had the author never noticed the difference in color between his mother and his father?

Understanding Technique

Santiago opens his essay with a question. Discuss the effectiveness of this strategy as a means of starting the essay.

Thinking Critically

1. Is there a tendency in our society to label or compartmentalize people? Why do you think people do this, and what are its positive and negative effects?
2. When the author had his first encounter with prejudice, why do you think he chose to tell his aunt but not his parents?

3. What part did the author's aunt play in shaping his life—particularly with regard to ideas about race?
4. What does the last sentence of the reading reveal about discrimination in our country?

Writing About the Reading

A Journal Entry

Write a journal entry describing what you know about your ethnic origins. Are they important to you?

A Paragraph

1. Santiago experiences conflict about his ethnic origins. Write a paragraph describing a conflict, ethnic or otherwise, that you have experienced. Explain how you resolved it.
2. Santiago read an autobiography of a man who shared his confusion about race. Have you ever read a book or watched a movie or television program that dealt with a problem you were experiencing? Write a paragraph explaining whether seeing others deal with a problem helps you cope with it.

An Essay

1. Santiago felt that people wanted him to be either black or Puerto Rican; they wanted him to choose sides. Many times in our lives, we are asked or forced to take sides. Write an essay discussing a situation in which you were asked or forced to take sides or to take a stand on an issue.
2. Santiago asks, "I am black, so why do I need to prove it?" Often, in our culture, we are called upon to prove who or what we are. Write an essay describing a situation in which you were called upon to prove yourself.
3. Imagine that you are black raised in a white family or white raised in a black family. Write an essay discussing the problems you would face.

A Creative Activity

Suppose Santiago, in adulthood, were to meet the woman on the horse. What do you think he would say to her?

Fifth Chinese Daughter

▸ Jade Snow Wong

*Traditional Chinese families hold to a culture in which children
must obey their parents and seek permission for what they do. In
this essay, the author describes her breaking from this cultural
tradition. This essay was taken from a book titled* The Immigrant Experience.

Reading Strategy

Highlight words, phrases, and descriptions that reveal how
Wong's parents felt about her actions.

Vocabulary Preview

impulsively (1) without thinking or planning
incredulous (5) not believing
unfilial (5) against family
revered (5) admired and respected
denounced (5) spoke out against
ingrate (5) ungrateful person
whims (5) sudden, fanciful ideas
proclamation (6) announcement
innuendoes (7) subtle or indirect negative comments
underscored (7) made the point more clear
devastated (8) stunned; overwhelmed
conceding (9) acknowledging; admitting

One afternoon on a Saturday, which was normally occupied with my   1
housework job, I was unexpectedly released by my employer, who was
departing for a country weekend. It was a rare joy to have free time
and I wanted to enjoy myself for a change. There had been a Chinese-
American boy who shared some classes with me. Sometimes we had
found each other walking to the same 8:00 A.M. class. He was not a spe-

cial boyfriend, but I had enjoyed talking to him and had confided in him some of my problems. Impulsively, I telephoned him. I knew I must be breaking rules, and I felt shy and scared. At the same time, I was excited at this newly found forwardness, with nothing more purposeful than to suggest another walk together.

He understood my awkwardness and shared my anticipation. He asked me to "dress up" for my first movie date. My clothes were limited but I changed to look more graceful in silk stockings and found a bright ribbon for my long black hair. Daddy watched, catching my mood, observing the dashing preparations. He asked me where I was going without his permission and with whom. 2

I refused to answer him. I thought of my rights! I thought he surely would not try to understand. Thereupon Daddy thundered his displeasure and forbade my departure. 3

I found a new courage as I heard my voice announce calmly that I was no longer a child, and if I could work my way through college, I would choose my own friends. It was my right as a person. 4

My mother heard the commotion and joined my father to face me; both appeared shocked and incredulous. Daddy at once demanded the source of this unfilial, non-Chinese theory. And when I quoted my college professor, reminding him that he had always felt teachers should be revered, my father denounced that professor as a foreigner who was disregarding the superiority of our Chinese culture, with its sound family strength. My father did not spare me; I was condemned as an ingrate for echoing dishonorable opinions which should only be temporary whims, yet nonetheless inexcusable. 5

The scene was not yet over. I completed my proclamation to my father, who had never allowed me to learn how to dance, by adding that I was attending a movie, unchaperoned, with a boy I met at college. 6

My startled father was sure that my reputation would be subject to whispered innuendoes. I must be bent on disgracing the family name; I was ruining my future, for surely I would yield to temptation. My mother underscored him by saying that I hadn't any notion of the problems endured by parents of a young girl. 7

I would not give in. I reminded them that they and I were not in China, that I wasn't going out with just anybody but someone I trusted! Daddy gave a roar that no man could be trusted, but I devastated them in declaring that I wished the freedom to find my own answers. 8

Both parents were thoroughly angered, scolded me for being shameless, and predicted that I would some day tell them I was wrong. But I dimly perceived that they were conceding defeat and were perplexed at this breakdown of their training. I was too old to beat and too bold to intimidate. 9

Examining the Reading

Finding Meaning

1. How did Wong's father respond when she refused to tell him where she was going and with whom?
2. What was the argument between father and daughter really about?
3. What rules was Wong breaking?
4. Summarize the father's argument.
5. What was Wong's mother's reaction when she heard the argument between her husband and her daughter?
6. In the end, how did Wong win the argument?

Understanding Technique

1. Although Wong recounts a family dispute, she does not include dialogue. How would her essay have been changed by including it? Suggest places where dialogue could be added.
2. Describe how the essay is organized.
3. Wong's sentence structure is varied and therefore interesting. Cite several examples.

Thinking Critically

1. Why did the author assume that her father would not understand even before she attempted to explain the situation?
2. Why do you think the author's parents were so upset by her need for privacy and independence?
3. In what way was this incident a turning point in the author's life?
4. To what extent and in what ways do you think this incident shaped Wong's future actions in going against cultural traditions?

Writing About the Reading

A Journal Entry

Write a journal entry on how you feel after having a heated argument with a family member or close friend.

A Paragraph

1. Write a paragraph explaining a conflict between you and your parents or an incident in which you disagreed with them about "the way to do things" (cultural traditions).
2. Sometimes it's necessary to do the opposite of what you know your

family or friends want you to do. Write a paragraph describing a time when you felt that way or when you observed someone else doing so.

An Essay

At some point, we have all decided to act against a cultural tradition. Write an essay describing a situation in which you acted against tradition. Explain how other people responded to your decision and how you attempted to resolve any conflicts.

A Creative Activity

Write a paragraph describing what you think happened between Wong and her parents the day after her movie date.

Through Tewa Eyes

▶ **Alfonso Ortiz**

Different cultures have different ways of marking important life events. This essay describes rituals celebrated by the Tewa tribe. It was originally published in National Geographic *magazine.*

Reading Strategy

As you read, highlight each ceremonial event in a Tewa's life. For each, write an annotation that summarizes its purpose.

Vocabulary Preview

proffered (1) held out; presented
evokes (2) calls to mind
duality (3) twofoldness
moieties (7) halves; parts
deities (11) gods
kiva (11) ceremonial structure
cicada (15) insect whose wings produce high-pitched sounds
admonishes (15) warns; advises

I do not remember the day, of course, but I know what happened.   1
Four days after I was born in the Pueblo Indian village of San Juan in the Rio Grande Valley in New Mexico, the "umbilical cord–cutting mother" and her assistant came to present me to the sun and to give me a name. They took me from the house just as the sun's first rays appeared over the Sangre de Cristo Mountains. The cord-cutting mother proffered me and two perfect ears of corn, one blue and one white, to the six sacred directions. A prayer was said:

> *Here is a child who has been given to us. Let us bring him to manhood.* . . . *You who are dawn youths and dawn maidens. You who are winter spirits. You who are summer spirits.* . . . *Take therefore.* . . . *Give him good fortune, we ask of you.*

Now the name was given. It was not the name at the head of this   2
story. It was my Tewa name, a thing of power. Usually such a name evokes either nature—the mountains or the hills or the season—or a ceremony under way at the time of the birth. By custom such a name is shared only within the community, and with those we know well. Thus, in the eyes of my Tewa people, I was "brought in out of the dark-

ness," where I had no identity. Thus I became a child of the Tewa. My world is the Tewa world. It is different from your world. . . .

Remember my naming ceremony: There were two women attending, two ears of corn offered with me to the sun. This duality is basic to understanding our behavior.   3

When the Tewa came onto land, the Hunt Chief took an ear of blue corn and handed it to one of the other men and said: "You are to lead and care for all of the people during the summer." To another man he handed an ear of white corn and told him: "You shall lead and care for the people during the winter." This is how the Summer and Winter Chiefs were instituted.   4

The Hunt Chief then divided the people between the two chiefs. As they moved south down the Rio Grande, the Summer People traveled on the west side of the river, the Winter People on the east side.   5

The Summer People lived by agriculture, the Winter People by hunting.   6

From this time, the story tells us, the Tewa have been divided during their lives into moieties—Winter People, Summer People. Still today a Summer Chief guides us seven months of the year, during the agricultural cycle; a Winter Chief during the five months of hunting. There are special rituals, dances, costumes, and colors attached to each moiety. Everything that has symbolic significance to the Tewa is classified in dualities: Games, plants, and diseases are hot or cold, winter or summer. Some persons or things, like healers, are of the middle, mediating between the two. This gives order to our lives.   7

A child is incorporated into his moiety through the water-giving ceremony during his first year. The Winter Chief conducts his rite in October; the Summer Chief in late February or March. The ceremony is held in a sanctuary at the chief's home. There are an altar, a sand painting, and various symbols; the chief and his assistants dress in white buckskin. A final character appears, preceded by the call of a fox, as in the creation story. It is the Hunt Chief.   8

A female assistant holds the child; the moiety chief recites a short prayer and administers a drink of the sacred medicinal water from an abalone shell, thereby welcoming the child into the moiety.   9

The third rite in a child's life—water pouring—comes between the ages of six and ten and is held within the moiety. It marks the transition from the carefree, innocent state of early childhood to the status of adult, one of the Dry Food People. For four days the boys are made to carry a load of firewood they have chopped themselves, and the girls a basket of corn, meal they have ground themselves, to the homes of their sponsors.   10

A sponsor instructs each child in the beliefs and practices of the village. On the fourth night, the deities come to the kiva, and the child may go to watch. Afterward, the sponsor bathes the child, pouring wa-   11 ter over him. From this time, the child is given duties judged proper for his sex.

A finishing ritual a few years later brings the girls and boys to   12
adulthood. For the boys it is particularly meaningful, for they now become eligible to assist and participate in the coming of the gods in their moiety's kiva. Thus the bonds of the moiety are further strengthened.

It is at death that the bond of moiety is broken and the solidarity of   13
the whole society emphasized again. This echoes the genesis story, for after the people had divided into two for their journey from the lake, they came together again when they arrived at their destination.

When a Tewa dies, relatives dress the corpse. The moccasins are   14
reversed—for the Tewa believe everything in the afterlife is reversed from this life. There is a Spanish Catholic wake, a Requiem Mass, then the trip to the cemetery. There the priest completes the church's funeral rites: the sprinkling of holy water, a prayer, a handful of dirt thrown into the grave. Then all non-Indians leave.

A bag containing the clothing of the deceased is now placed under   15
his head as a pillow, along with other personal possessions. When the grave is covered, a Tewa official tells the survivors that the deceased has gone to the place "of endless cicada singing," that he will be happy, and he admonishes them not to let the loss divide the home.

During the four days following death, the soul, or Dry Food Who Is   16
No Longer, is believed to wander about in this world in the company of the ancestors. These four days produce a time of unease. There is the fear among relatives that the soul may become lonely and return to take one of them for company. Children are deemed most susceptible. The house itself must not be left unoccupied.

The uneasiness ends on the fourth night, when relatives gather again   17
to perform the releasing rite. There are rituals with tobacco, a piece of charcoal, a series of four lines drawn on the floor. A pottery bowl, used in his naming ceremony long ago and cherished by him all his life, is broken, or "killed." Then a prayer reveals the purpose of the symbols:

> We have muddied the waters for you [the smoke]. We have cast shadows between us [the charcoal]. We have made steep gullies between us [the lines]. Do not, therefore, reach for even a hair on our heads. Rather, help us attain that which we are always seeking: Long life, that our children may grow, abundant game, the raising of crops. . . . Now you must go, for you are now free.

With the soul released, all breathe a sigh of relief. They wash their   18
hands. As each finishes, he says, "May you have life." The others respond, "Let it be so." Everyone now eats.

The Tewa begin and end life as one people; we call the life cycle   19
poeh, or emergence path. As a Tewa elder told me:

"In the beginning we were one. Then we divided into Summer People   20
and Winter People; in the end we came together again as we are today."
    This is the path of our lives.   21

Examining the Reading

Finding Meaning

1. With what Tewa customs is this reading concerned?
2. Explain the importance of duality (twofoldness) in the Tewa culture.
3. What do Tewa names usually stand for?
4. What four rituals occur in a child's life? Explain their significance.
5. Why do the Tewa reverse the moccasins on their deceased relatives?

Understanding Technique

1. Ortiz includes two prayers within the essay. Why are they included? What purpose do they serve?
2. Ortiz uses transitional words and phrases to connect ideas and events. Highlight several that are particularly effective.

Thinking Critically

1. Who do you think the Hunt Chief is?
2. Discuss religious rituals that symbolize the passage from childhood to adulthood.
3. Discuss your beliefs about what happens to the soul after the body dies.
4. The Tewa follow a life cycle called a *poeh.* Do life cycles exist in American culture? If so, describe them.

Writing About the Reading

A Journal Entry

Brainstorm about your reaction to the Tewa practices. Do you wish your culture had more traditions to follow?

A Paragraph

1. Write a paragraph identifying an ethnic or religious ritual in which you participated or that you have observed. Explain its significance.
2. Write a paragraph agreeing or disagreeing with the following statement: Ceremonies or rituals occur at changing points in our lives. Support your paragraph with examples.

An Essay

1. In the Tewa culture, many things are divided into twos. The author explains that "this gives order to our lives." Write an essay discussing what values, beliefs, or traditions give order to your life.
2. Write an essay discussing the function or purpose of rituals or ceremonies. Why does each culture have them? What do they accomplish?

A Creative Activity

After a Tewa dies, the house is guarded so that the deceased may not return to claim the life of a relative. Assume that you are a Tewa child and that you and your parents are staying in your home immediately after the death of a close relative. Write a paragraph describing what you might do and feel when you are alone in your room at night.

Dumpster Diving

▶ Lars Eighner

*In this essay, the author, at the time homeless, describes how he
and others survived by scavenging for food and possessions in
Dumpsters. Through the essay you learn about Eighner's values
and attitudes toward others, as well as his survival techniques.
This essay first appeared in* The Threepenny Review.

Reading Strategy

Highlight factual information that Eighner provides about
Dumpster diving. Annotate your responses to these facts.

Vocabulary Preview

niche (3) position; place in life
pristine (6) pure; unspoiled
utility (7) usefulness
bohemian (8) unconventional (usually with an interest in the
                      arts)
dilettanti (9) amateurs; dabblers
contaminants (10) dirt; germs; unhealthy material
dysentery (12) a temporary intestinal disorder; extreme
                      diarrhea
transience (14) changeability; briefness
envisioning (15) picturing in one's mind
gaudy (16) flashy; showy
bauble (16) small ornament; piece of jewelry
sated (16) satisfied; taken care of
confounded (16) mixed up; confused

I began Dumpster diving about a year before I became homeless.   1

I prefer the term *scavenging*. I have heard people, evidently mean-   2
ing to be polite, use the word *foraging*, but I prefer to reserve that word
for gathering nuts and berries and such, which I also do, according to
the season and opportunity.

I like the frankness of the word *scavenging*. I live from the refuse of   3
others. I am a scavenger. I think it a sound and honorable niche, although if I could I would naturally prefer to live the comfortable consumer life, perhaps—and only perhaps—as a slightly less wasteful
consumer owing to what I have learned as a scavenger.

Except for jeans, all my clothes come from Dumpsters. Boom boxes, candles, bedding, toilet paper, medicine, books, a typewriter, a virgin male love doll, coins sometimes amounting to many dollars: all came from Dumpsters. And, yes, I eat from Dumpsters, too.   4

There is a predictable series of stages that a person goes through in learning to scavenge. At first the new scavenger is filled with disgust and self-loathing. He is ashamed of being seen.   5

This stage passes with experience. The scavenger finds a pair of running shoes that fit and look and smell brand-new. He finds a pocket calculator in perfect working order. He finds pristine ice cream, still frozen, more than he can eat or keep. He begins to understand: people do throw away perfectly good stuff, a lot of perfectly good stuff.   6

At this stage he may become lost and never recover. All the Dumpster divers I have known come to the point of trying to acquire everything they touch. Why not take it, they reason, it is all free. This is, of course, hopeless, and most divers come to realize that they must restrict themselves to items of relatively immediate utility.   7

The finding of objects is becoming something of an urban art. Even respectable, employed people will sometimes find something tempting sticking out of a Dumpster or standing beside one. Quite a number of people, not all of them of the bohemian type, are willing to brag that they found this or that piece in the trash.   8

But eating from Dumpsters is the thing that separates the dilettanti from the professionals. Eating safely involves three principles: using the senses and common sense to evaluate the condition of the found materials; knowing the Dumpsters of a given area and checking them regularly; and seeking always to answer the question "Why was this discarded?"   9

Yet perfectly good food can be found in Dumpsters. Canned goods, for example, turn up fairly often in the Dumpsters I frequent. I also have few qualms about dry foods such as crackers, cookies, cereal, chips, and pasta if they are free of visible contaminants and still dry and crisp. Raw fruits and vegetables with intact skins seem perfectly safe to me, excluding, of course, the obviously rotten. Many are discarded for minor imperfections that can be pared away.   10

A typical discard is a half jar of peanut butter—though nonorganic peanut butter does not require refrigeration and is unlikely to spoil in any reasonable time. One of my favorite finds is yogurt—often discarded, still sealed, when the expiration date has passed—because it will keep for several days, even in warm weather.   11

No matter how careful I am I still get dysentery at least once a month, oftener in warm weather. I do not want to paint too romantic a picture. Dumpster diving has serious drawbacks as a way of life.   12

I find from the experience of scavenging two rather deep lessons. 13
The first is to take what I can use and let the rest go. I have come to
think that there is no value in the abstract. A thing I cannot use or
make useful, perhaps by trading, has no value, however fine or rare it
may be.

The second lesson is the transience of material being. I do not sup- 14
pose that ideas are immortal, but certainly they are longer-lived than
material objects.

The things I find in Dumpsters, the love letters and rag dolls of so 15
many lives, remind me of this lesson. Now I hardly pick up a thing
without envisioning the time I will cast it away. This, I think, is a
healthy state of mind. Almost everything I have now has already been
cast out at least once, proving that what I own is valueless to someone.

I find that my desire to grab for the gaudy bauble has been largely 16
sated. I think this is an attitude I share with the very wealthy—we both
know there is plenty more where whatever we have came from. Between us are the rat-race millions who have confounded their selves
with the objects they grasp and who nightly scavenge the cable channels for they know not what.

I am sorry for them. 17

Examining the Reading

Finding Meaning

1. What is Dumpster diving?
2. Why does the author prefer the word *scavenging*?
3. What does the author say is the primary disadvantage of eating out
   of Dumpsters?
4. Summarize the three stages that Dumpster divers go through.
5. What two lessons has the author learned through Dumpster diving?

Understanding Technique

1. Eighner uses topic sentences to structure his paragraphs and help
   identify the main point in his paragraphs. Identify several topic sentences and note their placement.
2. Describe Eighner's tone (his attitude toward his subject).
3. Evaluate the title and its meaning.

Thinking Critically

1. How do you think the average person looks upon a Dumpster
   diver? Why?

2. Can you imagine yourself eating out of a Dumpster? Why or why not?
3. Do you think Lars Eighner would continue to acquire things from Dumpsters if he didn't need to? What in the reading might indicate that he would or would not?
4. What does the author mean by the statement: "I do not suppose that ideas are immortal"?
5. The author says he feels sorry for people who "scavenge the cable channels." Why do you think he feels this way?

Writing About the Reading

A Journal Entry

Think of a homeless person you've seen and write a journal entry describing him or her and what thoughts or feelings you had at the time.

A Paragraph

1. Eighner places little value on personal possessions. As he picks something up, he imagines throwing it out. Think of a personal possession that you could easily do without or one that you could never do without. Write a paragraph explaining why the object is or is not important to you.
2. Imagine that some people in your neighborhood that you didn't know were moving and left their unwanted, but useful belongings on the sidewalk. Write a paragraph describing the kinds of "treasures" you might expect to find.

An Essay

1. The author believes that the usefulness of material possessions is short-lived. He also describes this belief as a "healthy state of mind." Write an essay discussing whether you agree or disagree and why.
2. The number and variety of perfectly good items the author has found in Dumpsters emphasizes the amount of waste in our society. Write an essay explaining how this waste affects us and suggesting alternatives to just throwing out unwanted items.

A Creative Activity

Imagine that you were the author of this essay, finding "love letters and rag dolls of so many lives," as he does. Recall an object or letter and write an essay that re-creates the life of the person who threw it away.

Silenced Voices: Deaf Cultures and "Hearing" Families

▶ Richard Appelbaum and William J. Chambliss

This textbook excerpt, taken from Sociology, *describes one of many groups that have formed their own subculture. These authors take the position that deaf people prefer to share experiences with others who are deaf.*

Reading Strategy

Highlight the topic sentence of each paragraph and the key details that support each topic sentence.

Vocabulary Preview

heritage (2) background
simulated (4) imitated
virtually (4) practically
fraught (4) filled
wary (5) cautious; worried
confront (5) face; challenge
daunting (5) intimidating
confer (6) give; bestow
mainstream (6) integrate
fundamental (7) basic

*T*here are as many as 450,000 Americans who are completely unable 1
to hear; about 250,000 were born deaf. For them, family life poses
unique challenges. As a consequence, many deaf people prefer to practice endogamy, marrying others who are deaf and therefore share a
common experience.

There is a growing movement within the deaf community to 2
redefine the meaning of deafness not as a form of disability, but rather
as a positive culture. A growing number of deaf people see themselves
as similar to any ethnic group, sharing a common language (American

Sign Language, or ASL), possessing a strong sense of cultural identity, and taking pride in their heritage. One survey reported that the overwhelming majority would not even elect to have a free surgical implant that would enable them to hear.

Roslyn Rosen is an example of a person who takes great pride in   3
being deaf. Born of deaf parents and the mother of deaf children, Rosen is the president of the National Association of the Deaf:

> *I'm happy with who I am, and I don't want to be "fixed." Would an Italian-American rather be a WASP [White Anglo-Saxon Protestant]? In our society everybody agrees that whites have an easier time than blacks. But do you think that a black person would undergo operations to be a white?*

The desire for a deaf identity reflects the near impossibility of deaf   4
people ever learning to communicate with "hearing" people (people who are not deaf) through lipreading and simulated speech. People who have never heard a sound find it virtually impossible to utter sounds that most "hearing" people can recognize as words. Lipreading is equally problematic and is fraught with error. Reading, which depends on an understanding of the meaning of spoken words, can prove to be a frustrating experience. Yet for those who "hear" and "speak" ASL, a rich form of communication is possible, and with it comes a strong sense of shared identity.

Many deaf parents are wary when their deaf children get involved   5
in relationships with "hearing" people, preferring that they remain within their own community. Among those who marry, 90 percent choose spouses who are also deaf. Although many deaf people have succeeded in the "hearing" world, the problems that confront them can be daunting. Most will never be able to speak in a way that is likely to be understood by "hearing" people, and most of the "hearing" people they encounter will not know ASL. It is not surprising that when it comes to intimate relations, most deaf people choose to marry others who share their own language and culture.

Although families ordinarily confer their own ethnic status on   6
their children, this is not true for the nine out of ten deaf children who are born to "hearing" parents. Their parents are of one culture; they are of another. This can pose difficult choices for their families. On the one hand, "hearing" parents want the same sorts of things for their deaf children as do any parents: happiness, fulfillment, and successful lives as adults. Many would like their children to mainstream into the "hearing" world as best as possible. Yet they know that this will prove extremely difficult.

On the other hand, the deaf community argues that the deaf chil-   7
dren of "hearing" parents can never fully belong to the "hearing"

world, or, for that matter, even to their own "hearing" parents. Many leaders in the deaf community urge "hearing" parents to send their deaf children to residential schools for the deaf, where they will be fully accepted, learn deaf culture, and be with their own people. Fundamental questions about the meaning of "family" arise when the children and parents largely live in two different cultures.

Examining the Reading

Finding Meaning

1. What is endogamy?
2. According to the article, how do many deaf people wish to define themselves?
3. Why are deaf parents of deaf children wary when their children become involved with hearing people?
4. Why is it almost impossible for people who are deaf to speak?
5. Name one problem with lipreading.

Understanding Technique

1. Identify the authors' tone.
2. What type of evidence do the authors provide to support their thesis?

Thinking Critically

1. Explain what is meant by deaf people desiring a "deaf identity."
2. Discuss the advantages and disadvantages of deaf people learning American Sign Language.
3. Discuss the problems that confront deaf people when they mainstream into a hearing society.
4. What other groups of people have formed their own subculture?

Writing About the Reading

A Journal Entry

Write a journal entry discussing your reaction to the idea that many deaf people do not want to be able to hear.

A Paragraph

1. Suppose you had become deaf through illness or injury. Would you elect to read lips or learn American Sign Language? Write a paragraph explaining your choice.

2. Write a paragraph identifying what you think would be the major challenges in a relationship between a hearing person and a deaf person.

An Essay

1. If you had a child who was born deaf, would you choose a residential school for the deaf or a traditional school? Write an essay explaining your choice.
2. Deaf people develop their own language, which builds group identity. In a sense, groups of hearing people also develop language that establishes their identity. For example, teenagers use slang; medical doctors speak in medical jargon. Choose a group of people and describe the language that identifies them. (*Hint:* You might write about football fans, salespeople, computer hackers, car enthusiasts.)

A Creative Activity

Some deaf people have formed their own culture. Do you think other groups of people with physical illnesses and disabilities (blindness, cancer, muscular dystrophy, etc.) also have a separate culture? Write a paragraph describing the shared problems and concerns of a particular group.

Cultural Education in America

▸ Jonathan Wong
Student Essay

A college student from Hong Kong writes about his adjustment to life in America.

After merely a month of college in Oregon coming from Hong Kong, I could not endure the uninspiring cafeteria style cooking any longer. I longed for some good old-fashioned Chinese food. Therefore, I convinced my roommate to venture out with me to the lone, local Asian restaurant in the rural town of McMinnville. Without any preconceived notions or expectations regarding the authenticity of the cooking, my taste buds even so were quick to protest this imposter Chinese food—at the first bite! Then came dessert, the fortune cookie, and while the tradition did not originate in China, but rather in America, it foretold the fortune of excellent food and great company. Alas, it was only half true—the great company part. Deep within the secret recesses of my self-indulgent, hungry heart, lay the temptation to bargain my friend's company for the fortune of some tasty, genuine Chinese food! So that was how my cultural education had its humble beginning . . . with this first Chinese dinner and with this tiny piece of an after-meal dessert. It was the food that was not Chinese and the fortune cookie that was American that seemed to predetermine a certain discovery and a certain destiny.

If food adjustment were the only discovery, life would have been simple. There are many more. For example, 5 feet 8 inches tall is an admirable height for men back home but relatively short when compared with most American men. This "shortness" becomes even more painfully evident on the volleyball court each time I attempt to spike the ball above the towering wall of blocking hands. I find solace, however, on the soccer field. Unknowingly gifted in agility due to my small stature in the United States, I easily dribble the ball around and outrun those taller, but sluggish, husky soccer opponents, just like a seasoned fighter pilot who skillfully dodges around the charging missiles without getting hit.

Hitting the overweight category is another unpleasant surprise. One can blame this on the American diet as well as the sedentary lifestyle or alternatively perhaps, on the prevalent indulgent attitude here which often overrides my self-discipline and an upbringing that would prompt me to say "no" to dessert. Consequently, my sparkling commercial quality white teeth have fallen victim to the cavity filled teeth of a sweets lover. This is costly in terms of dental health and personal finance. Furthermore, I have transformed myself from a traditional, lean Asian to a typical, obese American. No self-respecting lover would want to handle these "love handles" of mine. Celibacy is not exactly what I have in mind! Was coming to the States a mistake of Titanic proportions? This is a question I have found myself asking repeatedly.

Regardless of the negatives thus far, one of the biggest advantages 4 of living here is freedom of choice. Coupled with clever word manipulation, one can choose to elevate oneself from an unglamorous state of existence to a grandiose state, and there is no shame. For instance, housewife is analogous to household executive, while custodian becomes an environmental service engineer. Today, I can proudly proclaim (that which I dare not assert back home) that I am a bionic toothed, financially unique, and physically challenged (both height and width) American. Moreover, I am proud of it! Isn't life in the English language grand here?

Another interesting, positive discovery is the eating etiquette—it is 5 proper to eat with lips closed and to converse after the food is swallowed. In Hong Kong, it is customarily acceptable to eat with the lips open while talking with the mouth full. Although I have adjusted to this new custom quite well, environment still dictates behavior. Quite unconsciously and predictably, Miss Manner's advice on table manners is inevitably left behind every time I visit China. My natural form of ingestion instinctively takes control. Yet, I would instantly notice my overseas relatives' vulgar table manners here. Embarrassment is an understatement, especially when I have American guests at the dining table. I watch in horror but am too polite to correct my overseas guests as the food particles fly across the table between bites, and they gleefully engage in their lively conversation in absolute oblivion.

Bite by bite and little by little, I have gradually assimilated this cul- 6 ture while retaining my own, or so it seems. Nevertheless, my friends here, on occasion, still tease me about my writing skills and my accent—a constant reminder of my foreign past. My relatives and Chinese friends, on the other hand, never fail to point out my American way of thinking as well as lifestyle—a personification of a yellow-skinned, white-cored "banana" they struggle to accept.

Struggling for acceptance by both cultures is apparently a com- 7 mon challenge shared by all new immigrants, and most of us somehow are able to resolve these (outer and inner) conflicts eventually. Many even gain invaluable insights about life in general and specific multi-cultural skills. I personally feel the formal education attained in America is literally pale in comparison to the colorful cultural experiences acquired here. Such experiences have become the cultural education I will treasure for the rest of my life.

Examining the Essay

1. Highlight and evaluate Wong's thesis statement.
2. Wong begins his essay by telling a story. Why is this an effective introduction? How clearly does it illustrate his thesis?
3. Evaluate Wong's use of humor. Is it effective? Did the humor help you understand the author's main points?
4. Examine the author's use of descriptive language. Highlight several particularly effective examples.
5. What is Wong's conclusion? How does he reach it?

Writing an Essay

1. Write an essay on manners. You might discuss whether there is too much emphasis on manners among people or groups of people you know. Or you might discuss which rules of etiquette are the most important and which violations are most offensive.
2. Write an essay explaining the importance of food in our culture.
3. Many people are judged by their height and weight. Write an essay describing this problem and some possible solutions.

 ## Making Connections

1. Compare the ways that Santiago in "Black *and* Latino" and Wong in "Cultural Education in America" deal with being in the middle of two cultures.

2. Both "Silenced Voices: Deaf Cultures and 'Hearing' Families" and "Dumpster Diving" deal with subcultures, groups with their own identity that create customs and behaviors. Write an essay comparing the two subcultures.

3. Customs and rituals are very important in the Tewa culture ("Through Tewa Eyes"). Do you sense that ritual and custom are important in any of the other cultures discussed in this chapter? Write an essay explaining the importance of ritual and custom in one of these other cultures.

Internet Connections

1. When people travel to other countries for business, they often seek advice on local customs. Visit this site: **http://www.webofculture.com/worldsmart/gestures.asp**. Read the information on gestures. Pick one country and write a paragraph comparing the body language of that country to ours. Why is this topic important for travelers to know?

2. Summarize the activities carried out by Creative Connections, as listed on their web site at **http://www. creativeconnections.org/01/**. How effective do you think these programs are in promoting cultural awareness and understanding?

3. Browse this fruitarianism site: **http://fruitarian.com/ao/ WhatIsFruitarianism.htm**. Write an essay evaluating the site and its content. How convincing are the arguments for eating fruit only? Do you think fruitarians are a type of subculture? Why?

   (If any of these web sites are unavailable, use a search engine to locate another appropriate site.)

Chapter 5

Others Who Shape Our Lives

Shopping Can Be a Challenge
   Carol Fleischman

The Promised Land
   Bill Cosby

Our Wounded Hearts
   Allison Bernard

Poppa and the Spruce Tree
   Mario Cuomo

Food from the 'Hood
   Lester Sloan

Bill Gates: Computer Wizard
   *Michael Schaller, Virginia Scharff,
   and Robert D. Schulzinger*

Do unto Others
   David Polmer

O ur lives are shaped by those around us, particularly our family and friends. We have vivid memories of fun-filled days spent with a close friend; we recall someone we could confide in; we treasure intimate moments with a mate or spouse; and we remember close, comforting times with a parent.

As important as friends and family may be, our lives are also shaped by those we do not know personally—a radio disk jockey who wakes us up each morning, a sports star we cheer for at each game, or a character we admire in a novel. Local, state, and national figures—presidents, senators, talk show hosts—may shape our lives through the issues they raise and the actions they take. And then there are the unsung heroes—people who may shape our lives without our directly knowing it or them. A local businessperson who donates food for a community fair, a medical researcher who develops a new vaccine or antibiotic, and people who selflessly volunteer their time by working in a local homeless shelter are examples.

In this chapter, the readings focus on people who have shaped the lives of others. You will read about how people—both friends and strangers, in the family and at work—influence one another, and the positive experiences that result from such influence. Examples can be found in the story of a woman who tries to offer advice to an uncle suffering from heart disease ("Our Wounded Hearts"), how a father's advice had long-lasting effects ("Poppa and the Spruce Tree"), and how Bill Cosby's parents shaped their lives so that they "fit" each other ("The Promised Land"). You will also read about people whose actions affect hundreds, even thousands, of other people, such as the group of teenagers who begin their own company in "Food from the 'Hood" and Bill Gates, the world's richest man, who started his own computer empire ("Bill Gates: Computer Wizard"). In addition, you will read about how others make shopping a difficult task for a blind woman ("Shopping Can Be a Challenge") and consider whether sports heroes should follow the golden rule ("Do unto Others").

Brainstorming About Others

Class Activity: Form groups of three to four students. Each group member should brainstorm a list of at least ten influential or important people in the news over the past week. Group members should compare lists and prepare a final list, which includes names that appeared on two or more individual lists. Groups then can compare lists and, again, identify recurring names.

Shopping Can Be a Challenge

▶ **Carol Fleischman**

This essay, published in the Buffalo News, *provides a fresh view-point of a common experience—shopping. The writer, who is blind, focuses on how her experience is shaped by those around her.*

Reading Strategy

In this essay, Fleischman reveals her attitude toward the sighted people around her in several different ways. As you read, highlight words, phrases, and sentences that reveal how the writer feels.

Vocabulary Preview

ritual (2) habit; routine
beeline (4) direct route; straight line
imposing (5) impressive; mildly threatening
chastised (19) scolded; criticized
composing (21) calming; controlling
preoccupied (23) busy; distracted
retrieve (23) get and bring back
reminiscent (24) reminding one of
foiled (24) stopped; prevented

*H*ave you ever tried to buy a dress when you can't see? I have, be-   1
cause I'm blind.

At one time, I would shop with friends. This ritual ended after the   2
time I happily brought home a dress a friend had helped me choose,
and my husband, Don, offered a surprising observation: "The fit is
great, but do you like all those huge fish?" The dress went back.

Now I rely on Don and my guide dog, Misty, as my shopping partners.   3

We enter the store and make a beeline for the dress department.   4
Don usually sees two or three salespeople scatter. The aisles empty as
if a bomber had come on the scene.

Then I realize I'm holding the "live wire." But I'm not judgmental—   5
once I, too, was uneasy around large dogs. Although Misty is better
behaved than most children, I know a 65-pound German shepherd is
imposing.

On one recent shopping trip, a brave saleswoman finally approached us. "Can I help you?" she said to my husband.   6

"Yes, I'm looking for a dress," I replied. (After all, I'm the one who will be wearing it.) "Maybe something in red or white."   7

"RED OR WHITE," she said, speaking very slowly and loudly even though my hearing is fine. I managed not to fall as Misty jumped back on my feet, frightened by the woman's booming voice.   8

Don was distracted too. I heard him rustling through hangers on a nearby rack. I called his name softly to get his attention, and another man answered my call. Bad luck. What were the chances of two Dons being in earshot?   9

"This is great!" Don said, holding up a treasure.   10

I swept my hand over the dress to examine it. It had a neckline that plunged to the hemline. "Hmmm," I said. I walk three miles daily with Misty and stay current with fashion, but I'm positive this costume would look best on one of the Spice Girls.   11

Finally, I chose three dresses to try on.   12

Another shopper distracted Misty, even though the harness sign reads: "Please do not pet. I'm working." She said, "Your dog reminds me of my Max, who I recently put to sleep," so I am sympathetic. We discussed her loss for 15 minutes. Some therapists don't spend that much time with grieving clients.   13

Don was back. He told me the route to travel to the dressing room. I commanded Misty: right, left, right and straight ahead. We wove our way past several small voices.   14

"Mom, why is that dog in the store?"   15

"Mom, is that a dog or a wolf?"   16

And my personal favorite: "But that lady's eyes are open."   17

I trust parents to explain: "The lady is giving her guide dog commands. Her dog is a helping dog. They're partners." I questioned whether this positive message had been communicated though, when I heard an adult say: "Oh, there's one of those blind dogs."   18

Other people, though well-intentioned, can interfere with my effective use of Misty. Guide dogs are highly trained and very dependable but occasionally make potentially dangerous mistakes. On my way through the aisles, Misty bumped me into a pointed rack, requiring my quick action. I used a firm tone to correct her, and she dived to the ground like a dying actress. Witnessing this performance, another shopper chastised me for being cruel.   19

I was shocked. Misty's pride was hurt, but I needed to point out the error in order to avoid future mistakes. If I did not discipline her, what would prevent Misty from walking me off the curb into traffic?   20

Composing myself, I was delighted by the saleswoman's suggestion: "Can I take you to your dressing room?" I was less delighted when   21 she grabbed me and pushed me ahead while Misty trailed us on a leash. I wriggled out of the woman's hold. Gently pushing her ahead, I lightly held her elbow in sighted-guide technique (called so because the person who sees goes first).

"This is better. Please put my hand on the door knob. I'll take it from here," I said.   22

In the room, Misty plopped down and sighed with boredom. I sighed with relief that she was still with me. On one shopping trip, I was so preoccupied with trying on clothes that Misty sneaked out beneath the dressing room's doors. I heard her tags jingling as she left but was half-dressed and couldn't retrieve her. Fortunately, Don was outside the door and snagged her leash.   23

I modeled the dresses for Don and, feeling numb, bought all three. As we left the store, Misty's magnetism, reminiscent of the Pied Piper's, attracted a toddler who draped himself over her. She remained calm, as he tried to ride her. The boy's fun was soon foiled by his frantic mother.   24

When we returned to our car, I gave Misty a treat and lots of praise. A good day's work deserves a good day's pay for both of us.   25

"Shop till you drop" or "retail therapy" could never be my motto. To me, "charge" means going into battle.   26

Examining the Reading

Finding Meaning

1. Summarize Fleischman's attitude toward shopping.
2. Why did the author stop shopping with friends?
3. According to Fleischman, what types of problems do blind people face?
4. What did the author do when Misty bumped her into a pointed display rack? Why?
5. Describe Fleischman's attitude toward those around her. Where in the essay are these attitudes revealed?

Understanding Technique

1. Evaluate the effectiveness of opening this essay by asking and answering a question.
2. Fleischman makes extensive use of dialogue and description to express her ideas. Identify several particularly effective examples of each.
3. How does Fleischman establish a humorous tone?

Thinking Critically

1. Why do you think the saleswoman spoke loudly to the author?
2. Why might some people find the writer's guide dog threatening?
3. According to the article, what can you infer is meant by "sighted-guide technique"?
4. What did the author mean when she said, "To me, 'charge' means going into battle"?
5. From this article, can you conclude that most people understand the partnership between blind people and their dogs? Why?

Writing About the Reading

A Journal Entry

Write a journal entry describing a time in your life when you were unable to carry out everyday activities without help from others. How did you feel about this situation?

A Paragraph

1. Write a paragraph explaining what a parent should teach a child about guide dogs.
2. Write a paragraph describing the disability of a family member, friend, or acquaintance.

An Essay

1. Write an essay explaining a situation in which you felt frustrated by those around you.
2. Write a letter to the salesclerk who assisted Fleischman, informing her about the needs and sensitivities of blind customers and suggesting how she might change her approach.

A Creative Activity

Imagine that Fleischman is deaf rather than blind, and that she has a hearing guide dog. What problems might she experience while shopping or elsewhere?

The Promised Land

▶ **Bill Cosby**

In this reading, actor and humorist Bill Cosby tells of the stage of ultimate marital bliss his parents have reached. This essay is taken from his book titled Love and Marriage.

Reading Strategy

This essay is intended to be light and entertaining. As you read it, highlight or annotate sections that contribute to Cosby's light, humorous tone.

Vocabulary Preview

residing (1) living
mellowness (1) the state of being toned down (by passage of
                     years)
Dalai Lama (1) religious and political Tibetan leader, known
                     for being wise and calm
ascended (2) gone up; risen
plane (2) level
rapport (9) relationship marked by harmony
literal (9) actual
planetarium (16) a building for viewing a model of the solar
                     system
lotus land (18) a place of extreme contentment
follies (24) silly actions or foolish decisions

Grow old along with me!
The best is yet to be.

When Browning wrote these lines, he wasn't thinking of my mother   1
and father or anyone else in North Philadelphia; but whenever I see my
mother and father together, I know they're residing in a state where I
want to live with Camille, a state of such blessed mellowness that they
make the Dalai Lama seem like a Type A personality.

I will never forget my first awareness that my mother and father had ascended to a matrimonial plane where only God knew what they were doing—perhaps. We were driving to Philadelphia from Atlantic City, with my father at the wheel, my mother beside him, and me in the back.   2

"Oh, there's a car from Pittsburgh," said my mother, looking at a license plate in the next lane.   3

"How do you know it's from Pittsburgh?" said my father.   4

"Because I couldn't think of Pennsylvania," she replied.   5

And I waited for my father to respond to this Einsteinian leap into another dimension, but he didn't speak. He simply continued to drive, a supremely contented man.   6

Because he had understood.   7

He had understood that my mother's Pittsburgh was a mythical place, located where the Monongahela entered the twilight zone. My mother also had not been able to think of Afghanistan, but she didn't say that the car was from Kabul. However, *had* she said that the car was from Kabul, my father would have understood it bore Afghans moving to Allentown.   8

For the next twenty minutes, I thought about fifty-three years of marriage and how they had bonded my parents in this remarkable Zen rapport; but then I was suddenly aware that my father had just driven past the exit for Philadelphia. Not the exit for Pennsylvania or for North America, but for Philadelphia, the literal city.   9

"Mom," I said, "didn't Dad just pass the exit we want?"   10

"Yes, he did," she replied.   11

"Well, why don't you *say* something?"   12

"Your father knows what he's doing."   13

Had *I* driven past the proper exit, my wife would have said, *Please pull over and let me out. I'd like to finish this trip by hitching a ride on a chicken truck.*   14

But if Camille and I can just stay together another twenty-five years, then we also will have reached the Twilight Zone, where one of us will do something idiotic and the other one not only will understand it but admire it as well.   15

You turned out the light where I'm reading, I will tell her. *Thank you for the surprise trip to the planetarium.*   16

You left your shoes in the bathtub, she will tell me. *Thank you for giving me two more boats.*   17

One morning a few days after that memorably roundabout trip to Philadelphia, I got another glimpse of the lotus land where my parents dwelled. My father came into the house, took off his hat, put it on a chair, gave some money to my children, and then went back and sat on his hat.   18

"You just sat on your hat," my mother told him.   19

"Of course I did," he replied, and then neither one of them said an- 20
other word about hat reduction. When the time came to leave, my
father picked up the crushed hat and put it on his head, where it sat
like a piece of Pop Art. My mother glanced at it, as if to make sure that
it would not fall off, and then she took his arm and they walked out the
door, ready to be the sweethearts of the Mummers Parade.

However, if *I* ever sat on my hat, Camille would say, *Can't you feel* 21
that you're sitting on your hat?

And I would reply, *It's a tradition in my family for a man to sit on his* 22
hat. It's one of the little things that my father did for my mother.

Yes, twenty-five years, happy as they have been, are still not 23
enough to have given Camille and me that Ringling Brothers rhythm
my mother and father enjoy. But we can hear the circus calling to us.

Love, what follies are committed in thy name, said Francis Bacon. 24

So far, most of marriage has been the Ziegfeld Follies for Camille 25
and me. And now we're getting ready to send in the clowns.

Examining the Reading

Finding Meaning

1. What is it about his parents' marriage that Cosby finds so endearing?
2. How did Cosby's father respond when his mother said the car was
   from Pittsburgh?
3. Why didn't Cosby's mother stop his father from driving past the correct exit?
4. How did Cosby's father respond when his mother informed him
   that he was sitting on his hat?

Understanding Technique

1. Evaluate the effectiveness of opening the essay with a quotation.
2. Describe the essay's organization.

Thinking Critically

1. How has Cosby's parents' marriage shaped the expectations Cosby
   now has in his own marriage?
2. Explain what Cosby means when he refers to his parents' marriage
   as having "that Ringling Brothers rhythm."
3. Discuss how Cosby views his own twenty-five years of marriage.
4. Explain Bacon's statement, "Love, what follies are committed in
   thy name."

Writing About the Reading

A Journal Entry

Write a journal entry about longlasting marriages. Why do some marriages last while others do not?

A Paragraph

1. Our lives are constantly being shaped by others' experiences. Write a paragraph on how a couple you know has influenced a relationship you have had.
2. Every individual has different "requirements" for a spouse. Write a paragraph identifying the requirements you have found essential— or would look for—in a spouse or potential spouse.

An Essay

1. Cosby's parents seemed to have reached a state of complete compatibility and understanding of each other. Have you ever reached that state in a relationship? Write an essay explaining why you have or have not reached it with another person.
2. Write an essay describing a couple you know. Explain the type of relationship they have. Use specific instances, events, or conversations to illustrate your points.
3. Cosby's parents readily accept each other's idiosyncrasies. Think of a person with whom you are close. Write an essay describing how you respond to that person's idiosyncrasies and how he or she reacts to yours.

A Creative Activity

What other crazy, zany, or inconsistent exchanges can you imagine might have occurred between Cosby's parents? Describe several in paragraph form.

Our Wounded Hearts

▶ **Allison Bernard**

What could you do about a relative whose personal habits are killing him or her? In this reading from Health *magazine, the author relates her experience with an uncle who suffered from heart disease.*

Reading Strategy

As you read, highlight the details that describe the uncle's original condition and those that reveal a change in his lifestyle following his second heart attack.

Vocabulary Preview

malice (3) ill will; evil intent
bypass (4) heart surgery that replaces clogged arteries
with clear ones
squelched (10) covered up; held back
momentous (11) eventful; important
abundance (12) large amount
bullied (12) forced; pushed
deteriorate (16) worsen; decline

*I*t didn't take a rocket scientist to see the problem. My uncle ate too   1
much, never exercised, threw few but awesome temper tantrums, and
was an on-again, off-again smoker. In fact, more than a decade before,
at the age of 40, he'd had a minor heart attack. After that there was a
lot of talk and activity: This cheese is fat-free, that omelette was made
with egg whites only. Always turkey breast, never lasagna. A new treadmill in front of the television—but little change in his habits.

It drove me nuts. Not necessarily him or his health, but the entire   2
situation. Everyone ate so much at my aunt and uncle's home in Con-
necticut. No one ever left the house, and the television was always on.
When I first came to the East Coast for college, I would visit them on
holidays and realize only on the way home, two or three days later, that
I hadn't gone outdoors the entire time. I found myself suggesting walks
and tentatively volunteering recipes for brown rice. I pointed out articles on nutrition, cooking, starting exercise programs. I wanted to
help; I was aching to help.

"We eat fat-free," my aunt would tell me impatiently. I got the message, though I felt like a bystander watching an accident in slow motion. During these visits my uncle didn't talk much. He watched sports on TV with my male cousins. He was always friendly if distant, not particularly interested in a young woman who didn't understand football. One day when I was visiting him and my aunt at the beach, a friend I'd brought along commented, "Your uncle is a very large person." It was said without malice, and I was about to point out that he was just tall and big-boned when I realized that, yes, he was fat.   3

So it wasn't a major shock when I heard he'd had a second heart attack. Initially everyone was calm. He seemed fine, was in the hospital, resting. Then tests showed that as much as 70 percent of his heart was dead. A bypass would be useless, and the alternatives narrowed to a transplant. Before he could get on the list for a new heart, however, he would have to lose 75 pounds.   4

I was visiting when the doctor gave him the news. My cousin asked about a possible genetic basis for his condition, but the doctor politely dismissed the idea. "Your father is very heavy," he said. "He must eat less and take drugs for his blood pressure." There wasn't much else to do.   5

After the doctor left, my uncle sighed. "I don't want to have to worry about what I eat for the rest of my life," he said.   6

"Tough," I heard my cousin mutter.   7

I followed her out of the hospital room and suggested that maybe he could learn to cook. If he prepared his own food, he would know what he could and couldn't eat. She looked at me as though I were a lunatic. "There is no way my father will ever set foot in the kitchen," she said.   8

I called my aunt a few days later to see how things were going. He was starting his diet, she reported, and she had finally figured out the trick. "Portion size," she said. "We ate fat-free for years when we should have been cutting down on how much we eat."   9

Did I know that? Well, yes, actually, I did. I'd even given her an article I'd written on portion control. I realized my aunt had never read past the first few sentences. I put a smile in my voice, squelched my frustration, and said that I was looking forward to helping at Christmas, only three weeks away.   10

That Christmas was a momentous one. My parents were visiting—having given up hope of my sister and me ever making it out west—and it was the first time the two families were to spend the holidays together. I'd heard my uncle had been losing weight, 15 pounds so far—but he still had 60 to go.   11

When we arrived at the house, my aunt immediately set us to preparing food: my mother to cutting up vegetables, my father to mashing potatoes with whole milk and butter. I wandered in and out of the kitchen, amazed at the abundance of rich, fattening food. I was   12 bullied into sprinkling cups of brown sugar and pouring pints of maple syrup over a small number of yams.

When we sat down to dinner, however, I noticed that my uncle ate   13
well: turkey, a plain potato, steamed green beans. I was impressed, even envious.

Earlier, during the food preparation, we'd had our first real con-   14
versation. He'd talked about his exercising, about the seven-minute stints he did on the treadmill, his determination to lose weight. For once I felt some hope that my prodding was justified, maybe welcome. Then he told me that his father—a sharp quiet man watching TV in the next room—didn't know he was waiting for a heart transplant. "Why worry him?" he said.

Why not: He's his *father*, after all. This sad secrecy, this willingness   15
to keep something as serious as a heart transplant from his own father, stunned me. So did the other things I heard a few weeks later: that my uncle had tried to cut up the Christmas turkey for us to take back to the city and was too weak to do it; that my aunt had thrown a tantrum before we arrived and stalked out of the house; that she was furious with my uncle for letting himself get so sick and with herself for not stopping him.

Now we all felt guilty—and angry—at how we'd watched my uncle's   16
health deteriorate. But was there really anything we could have done?

I called William Castelli, a cardiologist and former director of the   17
legendary Framingham Heart Study, who's responsible for much of what we know about the causes of heart disease, lung cancer, and stroke. Over 30 years he repeatedly interviewed 13,000 participants and gave them advice time and again about eating and smoking—advice that was mostly ignored.

"How did you keep from getting angry?" I asked him.   18

Castelli seemed surprised; anger hadn't occurred to him. "Well, you   19
don't want to be unpleasant. . . . It's a tough problem. You have to create a reality. Most people won't change unless some disaster strikes them.

"But once they see a benefit, even just a slight one, they begin to get   20
a feeling of what they can accomplish," he continued. "Otherwise, all families can do is show love and respect but also remind them what the evidence is, what the route is, and what's at the end of the tunnel."

It hit me just how vain my so-called help had been: Had I really   21
hoped to save my uncle? Had I felt obliged to? Or had I just wanted to be right after seeing my advice ignored for so long? In the thick of it, I couldn't tell. And gradually I pulled back. I'd go on giving feedback, but I stopped expecting it to matter.

Then, to my surprise, my uncle made the transplant list. He danced   22
and glowed at his daughter's wedding and became, for less than a year, a man full of hope and conversation and life. We talked more during those few months than we had in previous decades.

But it all came too late. In December he died of a third heart attack   23
while waiting for his transplant. I realized then, perhaps for the first
time, how being right can be a false reward. Being wrong, sometimes,
is so much better.

Examining the Reading

Finding Meaning

1. Describe the lifestyle of Allison Bernard's uncle.
2. Why was Bernard's uncle unable to have bypass surgery?
3. What did the doctor say her uncle should do after he had the second heart attack?
4. How did the author try to help her uncle?
5. According to Dr. Castelli, a cardiologist, what can families do for patients like the author's uncle?

Understanding Technique

1. Describe how this essay is organized.
2. Evaluate Bernard's conclusion. What additional information does it contribute to the essay?

Thinking Critically

1. Why was it so difficult for the author's uncle to change his lifestyle?
2. Why did Bernard say that she "felt like a bystander watching an accident in slow motion" when she visited her uncle?
3. How did the author feel about her uncle keeping his heart transplant a secret from his own father?
4. What did the author mean by "I realized then, perhaps for the first time, how being right can be a false reward"?
5. Is the title "Our Wounded Hearts" appropriate for this essay? Why or why not?

Writing About the Reading

A Journal Entry

Write a journal entry describing your lifestyle. How do you think it affects your health?

A Paragraph

1. Write a paragraph describing the attitudes of Bernard's aunt and cousin toward her uncle. Explain why you think they felt as they did.

2. Choose a friend or relative who is particularly close to you. Write a paragraph explaining why you admire that person.

An Essay

1. Write an essay describing a time you tried to help a friend or family member by offering advice. Did the person follow your advice? If not, explain what you think you should have done differently to help that person.
2. Imagine that you are Allison Bernard. Write a letter she might have written to her uncle after her Thanksgiving visit.

A Creative Activity

Imagine that Bernard's uncle had lived. How do you think he might have felt, thought, and lived his life? Rewrite the ending of this essay as if he had lived.

Poppa and the Spruce Tree

▶ Mario Cuomo

*In this essay Mario Cuomo, former governor of New York, recalls
an experience with his father that serves as an inspiration to
him. It was first published in the* Diaries of Mario M. Cuomo.

Reading Strategy

As you read, underline words, phrases, or statements that reveal Cuomo's attitude toward his father.

Vocabulary Preview

rummaging (2) looking through; searching
accumulate (2) collect; pile up
scale (5) climb
stakes (8) large sticks, usually sharpened, used for support
vengeance (10) great force

*P*oppa taught me a lot about life, especially its hard times. I remem-   1
bered one of his lessons one night when I was ready to quit a political
campaign I was losing, and wrote about it in my diary:

   Tired, feeling the many months of struggle, I went up to the den to   2
make some notes. I was looking for a pencil, rummaging through papers in the back of my desk drawer, where things accumulate for years,
when I turned up one of Poppa's old business cards, the ones we made
up for him, that he was so proud of: *Andrea Cuomo, Italian-American
Groceries—Fine Imported Products*. Poppa never had occasion to give
anyone a calling card, but he loved having them.

   I couldn't help wondering what Poppa would have said if I told him   3
I was tired or—God forbid—discouraged. Then I thought about how
he dealt with hard circumstances. A thousand pictures flashed through
my mind, but one scene came sharply into view.

   We had just moved to Holliswood, New York, from our apartment   4
behind the store. We had our own house for the first time; it had some

land around it, even trees. One, in particular, was a great blue spruce that must have been 40 feet tall.

Less than a week after we moved in, there was a terrible storm. We came home from the store that night to find the spruce pulled almost totally from the ground and flung forward, its mighty nose bent in the asphalt of the street. My brother Frankie and I could climb poles all day; we were great at fire escapes; we could scale fences with barbed wire—but we knew nothing about trees. When we saw our spruce, defeated, its cheek on the canvas, our hearts sank. But not Poppa's.

Maybe he was five feet six if his heels were not worn. Maybe he weighed 155 pounds if he had a good meal. Maybe he could see a block away if his glasses were clean. But he was stronger than Frankie and me and Marie and Mamma all together.

We stood in the street looking down at the tree. The rain was falling. Then he announced, "O.K., we gonna push 'im up!" "What are you talking about, Poppa? The roots are out of the ground!" "Shut up, we gonna push 'im up, he's gonna grow again." We didn't know what to say to him. You couldn't say no to him. So we followed him into the house and we got what rope there was and we tied the rope around the tip of the tree that lay in the asphalt, and he stood up by the house, with me pulling on the rope and Frankie in the street in the rain, helping to push up the great blue spruce. In no time at all, we had it standing up straight again!

With the rain still falling, Poppa dug away at the place where the roots were, making a muddy hole wider and wider as the tree sank lower and lower toward security. Then we shoveled mud over the roots and moved boulders to the base to keep the tree in place. Poppa drove stakes in the ground, tied rope from the trunk to the stakes, and maybe two hours later looked at the spruce, the crippled spruce made straight by ropes, and said, "Don't worry, he's gonna grow again. . . ."

I looked at the card and wanted to cry. If you were to drive past that house today, you would see the great, straight blue spruce, maybe 65 feet tall, pointing straight up to the heavens, pretending it never had its nose in the asphalt.

I put Poppa's card back in the drawer, closed it with a vengeance. I couldn't wait to get back into the campaign.

Examining the Reading

Finding Meaning

1. Describe Cuomo's father's reaction when the forty-foot blue spruce fell during the storm.
2. What actions did Cuomo's family take to get the tree to grow again?

3. What triggered Cuomo's recollection of the spruce tree story?
4. Compare Cuomo's emotional state before and after recalling the story of the spruce tree.

Understanding Technique

1. What is the thesis of the essay? Is it stated or implied (suggested)?
2. Study Cuomo's use of dialogue in paragraph 7. What did it contribute to the essay?

Thinking Critically

1. Why do you think Cuomo's father went to such great lengths to save the tree?
2. Based on the story, what kind of man do you think Cuomo's father was?
3. How did remembering this story about his father and the tree help Cuomo in his campaign?
4. Based on this reading, what do you know about how Cuomo feels about his father?

Writing About the Reading

A Journal Entry

Write an entry describing an event or experience that made you feel terribly discouraged.

A Paragraph

1. Write a paragraph describing a situation in which you felt like giving up. Include the outcome. Did you give up? If so, did you make the right decision? If not, how did you motivate yourself to continue?
2. Cuomo says his father taught him a lot about life, especially its hard times. Write a paragraph describing a hard time you experienced and what you learned from it.

An Essay

1. Write an essay describing something your mother, father, or another important person in your life once did or said that later inspired you.
2. By raising the spruce tree, Cuomo's father accomplished what Cuomo thought to be an impossible task. Write an essay describing an event or situation that you felt was impossible or unlikely but that actu-

ally happened. Include why it happened and explain your reaction
to it.

A Creative Activity

Suppose Cuomo's father were still alive and Mario called him on the
phone to announce that he was quitting his campaign. Write a dialogue re-creating what you think Cuomo's father would have said. Use
the following format, if you wish.

Mario: Dad, I've decided to quit the campaign.

Father:

Mario:

Food from the 'Hood

▶ **Lester Sloan**

This essay describes a student project that eventually became a national enterprise, producing funds for college scholarships. The account originally appeared in Newsweek.

Reading Strategy

As you read, highlight the key details that describe how Food from the 'Hood began and what it has accomplished.

Vocabulary Preview

reclaim (1) take back
mural (1) wall painting
oasis (1) fertile area
buoyed (2) lifted up; inspired
roster (2) list
diversify (2) create more variety; branch out
burgeoning (2) rapidly expanding; blossoming
catapulted (2) hurled; quickly raised up or over
franchise (3) to sell rights to market a product in a different
              area
logo (3) identifying symbol
mentor (3) an experienced person who advises and guides a
              novice
incarcerated (3) imprisoned

*I*t may not be history's biggest victory garden, but don't underestimate   1
the size of the victory. Shortly after the Los Angeles riots in 1992, a
group of 40 students at Crenshaw High School and their energetic biology teacher decided to reclaim the weedy quarter-acre plot that had
long been abandoned behind the school's football field. The goal was
simple: to create a community garden that would bring life back to one
of the city's most battered neighborhoods while giving the students
some hands-on science experience. They planted flowers, herbs, lettuce, collard greens, and other vegetables. A colorful mural soon appeared on the back wall, with a brown hand reaching toward a white
one. In the middle of South-Central L.A., an oasis bloomed. The kids
donated some of the produce to needy families in South-Central and

sold the rest at local farmers markets. They called their project Food from the 'Hood.

And the ideas kept on sprouting. Buoyed by their success and aided by a growing roster of adult volunteers, the Crenshaw students decided to diversify. They had the herbs, they had the lettuce—what could be a better accompaniment than salad dressing? The Food from the 'Hood members created their own recipe and designed their own label for the brand, called Straight Out 'the Garden. Local business leaders helped with the marketing and manufacturing, and now the dressing is sold, for $2.59 a bottle, in more than 2,000 stores in 23 states. The burgeoning enterprise has catapulted the student farmers into student owners; they expect to earn $50,000 in profits this year, which will go toward funding college scholarships. Ten of the 15 seniors in Food from the 'Hood have been accepted at four-year colleges—a remarkable record for an inner-city public school. "When a kid gets an acceptance letter to college, that's our immediate payoff," says Melinda McMullen, a marketing consultant who worked with teacher Tammy Bird to steer the kids toward produce and profits.

Even more important than the money is the sense of accomplishment that has grown out of Food from the 'Hood. "We showed that a group of inner-city kids can and did make a difference," says freshman Terie Smith, 15. The students run all aspects of the business—from weeding and harvesting to public relations and computer logs. They've received inquiries from across the country about duplicating their business plan, and they may franchise their logo to a group of New York kids who hope to sell applesauce. Food from the 'Hood members also have set up a mentor system and an SAT preparatory program. "We all try to help each other in everything," says Jaynell Grayson, 17, who will attend Babson College on scholarship next year. Grayson doesn't know who her father is; her mother has been incarcerated most of her life. Food from the 'Hood has been a substitute family for her. "What comes from that garden is inspiration," says McMullen. "From anything—even the riots—amazing things can grow."

Examining the Reading

Finding Meaning

1. What was the goal of the students when they began the gardening project?
2. How did they continue the project after they grew vegetables?
3. How will they spend the $50,000 they expect to earn this year?
4. Explain how the group came to be named "Food from the 'Hood."
5. What activities have the students who began Food from the 'Hood designed to help one other?

Understanding Technique

1. Analyze Sloan's use of topic sentences.
2. What types of details does he use to support his main points?

Thinking Critically

1. Why do you think the biology teacher took a special interest in helping students coordinate Food from the 'Hood?
2. What do you think has been the most important result of Food from the 'Hood?
3. In what sense can the Food from the 'Hood members be considered heroes?
4. What did McMullen mean when she said, "What comes from that garden is inspiration"?

Writing About the Reading

A Journal Entry

Write a journal entry exploring your feelings toward getting involved in community projects. Have you done so? Why or why not?

A Paragraph

1. Both the name of the group and the name of the salad dressing use nonstandard English. Write a paragraph describing situations in which you feel nonstandard English should and should not be used.
2. Write a paragraph explaining what, if anything, you feel the scholarship recipients should give back to the project. (Should they be required to work on the project during the summer, for example?)

An Essay

1. Suppose you were given the opportunity to coordinate a fund-raising activity for college scholarships. Write an essay describing what product you would try to sell and how you would market it.
2. Suppose you were required, as part of your graduation requirements, to work in a community or college service program designed to help others. Write an essay describing the kind of project you'd like to get involved with and what you'd hope to accomplish.

A Creative Activity

Suppose Food from the 'Hood continues to expand. What types of foods do you think they might sell next? Write a paragraph describing their expansion. Include the names of the new products, and explain where they will get their ingredients and materials.

Bill Gates:
Computer Wizard

▶ **Michael Schaller, Virginia Scharff,
and Robert D. Schulzinger**

*This reading describes how Bill Gates, the world's richest man,
built his Microsoft computer company. Taken from a United
States history textbook,* Present Tense, *it traces his life from
age 12 to 1997. Gates has been troubled by legal battles since the
fall of 1997 when Microsoft was sued by the Justice Department
and eighteen states plus the District of Columbia for using illegal
means to expand its monopoly on computer-operating systems.
In April 2000, a ruling stated that Microsoft had indeed violated
antitrust laws. The company was not split in two as many had
hoped, but settlement talks ensued and a tentative agreement was
reached in November 2001.*

Reading Strategy

A time line is a diagram that shows events in the order in
which they happened. Draw a time line showing the major
events in Gates's life.

Vocabulary Preview

envisioned (1) saw in the mind; imagined
revolutionize (1) change completely
mainstream (1) normal; average
entrepreneurial (1) pertaining to one who turns an idea into
                        a business
insatiable (1) never satisfied; limitless
penchant (2) strong liking; tendency
municipalities (3) governments of cities, towns, or villages
dominated (5) controlled; had taken over
squelch (6) stamp out; do away with
contested (6) called into question; challenged

*I*n the mid-1960s, few Americans envisioned the ways in which com- 1
puters would later revolutionize American life. Even those who were
most familiar with the machines could not foresee the time when millions of American families would assume the necessity of owning, and
using daily, a personal computer. Being interested in computers then,
recalled William H. Gates III, was "not a mainstream thing. I couldn't
imagine spending the rest of my life at it." But by the 1990s, Bill Gates
would become America's richest man, an inventor and entrepreneurial
genius who built his vast fortune on the world's insatiable appetite for
computer technology.

The son of a well-to-do Seattle family, Gates first became fascinated 2
with computers as a child of twelve, in 1967, when he and three friends
from the exclusive Lakeside School formed the Lakeside Programming
Group. One of his first programs was a class schedule for the school,
which he engineered so that he would share classes with all the pretti-
est girls. The school paid him $4,200 for a summer's work. Soon, the
Lakeside students were doing consulting work for the Computer Center Corporation, but Gates's penchant for pulling pranks got him into
trouble when he hacked into, and crashed, Control Data Corporation's
CYBERNET computer system.

By the time Gates was 14, he was president of his own company, Traf- 3
o-Data. The firm earned $20,000 selling traffic-counting systems to mu-
nicipalities before its customers even found out that the company was
run by high school students. He interrupted a thriving career, however,
and enrolled at Harvard University in 1973, planning to become a lawyer.

At Harvard, Gates remained fascinated by the possibilities of com- 4
puter programs, operating systems, and software. In 1975, at the end of
his sophomore year, he dropped out, moved to Albuquerque, New Mexico, and with his old Lakeside friend Paul Allen, founded Microsoft. Securing a contract with the Tandy Corporation to develop software for
Radio Shack computers, Microsoft grew quickly and moved to Seattle.
The company hit the big time when IBM contacted Gates about creating an operating system for a new product, the "personal computer."
The result, the MS-DOS operating system, was eventually licensed to
more than one hundred companies producing IBM-compatible computers, and by 1981 Microsoft was earning $16 million a year.

Like Thomas Edison, Gates was the rare inventor who mastered the 5
marketplace as well as the laboratory. In the late 1980s, Microsoft introduced its Windows operating system, which allowed users to run IBM-
compatible computers with a handheld "mouse" and on-screen symbols.
Windows was as simple to use and "user-friendly" as the operating system

pioneered by arch-rival Apple Computer, and IBM "clones" were much less expensive than Apple's famous Macintosh model. Soon Windows dominated the market, and Gates, at the age of 32, became a billionaire.

An intensely competitive man, Gates has often been described as   6
aloof, sarcastic, and abrupt, but also as charming, funny, and able to inspire strong loyalty in his employees. The very model of a nineties corporate executive, he puts in long days and works weekends, and he expects employees who aspire to upward mobility to do the same. Microsoft has also earned a reputation as a cutthroat competitor: the Federal Trade Commission has investigated allegations that the company used its dominant position to squelch competition. But however contested his business practices, Gates undeniably had more to do with bringing the computer revolution into American homes and offices than any other individual.

Examining the Reading

Finding Meaning

1. What was Bill Gates's first professional computer experience?
2. How did Bill Gates get into trouble with a major computer corporation when he was young?
3. When Gates was the president of his first company, what did his company do?
4. Describe the development that made Gates a billionaire.
5. How has Gates influenced his employees?
6. How has Gates been described by others?

Understanding Technique

1. What is the essay's thesis? Which sentence in the conclusion refers to it again?
2. Although the essay is primarily factual, the writers' attitude toward Gates are revealed. Highlight those sections in which the authors' attitudes are revealed.
3. Highlight the transitions.
4. Evaluate the essay's introduction. How do the writers capture your interest?

Thinking Critically

1. How did Gates's contributions influence the computer world?
2. Why was the development of Windows perceived as a major contribution?

3. In the reading, Bill Gates is compared with Thomas Edison. Do you think this is a fair and reasonable comparison? Why or why not?
4. This reading was taken from a U.S. history textbook. Do you think Bill Gates has already become an important historical figure?
5. From the reading, what can you conclude about Gates's methods of doing business?

Writing About the Reading

A Journal Entry

Bill Gates is first and foremost an inventor. Brainstorm a list of inventions that have influenced your life.

A Paragraph

1. The frequent and extensive use of computers in this country has both a negative and a positive side. Write a paragraph explaining whether you believe the advent of the computer is more positive than negative or the other way around.
2. Since Gates works long days and weekends, he might be described as a workaholic. Are you a workaholic or do you know someone who is? Write a paragraph describing the traits and characteristics of a workaholic.

An Essay

1. Suppose someone was willing to loan you $20,000 to start your own business. Write an essay describing the product, service, or project you would focus on and how you would get started.
2. The introductory paragraph of this article states that computers have revolutionized American life. Write an essay presenting reasons why you think this statement is or is not true.

A Creative Activity

Select a point in this article at which Bill Gates's life could have gone in a different direction if he had made a particular decision differently. Rewrite the remainder of this article as if he had made a different choice at this point.

Do unto Others

▶ **David Polmer**
Student Essay

*In this essay, Polmer explains how his beliefs about sportsman-
ship have changed since childhood. He wrote this while he was a
student at Washington University in St. Louis.*

Remember life when you were ten years old? It was simple. Your   1
responsibilities were to obey the rules your mother repeatedly
preached—the foremost being, "Do unto others as you would have others do unto you"—and if you followed these rules, she would declare
you the best child in the world. The rules were basic, and while you
may not have grasped them all as quickly as your mother would have
liked, before too long you had managed to conquer not only the easy
rules, but even some of the tougher ones (including looking both ways
before crossing the street and keeping your elbows off the dinner
table). The one rule that seemed obvious from the second Mom explained it to me was "do unto others." It was catchy, concise and, most
of all, easy to accept. Yet at age ten I learned that not even professional
athletes always adhere to the rule I had considered the easiest of my
mother's to follow.

On one of my first days as a ball boy for the ATP tennis tournament   2
in Washington, D.C., I was assigned to work a doubles match involving
highly ranked Brad Gilbert. What I witnessed that day permanently
changed my perception of Gilbert. After a close line call went against
him, Gilbert turned to the linesman, unleashed a profanity-filled
tirade, then let loose a wad of spit meant only for him. The instant I
witnessed Gilbert's actions, I decided (as only a kid can) that this guy
was not only my least favorite tennis player in the world, but an undesirable person altogether.

Ten years later, a similar incident occurred. It involved the same   3
scenario—an official, umpire John Hirschbeck, making a close call
that does not go in the player's favor. The player, Roberto Alomar of the
Orioles, turns to the umpire and spits in his face. There was, however,
one significant difference for me in the Alomar incident—the athlete
played for a team I have passionately rooted for my entire life, a team
that has not reached postseason play since 1983. Furthermore, I knew

that for the Orioles to have a successful postseason, Alomar would be desperately needed. Because of these factors, I tried to rationalize why Alomar should be exempt from my mother's "do unto others" rule and thereby escape banishment from the playoffs because of his actions.

And I do have my reasons.   4

First, Hirschbeck clearly blew the call at a crucial time during a crit-   5
ical season-ending series. Second, he apparently egged on Alomar after the player had begun to walk back to the dugout. And third, Alomar is a fierce competitor whose job entails competing at the highest level possible every night. (Hirschbeck no doubt approaches his work in the same manner.) Not only did my mother refuse to accept any of my theories, she pointed out that most of them could have held true for Brad Gilbert.

So why was my reaction to the two events so different? Why, after   6
ten years, did I find myself trying to excuse a ballplayer's actions that a decade ago I would have acknowledged instantly as disgraceful for any individual?

Clearly, as long as fans create emotional ties to specific players and   7
teams, there will be some people willing to excuse misconduct involving their favorite players or teams, no matter how offensive their actions may be. When Albert Belle played for the Indians, his insolence usually was tolerated by Cleveland fans; now, it's different. Also, society bombards us with the message that winning must be achieved because the pain of losing is too great to handle. Most ten-year-olds have yet to establish emotional ties to specific players on teams. When a kid sees his team win or lose, he is affected for maybe half an hour.

Yet, as a boy grows up and becomes better acquainted with the ex-   8
pectations of society and the impact of money in pro sports (particularly as it relates to that great end-all, winning), the games he loves lose their purity.

Consider the New York media and Yankees fans who treated twelve-   9
year-old Jeff Maier like a king after his interference altered the outcome of Game 1 of the 1996 AL Championship Series. The next day, Maier was given box seats behind the Yankees' dugout, courtesy of the *New York Post,* and he became the star of every New York early-morning and late-night talk show. All this for a kid who, instead of going to school that day, assisted the Yankees in winning a big game. To every die-hard Yankees fan, Maier's actions were heroic; it was the victory that mattered, not how it was achieved. Thus, the lesson from society is evident. Simply enjoying the game, as you did as a child, isn't enough.

I have become a victim of these twisted rules. As I watch my fa-   10
vorite pro teams, I realize the fun is not in seeing them compete, but in seeing them win. And when I participate in sports, I find little satisfaction in the competition, or the exercise, or the skills I acquire. Winning is the must.

When I reflect on the simple "do unto others" rule my mother in-   11
stilled, I think of how much easier it was to believe in it back then.
When you're ten, the rule, like sports itself, is simple. Now that I have
grown, society has taught me—for better or worse—that my mother's
rule doesn't mix very well with today's sports world.

Unfortunately for Brad Gilbert, I had yet to be brainwashed by   12
society's crazy rules when I was a boy. Now that I am older, and
feel somehow trapped into accepting much of society's winning-is-
everything mentality, I try as best I can to excuse Roberto Alomar.
However, what I have learned most from these two spitting incidents is
that regardless of what society plants in my brain, my mother will love
me no matter what I choose to believe—although she would surely prefer that her kindness credo be a priority.

Examining the Essay

1. Identify and evaluate Polmer's thesis.
2. In what ways do Polmer's references to his mother's golden rule
   strengthen his essay?
3. Evaluate Polmer's introduction and conclusion.
4. Polmer bases his essay on two incidents, that of Brad Gilbert and
   Roberto Alomar. What other types of evidence would strengthen his
   thesis?

Writing an Essay

1. Write an essay about a belief or opinion you held as a child and describe how it changed as you grew older. Explain why you think the
   change occurred.
2. Besides the sports world, can you think of other situations in which
   winning seems to be the most important thing? Write an essay describing the situation.
3. Write an essay describing what you think are the most important
   aspects of playing or watching sports.

Making Connections

1. Compare Bernard's attitude toward her uncle in "Our Wounded Hearts" with Mario Cuomo's attitude toward his father in "Poppa and the Spruce Tree."

2. Both "The Promised Land" and "Poppa and the Spruce Tree" deal with family members who affect the writers' lives. Write an essay comparing the ways in which the different authors perceive family relationships and how they were affected by them.

3. Both "Bill Gates: Computer Wizard" and "Food from the 'Hood" discuss entrepreneurship. Write an essay comparing the two business ventures.

Internet Connections

1. Habitat For Humanity helps people who have difficulty affording housing by building them houses with donated materials and volunteer labor. Visit their web site at **http://www.habitat.org/default.html**. Identify the projects in progress where you live and write an essay describing three of them.

2. Many people do not realize the contributions that women have made to science throughout history. The web site 4000 Years of Women in Science, at **http://crux.astr.ua. edu/4000WS/4000WS.html**, contains information on over 100 of these individuals. Visit the site and read about some of these women. Are you surprised by any of the biographies on this site? For example, you might look at En Hedu 'Anna, Hypatia, or Mary Whiton Calkins. Write a summary of the contributions of one of the women whose achievements most surprised you. Be sure you do not copy information directly from the article.

3. Try a quiz about famous fathers and find out the origins of Father's Day at this site: **http://www.biography.com/ features/father/main.html**. Write a paragraph describing what you learned from the quiz about others who have influenced our lives.

   (If any of these web sites are unavailable, use a search engine to locate another appropriate site.)

Chapter 6

Media That Shape Our Lives

Oprah Winfrey
Deborah Tannen

My First Story
Patrice Gaines

Music 'n Moods
Carolyn Gard

Advertising: Institutionalized Lying
Donna Woolfolk Cross

Can TV Improve Us?
Jane Rosenzweig

How Much "Reality" TV Can We Survive?
Todd Leopold

Sporting the Fan(tasy) of Reality TV
Colleen Diez

Hardly a day goes by when we do not pick up a newspaper, look at a magazine, watch some television, listen to a radio, or spend some time with all four types of media. New forms of media are also developing: laser disks, CD-ROMs, videos, infomercials, closed-circuit and interactive television. Media include all means of communicating information, ideas, or attitudes to an anonymous public audience. And everywhere there are advertisements—on public transportation; in shopping carts, ball parks, hotel rooms, even public rest rooms; on cable shows that air in some high schools; and, increasingly, on nonprofit public broadcasting stations. In fact, we are bombarded by the media, whether we like it or not.

The media have a powerful impact on our beliefs and desires. Through advertising, the media influence what we buy. By choosing to follow certain stories and trends and ignoring others, the media focus our attention on particular topics. Talk shows, television series, and movies affect what we might talk about at the dinner table, dream about, or feel about ourselves and others. The readings in this chapter explore the impact of the media on the lives of others. Through them you will come to a fuller realization of how the media affect your life.

In this chapter, you will read about television, including the popularity of Oprah Winfrey and the issues she raises on her talk show ("Oprah Winfrey"). You will examine the new trend in television programming—reality TV ("How Much 'Reality' TV Can We Survive?" and "Sporting the Fan(tasy) of Reality TV") and consider the use of television as a vehicle for social change ("Can TV Improve Us?"). You'll read about the effects of advertising both products and events in "Advertising: Institutionalized Lying." You'll also hear from a journalist who discusses her first professional writing experience ("My First Story"). You will also read about how one form of media, music, affects our lives ("Music 'n Moods").

Brainstorming About the Media

Class Activities:

1. Working in pairs, brainstorm a list of all the types of media you have come in contact with in the past twenty-four hours.
2. Brainstorm a list of programs that have influenced or inspired you or led you to a decision or important change.

Oprah Winfrey

▶ Deborah Tannen

In this 1998 essay from Time *magazine, Deborah Tannen, a noted authority on human communication, examines Oprah Winfrey's rise to fame and her impact on talk shows and our society.*

Reading Strategy

As you read, highlight factors that account for Winfrey's popularity.

Vocabulary Preview

poised (1) self-confident
insouciant (1) carefree; unconcerned
beacon (2) guiding force
discourse (2) conversation; talk
solace (4) comfort; relief
overt (6) open; obvious
paradox (8) contradiction; puzzle
legacy (8) gift; something left to future generations
permeate (8) spread throughout

*T*he Sudanese-born supermodel Alek Wek stands poised and insouciant   1
as the talk-show host, admiring her classic African features, cradles Wek's
cheek and says, "What a difference it would have made to my childhood if
I had seen someone who looks like you on television." The host is Oprah
Winfrey, and she has been making that difference for millions of viewers,
young and old, black and white, for nearly a dozen years.

  Winfrey stands as a beacon, not only in the worlds of media and en-   2
tertainment but also in the larger realm of public discourse. At 44, she
has a personal fortune estimated at more than half a billion dollars. She
owns her own production company, which creates feature films, prime-
time TV specials, and home videos. An accomplished actress, she won
an Academy Award nomination for her role in *The Color Purple,* and
this fall will star in her own film production of Toni Morrison's *Beloved.*

  But it is through her talk show that her influence has been greatest.   3
When Winfrey talks, her viewers—an estimated 14 million daily in the
U.S. and millions more in 132 other countries—listen. Any book she
chooses for her on-air book club becomes an instant best seller.
When she established the "world's largest piggy bank," people all over

the country contributed spare change to raise more than $1 million (matched by Oprah) to send disadvantaged kids to college. When she blurted that hearing about the threat of mad-cow disease "just stopped me cold from eating another burger," the perceived threat to the beef industry was enough to trigger a multimillion-dollar lawsuit (which she won).

Born in 1954 to unmarried parents, Winfrey was raised by her grandmother on a farm with no indoor plumbing in Kosciusko, Miss. By age 3 she was reading the Bible and reciting in church. At 6 she moved to her mother's home in Milwaukee, Wis.; later, to her father's in Nashville, Tenn. A lonely child, she found solace in books. When a seventh-grade teacher noticed the young girl reading during lunch, he got her a scholarship to a better school. Winfrey's talent for public performance and spontaneity in answering questions helped her win beauty contests—and get her first taste of public attention.

Crowned Miss Fire Prevention in Nashville at 17, Winfrey visited a local radio station, where she was invited to read copy for a lark—and was hired to read news on the air. Two years later, while a sophomore at Tennessee State University, she was hired as Nashville's first female and first black TV-news anchor. After graduation, she took an anchor position in Baltimore, Md., but lacked the detachment to be a reporter. She cried when a story was sad, laughed when she misread a word. Instead, she was given an early-morning talk show. She had found her medium. In 1984 she moved on to be the host of *A.M. Chicago,* which became *The Oprah Winfrey Show.* It was syndicated in 1986—when Winfrey was 32—and soon overtook *Donahue* as the nation's top-rated talk show.

Women, especially, listen to Winfrey because they feel as if she's a friend. Although Phil Donahue pioneered the format she uses (mike-holding host moves among an audience whose members question guests), his show was mostly what I call "report-talk," which often typifies men's conversation. The overt focus is on information. Winfrey transformed the format into what I call "rapport-talk," the back-and-forth conversation that is the basis of female friendship, with its emphasis on self-revealing intimacies. She turned the focus from experts to ordinary people talking about personal issues. Girls' and women's friendships are often built on trading secrets. Winfrey's power is that she tells her own, divulging that she once ate a package of hot-dog buns drenched in maple syrup, that she had smoked cocaine, even that she had been raped as a child. With Winfrey, the talk show became more immediate, more confessional, more personal. When a guest's story moves her, she cries and spreads her arms for a hug.

When my book *You Just Don't Understand: Women and Men in Conversation* was published, I was lucky enough to appear on both *Donahue* and *Oprah*—and to glimpse the difference between them.

Winfrey related my book to her own life: she began by saying that she had read the book and "saw myself over and over" in it. She then told one of my examples, adding, "I've done that a thousand times"—and illustrated it by describing herself and Stedman. (Like close friends, viewers know her "steady beau" by his first name.)

Winfrey saw television's power to blend public and private; while it [8] links strangers and conveys information over public airwaves, TV is most often viewed in the privacy of our homes. Like a family member, it sits down to meals with us and talks to us in the lonely afternoons. Grasping this paradox, Oprah exhorts viewers to improve their lives and the world. She makes people care because she cares. That is Winfrey's genius, and will be her legacy, as the changes she has wrought in the talk show continue to permeate our culture and shape our lives.

Oprah Winfrey

Examining the Reading

Finding Meaning

1. What was Winfrey's childhood like?
2. How did Winfrey first become a public figure?
3. What was the purpose of the "world's largest piggy bank"?
4. According to Tannen, what is the difference between the interview styles of Winfrey and Phil Donahue?
5. What did Winfrey do when she interviewed the author on her television show?

Understanding Technique

1. Identify Tannen's thesis statement.
2. Describe the organization of the essay.
3. The title of the essay identifies its subject, but it does little to capture the readers' interest or suggest its thesis. Suggest several possible alternative titles that might be more effective.

Thinking Critically

1. What did Winfrey mean when she told model Alek Wek, "What a difference it would have made to my childhood if I had seen someone who looks like you on television"?
2. Why was Winfrey sued by the beef industry? Why do you think the author included this incident in the article?
3. Why does the author describe television as a "paradox"?
4. What do you think makes Winfrey so different from others in her business?
5. The author believes that talk shows "shape our lives." Do you agree or disagree with her? Why?

Writing About the Reading

A Journal Entry

Write a journal entry about a book or article you have read or a movie you have seen that was so much like your own life that you saw yourself over and over in it.

A Paragraph

1. Write a paragraph explaining why you think Winfrey has become so influential.

2. Talk shows deal with various issues. Write a paragraph describing an issue that is of major importance to you.

An Essay

1. Write an essay about a public figure (a television personality, musician, politician, author, etc.) who has made a difference in your life. Describe how this person has influenced you and why.
2. Do you agree with Tannen that men and women speak to each other differently? Explain why you agree or disagree and give some examples to back your opinion.

A Creative Activity

Imagine you have been chosen to be interviewed on Winfrey's show. What would you like to discuss with Winfrey?

My First Story

▶ **Patrice Gaines**

Patrice Gaines, a successful journalist and writer, describes how her career began with a page filled with corrections and criticisms. This essay is taken from Gaines's autobiography, Laughing in the Dark.

Reading Strategy

As you read, highlight words, phrases, and sentences that reveal Gaines's attitude toward her job and toward writing. Write annotations of any personal experiences about jobs or writing that the essay brings to mind.

Vocabulary Preview

muster (2) call forth; gather
fate (2) a force beyond one's control that directs events
excel (2) be better than others
confidant (3) one with whom secrets are shared
fretting (5) worrying

*D*iscovering I was the only black secretary at the paper didn't make   1
me angry, as it would today; it boosted my self-esteem—at least as
much as I would allow. Even though I loved to write, I wasn't excited
about working for a newspaper; I didn't have any desire to become a
newspaper reporter. I wrote short stories and poetry, not journalism. I
had written enough poems now to fill a book, which I kept tucked in
my underwear drawer. I wrote short stories with a heavy moral message. One story was about three soldiers killed in Vietnam, their bodies
destroyed beyond recognition by a grenade. Their remains were
shipped in one casket, and the families—Jewish, Baptist, and atheist—
had to hold one funeral. One soldier was black. I wrote a poem about
the attention paid to pregnant women and the lack of care given the

environment. It ended: "Would things have been different if the fathers of this country had been mothers instead?"

I wrote about matters of the heart and I couldn't see yet that jour-   2
nalists did this, too, with more skill and sense of communication than I could yet muster. Still, if there is such a thing as fate, it had acted on my behalf, to put me in a place where when I woke up I would have before me what I had wanted all the time, where, even though I hadn't been in the upper half of my graduating class, I could still learn to be a writer and, perhaps, have a chance to excel.

My new boss, Peter, was a white guy barely a year older than I was.   3
We immediately struck up a comfortable friendship. He was a member of the new, young, white South, those who tried to build the bridge between the Confederate tradition of Jim Crow and the more integrated future of Martin Luther King, Jr. I became Peter's close confidant and assistant, in many ways no different from the scores of secretaries who in the course of their office duties compose personal as well as business letters, serving as human calendars, remembering flights and meetings, birthdays and anniversaries, covering for bosses who sneak off to play golf. Secretaries can be like members of the family, and with most of them being female, they often become the nurturing mother-wife and sister-friend. It was a position that suited me well for many years, and Peter was as near-perfect a boss-mate as possible.

He arranged for me to have my first chance to write for others, a   4
position on the monthly employee newsletter, which I helped write during my extra time. This was a big deal to me. It was as close as I could get to imagining myself as a writer. Becoming a reporter was too big a dream; just writing for the employee newsletter frightened me to near paralysis.

My first story was about pets—talking birds, big snakes, and show   5
dogs. The editor returned my draft covered with red marks, noting misspelled words, slang, wordiness, and whole paragraphs that needed to be rearranged or dropped. Accompanying his critique was a note: "An ego is too big to fit into a typewriter." I understood immediately what he was saying and dropped my initial feelings of embarrassment and disappointment. I stayed awake that night fretting, but by day my normally oversensitive self, who hurt at any hint of not being accepted, wrote with the attitude that every red mark was an opportunity to learn.

I discovered I thought differently when I wrote; I was smarter on   6
paper. I saw where the mistakes were made and I corrected them. It took a while—maybe six months—but eventually there were fewer red ink marks and among the lines of criticism were a few compliments. For me, it was nothing short of magic to string together words in a way that made people notice and care. This was the answer to my prayers,

to be able to touch people in a way that I had not been able to with my actions or the words from my mouth.

Examining the Reading

Finding Meaning

1. Given that the author wanted to be a writer, why was she not excited about working on a newspaper?
2. How did Gaines's boss help launch her career as a writer?
3. Describe Gaines's relationship with her boss.
4. Describe the types of stories Gaines enjoyed writing for herself.
5. Describe how Gaines improved her writing skills.

Understanding Technique

1. Describe this essay's organization.
2. Evaluate Gaines's sentence structure. How does she make sentences lively and interesting?

Thinking Critically

1. How did Gaines use the criticisms of her first story as a positive experience?
2. In what sense is journalism about "matters of the heart"?
3. Explain the meaning of the editor's note: "An ego is too big to fit into a typewriter."
4. Why did Gaines keep her short stories and poems in her underwear drawer?

Writing About the Reading

A Journal Entry

Write a journal entry describing your attitude toward your writing. Include likes, dislikes, rewards, problems, and so forth.

A Paragraph

1. Did you ever write something that was seriously criticized? Write a paragraph describing whether this was helpful or harmful to you.
2. Gaines enjoyed writing stories with moral messages. She wrote about "matters of the heart." Write a paragraph describing the kinds of writing or topics that are easy for you or that you enjoy.

An Essay

1. Write an essay describing someone's criticism of something other than your writing and explaining why or why not it was justified.
2. Gaines feels that fate acted on her behalf. Has fate ever worked on your behalf or against you? Write an essay describing a situation in which luck or fate seemed to be involved.

A Creative Activity

Write a paragraph describing what you think happened in Gaines's story about the funeral of the three soldiers.

Music 'n Moods

▶ **Carolyn Gard**

*Music not only stirs up your emotions, it also can be beneficial.
This article from* Current Health *examines the wide-ranging effects of music.*

Reading Strategy

As you read, make a list of the beneficial effects of music and
the evidence Gard offers to substantiate each effect.

Vocabulary Preview

evokes (5) brings out; stirs up
instills (6) builds up; leads to
discordant (6) harsh; unpleasant
cardiovascular (9) of the heart and blood vessels
neurological (10) pertaining to the nervous system
cadence (10) beat; rhythm
synchronized (10) timed; joined
verbalize (13) express in words
autistic children (14) mentally disturbed children who have
extreme difficulty learning language,
playing normally, and interacting with
others
Alzheimer's disease (14) a brain disorder that causes
memory loss, confusion, and
disturbance of speech and
movements.
baroque music (15) a form of classical music created in
seventeenth- and eighteenth-century
Western Europe; composers include
Bach, Handel, and Vivaldi
conducive (16) helpful

You've seen *Psycho* many times. You know exactly what's going to hap- 1
pen in the shower scene—but you're still on the edge of your seat.
   You're watching *Jaws* again. You know exactly when the shark is 2
going to appear—and you're still anxious.

Now rewind the movies and turn off the sound. Janet Leigh steps   3
into the shower, but this time she's just another tired tourist getting
ready for bed. Now do the same when watching *Jaws,* and the people
on the boat are simply sightseers out for an afternoon sail.

It's hard to imagine any movies without music, but originally Al-   4
fred Hitchcock didn't want any music in the shower scene in *Psycho.*
After he saw what screeching violins could do, he raised the composer's salary.

Movie music always evokes strong emotions in the audience—   5
from fear and panic to tenderness and love.

The power of music to set the mood in a movie depends on the fact   6
that most people react in the same way to the same music. Low-
pitched, repetitive sounds suggest fear. A single tone that gets louder
and louder instills anxiety. Kettle drums provoke anger, and a shrill
blast of high notes with a discordant blare of bass notes will drive you
to panic.

Why Does Music Affect Our Emotions?

Although researchers know that music can comfort, delight, convince,   7
frighten, or move us, they don't know how it does this.

One theory is that a fetus responds to sounds. Because of this early   8
association, hearing may evoke a more emotional response than sight.
Music also triggers memory, allowing you to remember a past experience.

According to Don Campbell, the founder of the Institute for Music,   9
Health, and Education, music is linked to many measurable changes
in body function. Music can relax and energize, release anger and
mask pain, cause muscles to tense, change skin temperature, and improve circulation and cardiovascular function. Every thought, feeling,
and movement has its own musical qualities. Your pulse and heartbeat
have a rhythm and tempo, your breath has pattern and flow.

Moving to Music

Music may produce a neurological effect that improves motor control.   10
The brain is organized in a complete pattern—your stride length, step
cadence, and posture are all centrally located. When muscle activity is
synchronized to rhythm, it becomes more regular and efficient. When
one part improves, everything improves.

Music can help you get more out of exercise. If you do jumping   11
jacks you may get tired after 100. With music in the background, you
may do 200 jumps before you get tired. The continuous rhythmic patterns in music increase the body's endurance and strength.

Music chosen specifically for exercising uses the natural rhythms   12
of the body. One company offers tapes of computer-generated music

that encourage you to regulate your walking from a 30-minute walk at 110 steps per minute to a race walk of a 10-minute mile at a rate of 170 steps per minute.

Music Communicates

Music lets you express emotions that are difficult to verbalize. Think   13
about the difference between saying the pledge of allegiance and singing the national anthem. Which one is more likely to give you a thrill? For the same reason, high schools and colleges have fight songs to excite the fans at sports events.

The idea of using music to heal goes back to the ideas of Aristotle   14
and Plato. In music therapy, music is the instrument of communication between the therapist and the patient; the patient doesn't need any particular musical skills to benefit. Music helps people come to an understanding of the inner self. Music therapy is extremely valuable in helping disturbed and autistic children, as well as people with Alzheimer's disease.

Making Music Work for You

You've got a final tomorrow—how can music help you study? Don   15
Campbell suggests that you start with 10 minutes of good, energetic dancing to pop music to get your body oxygenized. When you sit down to study, listen to slow baroque music, such as Bach, that has fewer than 60 beats per minute. This speed allows you to focus and concentrate. The best music for study has no words; words distract you by encouraging your brain to sort them out and make sense of them.

New Age music with a slow pulse is conducive to sleep. And music   16
with a fast beat, above 90 beats per minute, will give you energy for getting things done.

A recent study conducted at the University of California at Irvine   17
indicates that listening to the music of Mozart can raise a person's IQ. It seems that Mozart's music speaks directly to the parts of the brain that enhance learning.

On an even more personal level, music can help you become more   18
aware of your inner self and your feelings.

Suppose you're in a major slump—you flunked a test or you ended   19
a relationship. Campbell finds that there is a therapeutic strain in certain music that helps you get in touch with your emotions. He suggests you find five tapes or CDs that make you feel "safe" and calm so you can feel your own emotions. Play the soundtrack from *Out of Africa* or a symphonic piece such as "A Little Night Music" by Mozart, and write or draw how you're feeling. The music helps you relax, allowing the emotion to come out. When you've worked through your sadness, you'll be ready to face the world again.

Examining the Reading

Finding Meaning

1. How do soundtracks affect audience reaction to films?
2. What kind of music evokes each of the following emotions: fear, anxiety, anger, and panic?
3. How can music help people exercise better?
4. What is music therapy?
5. According to this article, what type of music is best to listen to while you study? To help you fall asleep? To raise your IQ?

Understanding Technique

1. The thesis of this essay is suggested in the title, but it is not directly stated anywhere in the essay itself. Discuss whether you feel a thesis statement is needed. If so, write a possible thesis statement for this essay.
2. What types of evidence does Gard offer to support her claim that music affects us?

Thinking Critically

1. Why do you think Alfred Hitchcock gave the soundtrack composer of the movie *Psycho* a raise?
2. Why do you think music therapy might be helpful for autistic children or for Alzheimer's patients?
3. What did the author mean by "music can help you become more aware of your inner self and your feelings"?
4. Do you agree that classical music is the best music to listen to while studying? Why or why not?

Writing About the Reading

A Journal Entry

Write a journal entry about a favorite song or musical piece. Explain why you like it and how it makes you feel.

A Paragraph

1. Choose an activity you like to do while listening to music. Write a paragraph describing the type of music you prefer while doing this activity and how you think the music affects your performance.

2. You probably react differently when you hear a poem read and when you listen to a song. Write a paragraph explaining the difference.

An Essay

1. Write an essay about a movie you saw recently. Describe the sound-track and explain how the music added to, or detracted from, your enjoyment of the movie. Be sure to use specific examples.
2. Write a letter to your college president, proposing that students should be allowed to listen to music while taking exams. Use the information presented in this article to back your argument.

A Creative Activity

Imagine that you just had a fight with your best friend and you are very upset about it. Name five CDs or individual pieces of music you think would be helpful to listen to at this time. Explain why you chose this music.

Advertising: Institutionalized Lying

▶ Donna Woolfolk Cross

Are advertisements true? Can you believe their claims? This essay explores the issue of false and misleading advertising. It is an excerpt from a book titled Mediaspeak.

Reading Strategy

This reading contains several examples of misleading advertising. Highlight or annotate why each is misleading. Also, highlight or annotate what the mouthwash story is intended to demonstrate.

Vocabulary Preview

inferential (1) implied; arrived at by drawing your own conclusion
rebuked (2) reprimanded
undaunted (2) not discouraged
purport (2) to claim, often falsely
deterred (5) discouraged from acting
eliciting (6) bringing forth
halitosis (6) bad breath
smiting (7) afflicting
ensued (7) resulted
discourse (7) discuss in detail

*T*he fact is that advertising is institutionalized lying. The lies are tol-   1
erated—even encouraged—because they serve the needs of the corporate establishment. . . . By now the falsity—either direct or inferential—of most television commercials is a matter of well-documented fact. Most people accept that ads are not true and yet, because they do not un-

derstand the methods by which they are influenced, are still taken in. Can *you* detect the deception behind the following statements?

- *"All aspirin is not alike. In tests for quality, Bayer proved superior."*

Most people assume this means that Bayer aspirin has been shown to relieve pain better than other aspirin. In fact the "tests for quality," which were conducted by Bayer and not an independent testing agency, showed that Bayer was superior, in its own manufacturer's opinion, because the tablets were whiter and less breakable than the other aspirins tested. Nevertheless, this claim is so effective that a recent FTC [Federal Trade Commission] survey revealed that forty percent of consumers believe Bayer is the most effective aspirin.

- *"Sominex makes you drowsy so you can sleep."*

Time and again the advertising agencies peddling over-the-counter remedies for insomnia have been rebuked for stating or implying that these products insure a good night's sleep. Undaunted, the nimble admen simply found a new way of making the same claim: The remedies still do not insure a good night's sleep, but they purport to make us drowsy so we *can* sleep. Reading a dull book or watching an uninteresting TV show would probably have the same effect. It is even possible that ads for insomnia cures can put you to sleep sooner than their product will. ２

- *"Gallo: because the wine remembers."*

If true, this should put a crimp in dinnertime conversations: "Hush, dear, not in front of the Hearty Burgundy."

The late August Sebastiani, who scorned selling techniques such as this, would not allow his wines to be advertised on TV, saying, "If you spend enough on advertising, you can get people to drink sauerkraut juice, juice you couldn't get a thirsty hog to drink." ３

If there is absolutely no need for a particular product, the adman must invent one. He must convince you that your health and happiness will be in jeopardy if you don't buy his product. ４

Believe it or not, In the Beginning there was no mouthwash. Proper oral hygiene consisted of a thorough brushing with a good toothpaste. Then one day an enterprising stranger rode into town peddling a new product, a liquid made of water, alcohol, and assorted additives that would "freshen your breath." People weren't interested. "What can this stuff do for me that toothpaste can't?" they asked. Not to be deterred, the stranger hired himself an advertising agency. ５

Soon the television disease-control center was informing people about a new and terrible disease. No one was immune from it: House-wives and clerics, teenagers, cab drivers, lawyers, new mothers, were ６ being struck down with a devastating malady. Far from eliciting sympathy, a person who contracted this disease was sure to lose his promotion, friends, loved ones, and paper boy. The sufferer himself was always the last to learn, usually from a hastily departing relative, that his affliction was . . . *halitosis*.

Bad breath was smiting the land, the righteous along with the sin-   7
ners. A great panic might have ensued but for the miraculously timed appearance, at that very moment, of a cure: *mouthwash*. Soon Americans were buying bottles of it by the millions, and many could discourse knowledgeably about the virtues of various brands: "mediciney" versus "sweet," etc. Skeptical about claims for the product, the American Dental Association and the National Academy of Sciences, after several intensive studies, issued a report stating that mouthwash has no lasting effect on bad breath, and that rinsing one's mouth with salt water is just as beneficial as using mouthwash. But medical science delivered its verdict too late. People had been taught to *believe* in mouthwash. The stranger rode out of town a very rich man.

Examining the Reading

Finding Meaning

1. How does Cross define advertising?
2. According to this reading, do most people believe ads are true or false?
3. In the "tests for quality," give one reason why Bayer was considered superior to other aspirin.
4. If the public has no need for a specific product, how do the advertisers "sell" the product?
5. After many studies on mouthwash, what did the medical organizations conclude about it?

Understanding Technique

1. How does Cross make the transition from examples of misleading advertising to a discussion of how advertisers create a so-called need for a product?
2. Evaluate the essay's final paragraph. How does it summarize the essay?

Thinking Critically

1. If the public recognizes that television ads are false, why do they continue to buy the products advertised?
2. Is there such a thing as advertising that is true but misleading? Explain.

3. Discuss how ads for Sominex and other anti-insomnia products may affect our thinking.
4. How does false advertising shape our lives?
5. Identify an example of false advertising not given in the reading and explain why it is false or deceptive.

Writing About the Reading

A Journal Entry

Explore your reaction to advertising by freewriting or brainstorming about ads and whether they can or should be believed, disbelieved, or ignored.

A Paragraph

1. Mouthwash is an example of a product that was sold to the public by advertising agencies. What other products do you think are popular because of the advertising attention they receive? Write a paragraph identifying these products and explaining how advertising makes them popular.
2. Write a paragraph describing the worst commercial you have ever seen. Explain why it was the worst.

An Essay

1. If advertising is false and/or misleading, should our legal system allow it to appear? Write an essay answering this question. Justify your position.
2. Do you ever buy a certain product simply because you liked the commercial? Write an essay on whether commercials influence what you buy. Include examples in your essay.

A Creative Activity

Find an ad that you think is false or misleading and add it to the essay. Write a paragraph explaining what is wrong with the advertisement.

Can TV Improve Us?

▸ Jane Rosenzweig

Jane Rosenzweig explores the possibility of television being used as a tool for individual and social change. This article originally appeared in The American Prospect *in 1999.*

Reading Strategy

As you read, highlight the questions posed by the author.

Vocabulary Preview

wedlock (1) marriage
photogenic (2) always looks good in a photograph
disintegrating (2) breaking apart
nuclear families (2) family groups made up of a father, mother, and children
liberal (2) not strict; broad-minded
pathology (2) something that is not normal
glean (2) find out
emulate (3) imitate; try to be like
cottage industry (3) small, informal business
parlance (5) speech
tangible (5) real; identifiable
advocacy (7) supporting and fighting for a certain cause

*I*t's eight o'clock Wednesday evening and a rumor is circulating at a   1
small-town high school in Massachusetts that a student named Jack is
gay. Jack's friends—one of whom is a 15-year-old girl who has been
sexually active since she was 13, and another of whom has a mother
who has recently committed adultery—assure him it would be okay
with them if he were, but admit their relief when he says he isn't. An
hour later, in San Francisco, a woman named Julia is being beaten by
her boyfriend. Meanwhile, in Los Angeles, a young stripper who has
given birth out of wedlock learns that her own mother locked her in a
basement when she was three years old, an experience that she thinks
may explain her inability to love her own child.

A typical evening in America? If a visitor from another planet had   2
turned on the television (specifically the WB and Fox networks) on the
evening of Wednesday, February 10, 1999, with the aim of learning

about our society, he would likely have concluded that it is made up pretty exclusively of photogenic young people with disintegrating nuclear families and liberal attitudes about sex. It's obviously not an accurate picture, but what might our visitor have learned from the programs he watched? Would all the sex, violence, and pathology he saw teach him antisocial behavior? Or might he glean from prime-time dramas and sitcoms the behavior and attitudes that he would do well to adopt if he intended to go native in America?

This is not an idle question—not because aliens might be watching   3
American television, but because people are, particularly impression-able children and teenagers. In a time when 98 percent of U.S. house-holds own at least one television set—a set which is turned on for an average of nearly seven hours a day—the degree to which people learn from and emulate the behavior of the characters they see on TV is an academic cottage industry. Some evidence does support the widespread belief that children and teenagers are affected by violence and other an-tisocial behavior in the media. When Dan Quayle made his infamous comments in 1992 about Murphy Brown having a baby out of wedlock, he was merely doing what numerous concerned parents, ethnic groups, religious organizations, gun-control advocates, and others were already doing—blaming television for encouraging certain types of behavior.

But if television contributes to poor behavior, might it also be a ve-   4
hicle for encouraging good behavior? In 1988, Jay Winsten, a professor at the Harvard School of Public Health and the director of the school's Center for Health Communication, conceived a plan to use television to introduce a new social concept—the "designated driver"—to North America. Shows were already dealing with the topic of drinking, Win-sten reasoned, so why not add a line of dialogue here and there about not driving drunk? With the assistance of then–NBC chairman Grant Tinker, Winsten met with more than 250 writers, producers, and exec-utives over six months, trying to sell them on his designated driver idea.

Winsten's idea worked; the "designated driver" is now common par-   5
lance across all segments of American society and in 1991 won entry into a Webster's dictionary for the first time. An evaluation of the cam-paign in 1994 revealed that the designated driver "message" had aired on 160 prime-time shows in four seasons and had been the main topic of twenty-five 30-minute or 60-minute episodes. More important, these airings appear to have generated tangible results. In 1989, the year af-ter the "designated driver" was invented, a Gallup poll found that 67 percent of adults had noted its appearance on network television. What's more, the campaign seems to have influenced adult behavior: polls conducted by the Roper Organization in 1989 and 1991 found sig-nificantly increasing awareness and use of designated drivers. By 1991, 37 percent of all U.S. adults claimed to have refrained from drinking at

least once in order to serve as a designated driver, up from 29 percent in 1989. In 1991, 52 percent of adults younger than 30 had served as designated drivers, suggesting that the campaign was having greatest success with its target audience.

In 1988 there were 23,626 drunk driving fatalities. By 1997 the number was 16,189. While the Harvard Alcohol Project acknowledges that some of this decline is due to new laws, stricter anti–drunk driving enforcement, and other factors, it claims that many of the 50,000 lives saved by the end of 1998 were saved because of the designated driver campaign. (The television campaign was only a part of the overall campaign; there were strong community-level and public service components as well.) As evidence, the project cites statistics showing the rapid decline in traffic fatalities per 100 million vehicle miles traveled in the years during and immediately following the most intensive period of the designated driver campaign. Officials at the National Highway Traffic and Safety Administration have stated that the only way to explain the size of the decline in drinking-related traffic fatalities is the designated driver campaign.   6

Following the success of the Harvard Alcohol Project's campaign, various other advocacy groups—the majority of them with progressive leanings—have begun to work within the existing structures of the television industry in a similar fashion, attempting to influence programming in a positive direction. In truth, there are limits to the effect any public interest group can have on what gets broadcast. Commercial television's ultimate concerns are Nielsen ratings and advertisers. Thus there will always be a hefty quantity of sex and violence on network television. As Alfred Schneider, the former vice president of policy and standards for ABC, asserts in his contribution to the forthcoming anthology *Advocacy Groups and the Television Industry*, "While [television] can raise the consciousness of the nation, it should not be considered as the major vehicle for social relief or altering behavior."   7

But why not?   8

Examining the Reading

Finding Meaning

1. What types of behavior did the author see one night on television?
2. Which networks does Rosenzweig single out?
3. Who is being affected by watching sex and violence on television?
4. Who is blaming television for encouraging unwanted behaviors in Americans?
5. How did the designated driver campaign get its start?

6. Name some of the organizations that were studying and doing polls on drunk driving.
7. In addition to the television campaign, what has contributed to less drunk driving?
8. What are the "ultimate concerns" of commercial television?

Understanding Technique

1. What is Rosenzweig's thesis? How does she support it?
2. Evaluate the opening paragraph. What effect does it have on the reader?
3. How does Rosenzweig's discussion of the designated driver campaign contribute to the article?

Thinking Critically

1. Why don't the television shows of February 10, 1999, give an "accurate picture" of life in America?
2. What does the author mean by "other antisocial behavior" in paragraph 3?
3. Why do other advocacy groups want to work with the television industry?
4. Why are there limits to what advocacy groups can put on television?
5. Why will there always be a "hefty quantity of sex and violence on network television"?
6. What does Rosenzweig mean in the last line of the article when she asks, "But why not?"

Writing About the Reading

A Journal Entry

Write a journal entry describing the types of violence you have viewed on television recently and indicate whether you feel it is appropriate or inappropriate for children to watch programs with these types of violence.

A Paragraph

1. Many people are concerned about what children watch on television. Write a paragraph explaining and describing what types of television programs that you feel children should be watching.
2. Television commercials can also affect behavior. Write a paragraph explaining what types of products should not be advertised on television and why.

3. Evaluate your television-watching habits. For example, do you watch more or less television now than before you started college? What types of programs do you watch? Why?

An Essay

1. Choose s controversial issue. Write an essay explaining how a message expressing your position on the issue can be written into a specific television show that you watch.
2. Many children and teenagers watch too much television. What are the possible solutions to this problem? How can parents and teachers help?
3. We are constantly faced with advertising. Write an essay describing the many places where ads appear, how the ads affect us, and why we should (or should not) be concerned.

A Creative Activity

Imagine that you are an alien visiting the United States. What would strike you as most unusual about American daily life? Why? Another suggestion for this activity is to create a list of projects that children, teenagers, and adults can do during a day without television.

How Much "Reality" TV Can We Survive?

▶ **Todd Leopold**

Entertainment writer Todd Leopold explains why reality TV programs are here to stay. His article first appeared on the CNN (Cable News Network) web site in 2001.

Reading Strategy

As you read, keep track of the reasons the author gives for the success of reality TV.

Vocabulary Preview

stalwart (1) something that is strong and unwavering
heist (1) robbery; theft
chump change (4) an insignificant amount of money
contrived (6) artificial; made up
artifice (6) clever trick; false or insincere
doldrums (8) period of inactivity or sluggishness
homogeneous (10) same kind; sharing similar characteristics
provocative (10) causes excitement
wag (15) witty person
venerable (16) respected because of its age
glut (17) oversupply

*R*eal life pays real well. Or so the broadcast networks have discovered. As it heads into its finale Thursday night, CBS's "Survivor: The Australian Outback" is the No. 1 show on television, regularly whipping longtime NBC stalwart "Friends" in its timeslot. Not long ago, Fox's "Temptation Island" and ABC's "The Mole" concluded runs with solid, if not blockbuster, ratings—good enough for both networks to order new episodes. And don't touch that remote, because there's more: the already debuted "Chains of Love," a Robin Hood–style heist series tentatively titled "Break In!," something currently called "Real People TV," a PBS version of "The 1900 House," more "Popstars," more "Making the Band" . . . the list seems as endless as cable reruns.

Can this still be called a trend, a phase of the airwaves? Or is it   2
something more? "I think it's now beyond a trend," says Robert
Thompson, director of Syracuse University's Center for the Study of
Popular Television. "It's now a form, just like soap operas, doctor
shows, or legal shows. I doubt you, me, our children, or our grandchildren will know a time without it."

A Lucractive Idea

For networks, the reality show's appeal is obvious. Every show is cheap—   3
no having to shell out millions in salary to keep cast members happy—
strike-proof (something to keep in mind with the possibility of writers'
and actors' strikes), and, says Thompson, "it perfectly fits the artistic
capabilities of the medium."

Reality shows are also incredibly profitable. ABC and its parent   4
company, Disney, recently acknowledged that "Who Wants to Be a Millionaire," a quiz show lumped into the reality genre because of its use
of regular joes and janes, is the most lucrative program in television
history. It's earned almost $1 billion in a little more than 18 months.
The show also has spun off a CD-ROM game, "Millionaire" clothes,
and an attraction at Walt Disney World. "Survivor" hasn't exactly produced chump change, either. Thirty-second spots for the August finale
of "Survivor I" were reportedly going for the blockbuster sum of
$600,000 a piece. Stack that against the show's major costs: the $1 million prize and creator Mark Burnett's salary.

All this for an idea as old as motion pictures, and one that has al-   5
ways had a place in the television universe. "Before the current crop
there was 'Cops' and 'America's Most Wanted,'" observes Dwight E.
Brooks, a professor of journalism and mass communications at the
University of Georgia. "Before that there was the video reality craze—
'America's Funniest Home Videos.' (And) prior to that we had 'Candid
Camera.' We've always had 'reality' TV, just in different forms."

This is not to say that reality programming is merely an update   6
of the classic documentary form. This new genre thrives on reality
that's contrived, Thompson notes. "The universe is all artifice, and you
populate that universe with non-actors," he says. "So it's half fiction,
half reality."

The shows' success is no surprise to cultural commentator Neal   7
Gabler, who traces reality-mania to what he calls "a deep crisis in narrative." "Reality programming not only provides suspense that conventional narratives have a difficult time matching; it seems to vanquish
the threat of (writerly) manipulation altogether," he wrote in a March
New York Times column.

A "Real World" and "Millionaire"

With the hindsight a TV season brings, it's amazing that the broadcast networks took so long to catch on. Thompson dates reality programming's modern genesis to MTV's "The Real World," which debuted in 1992 and had the market entirely to itself for almost eight years. Then came "Who Wants to Be a Millionaire." "Millionaire" slid into ABC's schedule during the 1999 late-summer doldrums and (much to the network's surprise) rolled up huge ratings. It proved no fluke when it was brought back during the November "sweeps" period. Editions of the show ended up No. 1, 2, and 3 for the 1999–2000 season.

"Millionaire" wasn't a reality show in the "Survivor" sense, but it had many of the elements of the reality show—real people, contrived situation (answer quiz questions to win $1 million), low costs. And the kicker was that it had originated in Europe. "Executives looked across the Atlantic for *anything*, and they discovered ripoffs of 'The Real World,'" says Thompson. "It's kind of like rock 'n' roll—it started here, crossed (the ocean), and came back here with the British Invasion."[1]

Not a single show, he adds, has been a failure. Even the relatively low-rated shows have made money and brought in the desirable adults 18–49 demographic. "The shows stand out in a rather homogeneous marketplace," Brooks says. "With all the competition, programmers needed innovative, provocative shows—something different to distinguish their product from all the others," he says.

Advertisers and Audiences

American producers have toned down the European shows, which often feature R-rated material that American broadcasters deem inappropriate. But, even watered-down for U.S. tastes, the shows have prompted cultural critics to wring their hands. For example, "Temptation Island," a test-their-devotion show that dangled the possibility of on-camera hanky-panky among four couples at a Caribbean resort, got skewered regularly on radio, in print, and on higher-brow TV.

Despite the critics' concern, Brooks believes there's a place for a variety of realities on American TV. "There will always be a place for risqué content on American television," he says. "How far our commercial networks take it remains to be seen. I don't think it will ever

---

[1]The name for a time in music history during the 1960s when music by British bands was imported into the United States. Most of these British bands were influenced by earlier American musicians.

reach the level of Europe. . . . Advertisers want audiences, but they don't want to be associated with the type of controversy that sexual poor taste in programming will surely bring."

On the other hand, says Yvonne Tocquigny, president of Austin, Texas–based Tocquigny Advertising, advertisers are likely to worry more about cash than content. "There will be advertisers who want any viewer," she says. "You can't really categorize viewers as undesirable as long as they are quantifiable." 13

Advertisers have made the most of the current reality craze. The retail giant Target, in particular, has a highly visible tie-in deal with "Survivor." Marketers could get even more involved in the future, along the lines of the U.S. soap operas owned by corporate titans such as Procter & Gamble, suggests Tocquigny. 14

No Crash in Sight

In the meantime, reality TV is the hottest thing going. According to an executive at a major production company, the frenzy is particularly furious right now, a mad market with networks commissioning shows from production companies and production companies selling shows to networks. One industry wag has called it the "NASDAQ reality bubble." And like tech stocks, the market for reality TV could crash, but Thompson doesn't see it. "It's (unpredictability) that makes these things work," he says. "We don't know what will happen." The fact that recent movies, such as "15 Minutes" and "Series 7," have exploited reality programming underscores how vital it is, he adds. 15

Tocquigny agrees. "With technology creating more and more isolation between people, I believe you can expect to see an increasing appetite for programming that approximates real human responses," she says. "I see reality shows maturing into programming that appeals to different audiences," from teens to middle-aged professionals. The venerable sitcom won't die, she says, but it will have to compete. 16

So, if you haven't already, get used to these newcomers on the box. Some reality shows may provide incredible drama; others may fall below the line of bad taste. The genre will likely have a shakeout after the current glut, but it will be as much a part of your TV as John Wayne shooting at bad guys on late-night movies. "We'll see reality in syndication, reality in daytime, reality news," says Brooks. "It's just another innovative way to tell stories. That's what TV must do to survive, find new ways of telling basically the same stories: about conflict, love, and—heaven forbid—survival." 17

Examining the Reading

Finding Meaning

1. What made the networks want to order new episodes of their reality TV shows?
2. What has the reality TV trend turned into?
3. Why are reality TV shows profitable for the networks?
4. Why is reality TV appealing to viewers?
5. Explain the history of reality TV. What television shows that came before it contained elements of reality TV?
6. What is different about the new style of reality television programs?
7. What show started the new type of reality TV show?
8. What does Brooks say are the basic elements of all stories?

Understanding Technique

1. What is Leopold's thesis? How does he support it?
2. How does the title relate to the conclusion drawn in the last paragraph?
3. What is the tone of the article? How is this tone conveyed?

Thinking Critically

1. Do you think people will be watching reality TV in twenty years? Explain your reasons.
2. Why were advertising spots so expensive for the finale of *Survivor I*?
3. What does Neal Gabler mean when he says there is "a deep crisis in narrative" (paragraph 7)?
4. Why do you think MTV had the only reality TV show for so long?
5. Explain how technology can create isolation between and among people.

Writing About the Reading

A Journal Entry

Create a list of words describing how you would feel about someone watching your every move during your daily routine.

A Paragraph

1. Write a paragraph explaining how reality TV might be useful in our lives, or why it is not useful.
2. Robert Thompson mentions soap operas, doctor shows, and legal shows. Write a paragraph explaining what these types of programs have in common that appeals to so many people.

An Essay

1. Write an essay explaining how television defines and continues to change the American idea of "entertainment."
2. Write an essay about a time you had to "survive" something. Include any similarities or differences between that incident and what is shown on reality TV.
3. Write an essay explaining why you would or would not want to participate in a reality TV show.

A Creative Activity

Create a new reality TV show. What would happen?

Sporting the Fan(tasy) of Reality TV

▶ **Colleen Diez**
Student Essay

Colleen Diez, a college student, explains the popularity of so-called reality TV shows.

"*A*aaagh!" my friend Mary screams at the television. "I can't believe   1
the tribal council kicked him off! He was my favorite!" She is referring,
of course, to *Survivor,* one of a slew of reality shows on current prime-
time TV. Everywhere, these "reality" shows appear to capture the
imagination of viewers. The media pretends this concept is a new idea,
but many MTV watchers recall the popular first seasons of *The Real
World* and *Road Rules.* We are fascinated by shows that cast "real" people, or nonactors, in the main roles. These shows have created a new
kind of entertainment, a new type of sport, and the reasons for the
popularity of this new form of entertainment are easy to identify.

Reality TV feeds our desire to know about and control other people.   2
We want to know the details about other people's lives because we are
curious, and because we have a need to identify with others. We buy
tabloid newpapers about movie stars in order to read about intimate
details that make the star seem closer to earth and to us. These personal,
sometimes flawed, characteristics make an actor seem more human.
Such details are plentiful in a reality show. We learn about someone's
children, spouse, or even sex life. By seeking similarities in another's situation, we feel closely tied to a person we've never met. A reality show
also gives us a sense of power over the people on the show. For example, in *Big Brother,* the viewer at home may see into people's lives without being seen. This watching while unseen can be called voyeurism.
The *Big Brother* voyeuristic audience also claims the right to determine
the outcome of the show. Each week, viewers may call in or vote online
to decide which group member will be removed. Reality TV makes us
feel powerful and superior to the cast, one of its big attractions.

The primary attraction of television is escapism, that is, escape   3
from reality. While television may be educational, most of us watch TV
to relax and to be entertained after a hard day at work or school. Escaping from the negative, repetitive aspects of our everyday lives appeals to us. Television stimulates us with exciting, new experiences.
Reality TV specifically helps us to escape, but makes us unaware that
we are escaping. This is part of the appeal. Shows like *Survivor* and
Temptation Island bring us to exotic, fantasy locations, but because the
people are not actors, we accept the situation as more realistic. We feel
that we are watching something real, not artificial. These shows make
fantasy, like being lost on a desert island, into reality. We escape into
this fantasy, while thinking that we actually confront reality in the cast
of "real" people. We willingly allow ourselves to be fooled by TV into
thinking that we are not escaping. That in itself is escapism.

Finally, this new generation of reality TV appeals to us as a new   4
kind of sport. All of the new shows feature competition, either against
oneself or others, to win a highly valued prize. *Survivor* displays competition first between teams, and then among individuals, while on
Fear Factor, contestants subject themselves to their greatest fears (like
being locked in a coffin with rats) in order to win money. As an audience to this kind of entertainment, we side with certain contestants,
and root them on, just as one would during a football game or any
other sport. My friend Mary, who I mentioned earlier, was one of numerous TV viewers who threw a *Survivor* final-episode party in her
dorm room. The number of guests could only be compared to a Super
Bowl party.

These shows make us feel as if we are participating or even inter-   5
acting with the cast on the reality TV show. This participation also
gives us both power and identity connected with the show. Reality television shows appeal to us because they feed our desire to know about
other people, and they provide us the ability to escape into an exotic
world where we participate in a new sport. Whether it's surviving in
the Australian outback, testing one's greatest fears, or simply learning
to live with other people, the possibilities of reality television are endless. Networks constantly attempt to create new shows that sport the
fantasy of reality TV shows. As prime-time shows become more interactive, what we watch helps to define a new genre of TV dinner theater.

Examining the Essay

1. Highlight and evaluate Diez's thesis statement.
2. Highlight and evaluate Diez's topic sentences.
3. Explain and evaluate the essay's title.

4. Examine Diez's use of examples. What do they contribute to the essay?
5. Diez begins her first paragraph with dialogue. Evaluate the effectiveness of her introduction.

Writing an Essay

1. Write an essay about reality TV shows that you have watched. Did you find them appealing in the ways Diez describes? Why or why not?
2. Write an essay describing the differences and similarities between watching real people on TV and reading about them in biographies and memoirs.
3. Write an essay comparing reality TV to other types of sports. Discuss their similarities and differences.
4. Suppose some readers of Diez's essay had never watched a reality TV show. Evaluate whether Diez provides sufficient background information to make the essay understandable to these readers.

 ## Making Connections

1. Drawing upon the information presented in the readings by Tannen, "Oprah Winfrey," and Cross, "Advertising: Institutionalized Lying," as well as your own knowledge about talk shows and advertising, answer the following question: In what sense do both television talk shows and advertising influence the public?

2. "Advertising: Institutionalized Lying," and "Oprah Winfrey" discuss aspects of television viewing. Write an essay describing what attitudes or viewpoints the authors (Cross and Tannen) hold in common.

3. Compare the different predictions for the future of television as described in "Can TV Improve Us?" and "How Much 'Reality' TV Can We Survive?"

 ## Internet Connections

1. Many news web sites are available online. Browse the following web sites.

   http:// www.courier-journal.com/
   http://abcnews.go.com/
   http://www.eugeneweekly.com/
   http://news.npr.org/

Write an essay comparing these web sites to the news sources you rely on. Do you prefer news web sites or newspapers? Why?

2. Advertising can sometimes be misleading. Read over the information on this web site, **http://linz1.net/fraud3.html/**, and summarize the advice it gives about fraudulent Internet ads.

3. Visit the web site for Fairness and Accuracy in Reporting at **http://www.fair.org/**. Write a paragraph explaining the purpose of this site. Do you agree with this organization's mission? Why or why not?

(If any of these web sites are unavailable, use a search engine to locate another appropriate site.)

Chapter 7

Technology That Shapes Our Lives

The Seven Sustainable Wonders of the World
Alan Thein Durning

Stepping Through a Computer Screen,
Disabled Veterans Savor Freedom
N. R. Kleinfield

Log to Learn
Jodie Morse

Inventing the Future
Thomas J. Frey and Darby L. Frey

Dr. Dolphin
Richard Blow

The Case for Selling Human Organs
Ronald Bailey

Human Interaction
Christine Choi

How many tools, machines, or appliances have you used already today? Your list might include a clock radio, Walkman, coffeemaker, hair dryer, toaster, lock and key, computer, and car or bus. Most of us are so used to these inventions that we don't give them a second thought, but in fact all of these items are the result of study and research. Research has also produced daily conveniences such as no-iron clothing, Post-it notes, and orange juice from concentrate. The use of scientific research to create products or services is called *technology*.

In many cases, technology directly controls our lives. For instance, if your car does not start or the bus breaks down, you may miss classes. If your brakes malfunction, your life could be in danger. If a storm causes an electrical failure, your home may be without heat, light, or cooking facilities. People's lives may have been saved by medical technology, their hearts having stopped but been restarted by a machine.

In other situations, technology influences or shapes the quality of our lives. Without technology, we would not have many conveniences we take for granted: elevators, automatic teller machines, microwave ovens, and so forth. Technology affects our communication through radio and telephones; our diet with convenience and low-fat foods; our comfort with furnaces, air conditioners, and plumbing systems; our health with vaccines, genetic engineering, and drugs; and our jobs with computers, copiers, and fax machines. In fact, it is difficult to think of any aspect of daily life that remains untouched by technology.

In this chapter, the reading selections explore the effects of technology and examine specific instances in which technology has made an impact. The first reading presents one author's listing of the seven most valuable inventions ("The Seven Sustainable Wonders of the World"). Other readings discuss the contributions that computer technology has made or will make to education through the availability of online college courses ("Log to Learn") and research that suggests swimming with dolphins may improve human health ("Dr. Dolphin"). Another reading discusses the issue of the sale of human organs for organ replacement ("The Case for Selling Human Organs"). And yet another reading discusses the variety of inventions possible in the future ("Inventing the Future"). You'll read further about the influence of computer technology, both positive, such as computers that can simulate reality for disabled persons ("Stepping Through a Computer Screen, Disabled Veterans Savor Freedom"), and negative, as reflected in "Human Interaction."

Brainstorming About Technology

Class Activities:

1. Working in groups, brainstorm a list of inventions that were developed or that came into widespread use during your lifetime.
2. Working in groups, list inventions that you would eliminate to improve the quality of life.

The Seven Sustainable Wonders of the World

▶ **Alan Thein Durning**

Simple little things can make a big difference in one's life. In this reading, the writer casts his vote for the seven key inventions— most of them quite simple—that make the biggest difference in our lives. This reading first appeared in the Utne Reader *in 1994.*

Reading Strategy

Read the heading that introduces each invention. Before you read the section that follows it, predict why the writer feels the invention is important.

Vocabulary Preview

sustainable (title) capable of being used continually
thermodynamically (2) having to do with the use of heat energy
climes (4) climates
flotsam and jetsam (8) debris or wreckage and discards
scourge (12) affliction

I've never seen any of the Seven Wonders of the World, and to tell you the truth I wouldn't really want to. To me, the real wonders are all the little things—little things that work, especially when they do it without hurting the earth. Here's my list of simple things that, though we take them for granted, are absolute wonders. These implements solve every-day problems so elegantly that everyone in the world today—and everyone who is likely to live in it in the next century—could make use of them without Mother Nature's being any the worse for wear.

1. The Bicycle

The most thermodynamically efficient transportation device ever cre-ated and the most widely used private vehicle in the world, the bicycle lets you travel three times as far on a plateful of calories as you could walking. And they're 53 times more energy efficient—comparing food calories with gasoline calories—than the typical car. Not to mention the fact that they don't pollute the air, lead to oil spills (and oil wars), change the climate, send cities sprawling over the countryside, lock up half of urban space in roads and parking lots, or kill a quarter million people in traffic accidents each year.

The world doesn't yet have enough bikes for everybody to ride, but it's getting there quickly: Best estimates put the world's expanding fleet of two-wheelers at 850 million—double the number of autos. We Americans have no excuses on this count: We have more bikes per person than China, where they are the principal vehicle. We just don't ride them much. 3

2. *The Ceiling Fan*

Appropriate technology's answer to air conditioning, ceiling fans cool tens of millions of people in Asia and Africa. A fan over your bed brings relief in sweltering climes, as I've had plenty of time to reflect on during episodes of digestive turmoil in cheap tropical hotels. 4

Air conditioning, found in two-thirds of U.S. homes, is a juice hog and the bane of the stratospheric ozone layer because of its CFC coolants. Ceiling fans, on the other hand, are simple, durable, and repairable and take little energy to run. 5

3. *The Clothesline*

A few years ago, I read about an engineering laboratory that claimed it had all but perfected a microwave clothes dryer. The dryer, the story went, would get the moisture out of the wash with one-third the energy of a conventional unit and cause less wear and tear on the fabric. 6

I don't know if they ever got it on the market, but it struck me at the time that if simple wonders had a PR agent, there might have been a news story instead about the perfection of a solar clothes dryer. It takes few materials to manufacture, is safe for kids, requires absolutely no electricity or fuel, and even gets people outdoors where they can talk to their neighbors. 7

4. *The Telephone*

The greatest innovation in human communications since Gutenberg's printing press, telephone systems are the only entry on my wonders list invented in this century, and—hype of the information age notwithstanding—I'll wager that they never lose ground to other communications technologies. Unlike fax machines, personal computers and computer networks, televisions, VCRs and camcorders, CD-ROMs, and all the other flotsam and jetsam of the information age, telephones are a simple extension of the most time-tested means of human communication: speech. 8

5. *The Public Library*

Public libraries are the most democratic institutions yet invented. Think of it! Equal access to information for any citizen who comes inside. A lifetime of learning, all free. Libraries foster community, too, by 9 bringing people of different classes, races, and ages together in that endangered form of human habitat: noncommercial public space.

Although conceived without any ecological intention whatsoever, libraries are waste reduction at its best. Each library saves a forestful of trees by making thousands of personal copies of books and periodicals unnecessary. All that paper savings means huge reductions in energy use and water and air pollution, too. In principle, the library concept could be applied to other things—cameras and camcorders, tapes and CDs, cleaning equipment and extra dining chairs—further reducing the number of things our society needs without reducing people's access to them. The town of Takoma Park, Maryland, for example, has a tool library where people can check out a lawn mower, a ratchet set, or a sledgehammer.

6. The Interdepartmental Envelope

I don't know what they're really called: those old-fashioned slotted manila envelopes bound with a string and covered with lines for routing papers to one person after another. Whatever they're called, they put modern recycling to shame.

7. The Condom

It's a remarkable little device: highly effective, inexpensive, and portable. A few purist Greens might complain about disposability and excess packaging, but these objections are trivial considering the work the condom has to do—battling the scourge of AIDS and stabilizing the human population at a level the earth can comfortably support.

Examining the Reading

Finding Meaning

1. Why is the bicycle more efficient than the automobile?
2. In what ways are ceiling fans better than air conditioners?
3. Explain the statement, "Public libraries are the most democratic institutions yet invented."
4. In what ways do libraries "foster community"?

Understanding Technique

1. Evaluate the effectiveness of using a numbered list to organize the essay. Consider both the advantages and the disadvantages.
2. This essay lacks a conclusion. Suggest possible ways the writer could have concluded this essay.

Thinking Critically

1. Do you agree with the author that each library "saves a forestful of trees"?
2. What other kinds of libraries can you think of that the author didn't mention?
3. Do you agree with the author that the telephone is a better invention than, for example, a computer or a fax machine? Why or why not?

Writing About the Reading

A Journal Entry

Brainstorm about the author's choice of "wonders." Which ones do you agree with? Which do you disagree with? What others would you include?

A Paragraph

1. Write a paragraph explaining which of the wonders identified by the author you would rank as most important. Justify your choice.
2. Write a paragraph identifying what you believe is the best invention, old or new, other than those listed by the author. Justify your choice.

An Essay

1. Write an essay titled "Three *More* Sustainable Wonders of the World." Use Durning's organization as a model for your own essay.
2. Write an essay comparing your choices for the above assignment with Durning's choices. How did your choices differ? Would you substitute any of Durning's "wonders" for your own? Would you re-place any of his with yours? Which ones, and why?

A Creative Activity

This reading identifies the most important inventions of the world. Suppose it had been titled "The Seven *Least* Sustainable Wonders of the World" and had discussed the most useless, silliest, or most waste-ful inventions or gadgets ever invented. What do you think it might have included? Write an essay explaining your choices.

Stepping Through a Computer Screen, Disabled Veterans Savor Freedom

▶ **N. R. Kleinfield**

Virtual reality, a new computer technology, will probably affect all of our lives in the future. Journalist N. R. Kleinfield wrote this New York Times *article about what virtual reality is and how it is being used to help disabled veterans.*

Reading Strategy

As you read, highlight or annotate specific uses of virtual reality for those with physical disabilities.

Vocabulary Preview

savor (title) taste; enjoy
paraplegic (1) one who is paralyzed from the waist down
quadriplegic (2) one who is paralyzed from the neck down
full-fledged (5) fully developed; complete
provocative (6) exciting; stimulating
tantalizing (9) arousing desire; tempting
muscular dystrophy (11) a disease in which some muscles
                              lose the ability to function
troves (13) hoards
buoyant (17) cheerful
mobility (18) ability to move

The other day, Angelo Degree single-handedly lifted a couch and ef-   1
fortlessly hauled it into another room. He moved around a lamp, a
crate. He snatched hold of a man and ran outside with him. Ever since
he was shot in the head and spine while being robbed in 1981, Mr. Degree has been a paraplegic. His legs are a wheelchair. One day he is
hoping to play football. Tackle.

The man who plans to suit him up is William Meredith, who is not   2
a doctor with a miracle cure but a recording engineer with a black bag

flush with interactive computer technology. His subjects are the paraplegics and quadriplegics in the spinal cord injury ward at the Bronx
Veterans Affairs Medical Center.

For some 10 years Mr. Meredith has done volunteer work for the   3
Veterans Bedside Network, a 46-year-old organization made up largely
of show-business people who try to rally the spirits of sick veterans, engaging them in plays and song-and-dance routines.

"But I always felt there was one group who we weren't able to   4
reach that well, and those were the quadriplegics and paraplegics," Mr.
Meredith explained. "And so I thought about virtual reality."

Virtual reality, for those unfamiliar with the outer envelope of tech-   5
nology, enables people to feel, through interactive computers, as
though they are inside a three-dimensional electronic image. In full-
fledged systems, they can actually sense that they are moving and feel
virtual reality objects. To participate, all that is required is a working mind.
                                                                          6
The more Mr. Meredith, 52, chewed over the notion, the more
provocative it became. "These visions ran through my mind," he said.
"These people could fly, which they can't. They could walk, which they
can't. They could play sports, which they can't."
                                                                          7
After winning over officials at the Bronx Veterans Medical Center
and getting a $5,000 equipment budget from the Veterans Bedside Net-
work, Mr. Meredith was in business. In mid-October he got his idea off
the ground.
                                                                          8
Every Tuesday and Thursday afternoon, he lugs three laptop computers to the Bronx hospital. He is an Air Force man himself, and
teaches virtual reality at various schools as well as uses it in his recording work for films. He usually travels to the hospital with Michael
Storch, who recently joined Veterans Bedside Network and is studying
to enter the virtual reality field. They report to the first-floor spinal
cord injury unit, where there are about 50 patients, and set up their
equipment in the physical rehabilitation room.
                                                                          9
From 2 P.M. to 4:30 P.M., wheelchairs roll up to their corner and patients enter the tantalizing world of virtual reality.
                                                                          10
The patients use goggles in which they see a three-dimensional image
and a glove that is wired to the computer in a way that, when they move
their hand, they seem to grasp and move things on the computer screen.
Mr. Meredith has yet to incorporate equipment that enables patients to
feel and smell the virtual world they enter, though he hopes to do so soon.   11

It seemed only a matter of time for this to happen. Virtual reality is
being used by therapists to help treat children who have suffered child
abuse. It is being used to teach sufferers of muscular dystrophy how to
operate a wheelchair. It is being used to help people overcome a fear of
heights. They are ushered onto a virtual reality ledge, many stories in
the sky. Go on, they are told. Look down.

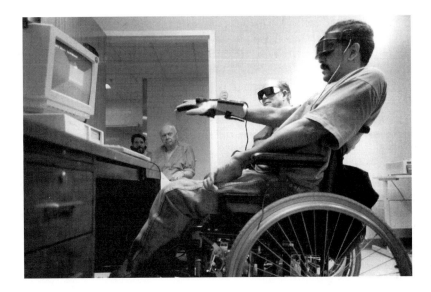

At this early stage in the program, Mr. Meredith is able to offer only   12
limited options to the patients. There are several virtual reality games,
including Heretic, which involves wandering through creepy dungeons
and staving off demons and menacing creatures. There is a program
that allows patients to redecorate a house by moving furniture around
through the use of a Power Glove. There is a chess game, which has
proved especially popular. And Mr. Meredith has designed his own virtual reality baseball game, where patients see the field from whichever
position they assume.

In addition, Mr. Meredith brings along various computer programs   13
that are not virtual reality but enable patients to look up vast troves of
information on the computers. One man has been researching the
places where he made bomber runs during World War II.

The other day, Mr. Degree, 39, finished rearranging the virtual re-   14
ality house and moved on to Heretic. He was reasonably accomplished. He destroyed quite a few knights and flying beasts before
mistakenly grabbing a gas bomb.

"You better work on your recognition," Mr. Meredith chided him.   15

"Next time, I'll give it to them real good," he promised.   16

Mr. Degree was buoyant about the program. "You know why a lot   17
of veterans are in and out of hospitals?" he asked. "Stress. If they want
to have any dreams, they have to get them from a bottle. Here, you can
have dreams without the bottle. All I can do is look here and see a lot
of potential. An angel with a lot of wings."

Mike Abelson, the chief of recreation services for the hospital, is   18
equally enthusiastic. "For these guys, it opens up a whole new world,"
he said. "Physical barriers don't matter. Mobility barriers don't exist."

Mr. Meredith has elaborate ambitions. Many veterans relish their   19
trips to the Intrepid Sea-Air-Space Museum aboard the aircraft carrier
permanently moored on West 46th Street. Spinal cord patients usually
don't go. Mr. Meredith is having a virtual reality tour of the Intrepid designed so patients can experience it from their beds. He hopes it will be
ready by July.

"Ultimately, I want to have interactive sports," Mr. Meredith said.   20
"I'd like to link up several hospitals and have leagues and everything.
They'll play baseball, football, whatever they want. They'll be able to
feel every hit."

Some patients have employed the computers to assist them in pro-   21
saic concerns. "One guy was having problems with the grass on his
lawn on Staten Island," Mr. Meredith said, "and so he looked up in one
of the data bases in the computer ways of dealing with Bluegrass diseases. I believe he found his answer."

Whatever use they make of the technology, the patients find their   22
bedimmed lives galvanized.

Wilfred Garcia, 55, was keen to gain knowledge. "I've been looking   23
up where I was stationed in Berlin in 1958," he said. "Brings back the
memories. I'm into biography. I looked up Christopher Columbus. I
looked up Marco Polo. He was born in the same city as Columbus. I
looked up Clark Gable. Man, what an actor."

In 1986, Mr. Garcia had an allergic reaction to a tuna sandwich   24
while he was driving on the New York Thruway. He blacked out and his
car crashed down an embankment. He was left an "incomplete paraplegic," meaning he can stand up and walk short distances on crutches,
but has no balance.

Now he immersed himself in chess. He was a novice. The com-   25
puter demolished him. "I might look into boxing on this," he said. "I
used to box. At the age of 16, I was going to join the Golden Gloves but
my mother wouldn't let me."

With limited resources and equipment, Mr. Meredith has been con-   26
fined to offering his program to those able to come to the rehabilitation room. His goal is to take systems to patient bedsides, which, after
all, is what Veterans Bedside Network is supposed to be about.

There are patients itchy to see that happen. Osvaldo Arias, 35, par-   27
alyzed from the neck down since being shot in the back by unseen as-
sailants in the Bronx in 1978, was lying in his room at the Veterans
hospital. Recovering from surgery, he could not get to the rehabilitation room.

"When you spend a lot of time in bed, you can go crazy," he said.   28
"Right now, I can't get out of bed. I'm bored. You watch TV for a while,
then you get tired of it. I try to write letters. An idle mind is the devil's

workshop. I want to see that system in here. It's meant for those who can't get out of bed to keep them from going stir crazy."

Examining the Reading

Finding Meaning

1. What is the specific purpose of the Veterans Bedside Network?
2. Describe the equipment used with virtual reality.
3. Name two activities in the world of virtual reality that Meredith has not yet incorporated.
4. Identify two ways in which therapists have used virtual reality.
5. How and why is virtual reality especially useful to patients with spinal cord injuries?

Understanding Technique

1. How does Kleinfield make the essay lively and interesting?
2. Evaluate the introduction and conclusion. Why are they effective?

Thinking Critically

1. Other than the examples cited in the article, name one way in which virtual reality can help people.
2. If you had a complete virtual reality system, how would you use it?
3. What did Degree mean when he said, "Here, you can have dreams without the bottle"?
4. What do you think the single most important use of virtual reality will be in the future?

Writing About the Reading

A Journal Entry

List the virtual reality events—real or imagined—that you would like to participate in.

A Paragraph

1. Suppose you became a paraplegic. Write a paragraph describing in detail three virtual reality activities you would enjoy.
2. Write a paragraph defining virtual reality for someone who has never heard of it.

An Essay

1. Write an essay explaining the process by which a virtual reality system could be used to lessen or eliminate a particular fear.
2. Many tasks are difficult to learn without hands-on experience (driving a car, using a computer, and so forth). In the future, virtual reality may take the place of hands-on training in many fields. Assume it is the year 2025. Write an essay predicting how training for a particular job, occupation, or profession might be different than it is now.

A Creative Activity

Assume that interactive sports using virtual reality became possible. Add a paragraph to the reading explaining the benefits and describing the veterans' reactions to playing interactive sports.

Log to Learn

> **Jodie Morse**

Jodie Morse investigates the world of online learning by enrolling in a cyberclass. This article was first published by Time Digital (**www.timedigital.com**) *in December 2000.*

Reading Strategy

As you read, note the pros and cons of online education as experienced by Morse.

Vocabulary Preview

lobbying (1) trying to influence
aspirations (1) strong desires
mores (2) customs; manners
evoked (5) called to mind
curmudgeon (5) cranky person
rapt (5) very moved and fully attentive
convening (6) meeting
in lieu of (6) in place of
garrulous (7) very talkative
allusions (9) references
engendered (11) created; gave birth to
attenuated (11) weakened
enthralled (12) interested; captivated
cataclysmic (12) devastating
apathy (13) lack of interest

I always dreaded the first day of school. My parents like to remind me 1
that I spent the first day of the first grade in denial, making repeated
trips back to my kindergarten classroom. On the first day of my junior
year in high school, after a summer of endless lobbying to be allowed
to drive myself to school, I found myself in the parking lot talking to
AAA when I locked my keys in the car with the engine running. During
my first day at college, I got lost while looking for a premed placement
test and wound up in a cemetery adjacent to the science complex. I took
this as a glaring sign and dropped my medical aspirations, promptly
enrolling in as many literature courses as possible.

So it was something of a relief to attend the first lecture of English 2
XB17, a survey course of Shakespeare's major plays offered by the Uni-

versity of California, Berkeley's extension program. Other than the short commute from my bed to the laptop at the other end of my 500-sq.-ft. studio apartment, no travel was necessary. To find my actual classroom, I simply clicked onto an area of AOL that Berkeley used, where I'd been preregistered, to read and complete my first assignment. And when I worried that I was wasting a sunny July Saturday immersed in an introduction to social and cultural mores of the English Renaissance, I just stepped outside for a walk. Then I returned to my desk, leisurely phoned a friend, and settled down to work.

I quickly learned why so many Americans are heading off to college without leaving their keyboards. They're logging on to sites set up by prestigious schools like Berkeley, Columbia, and Stanford, as well as to a new breed of cyber-only institutions, such as Jones International University and Western Governors University. Online learning is especially appealing at a time when traditional college students—those 18- to-22-year-olds who spend four years living on campus and attending classes and keg parties—make up just 16% of total university enrollment. The vast majority of today's students are time-crunched adults who must pencil in college diplomas and graduate degrees between hectic jobs and kids' soccer games. The upshot is during this academic year, some 2 million people will take online classes. . . . 3

I decided to conduct an unscientific study of my own and take a class. (I paid my $505 and enrolled like any other student, but at the end of the course I told the professor I was a journalist.) I gravitated to Berkeley mainly because of its reputation, but also because its online courses are still fairly low-tech, requiring nothing more than the 56K modem I have on my laptop at home. And I enjoyed the catchy motto: "Bringing the university to you." 4

I briefly considered Classics of Children's Literature and History of Film, but I settled on Shakespeare. The description boasted that the course was the "winner of the 1997 Helen Williams Award for Excellence in Collegiate Independent Study." Whatever that was, I was sold. Plus, as a one-time English major, I'd read more than my share of Shakespeare and felt I had a fairly good basis to judge the quality of the instruction. I also thought my background might enable me to skimp on some of the reading if I got busy. Finally, I could think of no educational experience that better evoked my own undergraduate years than my two semesters of Shakespeare. Once in a while, I still get flashbacks of my Shakespeare professor, an old-fashioned curmudgeon, hand to his heart, belting out an impassioned *Hamlet* soliloquy to a rapt class. 5

My online class was of the so-called asynchronous variety, meaning that instead of convening at an appointed time each week to learn and discuss material, each student works at his or her own pace. Lectures typically are downloaded from the Internet or, as in my case, ar- 6 rive in printed form through the mail. Discussions take the form of running commentaries snaking through topical message boards. Students are encouraged to arrange live chat discussions and, in lieu of weekly office hours, e-mail their professor whenever questions arise.

While it is a blessing for the eternally overbooked, like me, the asynchronous format did little to foster class unity. After reading each play, we were required to post a response on a message board and take up a question posed by one of our classmates. If a particularly spirited discussion was under way (example: cross-dressing Shakespearean actors), our professor, Mary Ann Koory, would send out an e-mail prodding us to log on. But other than those infrequent nudges, it was left up to us to decide how actively we participated. Asynchronicity was liberating in at least one sense, however. As an undergrad, I detested those class drones who always monopolized the discussion. They're just as garrulous and annoying over e-mail, tending to post their observations in loud colors like fire-engine red, but here they're easier to avoid. Just don't click on them. 7

I'd be hard-pressed to tell anything about my classmates or even how many were in the class at one time, since we were all chugging through the lessons at such varied paces. I'd often find myself responding to a posting by a student who had no intention of returning to that topic—he'd already moved on to the next lesson. And my attempts at starting a live group discussion in our class chat room were equally fruitless: only one other person showed up for my chat on Richard III's villainy. And it was the professor. 8

The quality of her teaching more than made up for the flat class dynamic. The "lectures" were learned, lively, and strewn throughout with 9

Where to Get Started

1. **geteducated.com** Home to a free monthly newsletter, the Virtual University Gazette, this site for distance-learning research and consulting also boasts an extensive catalog of online programs.
2. **detc.org** Log on to the Distance Education and Training Council and browse a directory of 74 accredited institutions and a list of subjects taught, from court reporting to Bible studies.
3. **learn.berkeley.edu** One of the most established online learning programs, featuring courses on such things as Buddhist philosophy and Irish culture; you can even take a guided tour before signing up.

entertaining pop-cultural allusions. (At one point, we were told to consider Shakespeare's folio of plays as a compilation of the best-ever Grateful Dead bootlegs.) Mary Ann (we were on a first-name basis from our very first e-mail) says she makes use of current events to connect with the varied backgrounds of her students. Most of the time the technique worked, though I could have done without the essay question asking us to compare and contrast Othello with O.J. Simpson.

The workload, as is often the case in online courses, was much   10
heftier—for both students and professor—than in a typical college course. Here, each reading assignment had an essay of several "screens" followed by a three-hour final. After netting a string of B's and lukewarm comments, I realized my skimp-on-reading strategy wouldn't cut it. Mary Ann perceptively tagged my early work a "little light on the logical argument," noting that "you were more interested in your prose than in Shakespeare's work." After that zinger, I stepped up my scholarship. And though I never took the final, I was pulling A's by the course's end.

Mary Ann's best response time was just one hour after I handed in   11
a paper, and her comments often engendered a string of follow-up e-mails. She says such one-on-one discussions are the norm—she often converses more with her online students than with those taking the in-person version. And those online discussions are often much more inclusive. "For shy people, the social barriers fall away online," she told me. "However attenuated, online conversations tend to be of higher quality and much more democratic in the best Jeffersonian sense of the word."

Even though my e-mails with Mary Ann were stimulating, I won-   12
dered if they would have been enough to keep me enthralled if I hadn't been writing this article. According to some estimates, the dropout rate from some online courses can be as high as 50%, compared with just 26% at traditional schools. "Older students' lives are full of disruptions," says Vicky Phillips, CEO of Geteducated.com, a distance-learning research and consulting firm. "Work responsibilities change, kids get sick, people get divorced." My disruptions were less cataclysmic (cable TV and phone calls), but they often proved urgent enough to pull me off an essay for several hours or days.

Many online proponents are looking to the more cutting-edge tech-   13
nologies, such as live streaming video, to curb online student apathy. Other online programs, like Duke University's well-regarded M.B.A. program, require students to come together for a certain number of in-person classes. But schools without a campus don't have that luxury and must find other ways to gin up school spirit: Jones International University has opened an online school store and sends its students

late-night snacks. Kentucky Virtual University is sponsoring a digital football league, and Kaplancollege.com has plans for online yearbooks and weekly mixers.

Class bonding is much less of an obstacle for students who progress   14
through a full-fledged online degree program together. Take Marilyn McKay, a marketing consultant in a two-year online M.B.A. program at the University of Maryland University College. McKay, who has a more than full-time job at her own firm and lives in the isolated California desert, chose online learning for its flexibility. "You really learn much more about people than in one of those crowded 200-person lectures where the professor uses the same notes he has for the past 10 years and no one speaks up," she says. Plus, she reminded me, meeting people in print can sometimes be more revealing than sharing small talk while filing into a classroom. "For starters," she says, "you learn quickly who knows how to spell and who uses bad grammar."

McKay is 53 and has grown children. For serious graduate stu-   15
dents like her—or even serious dabblers like me—online learning may work. But for the millions of wide-eyed 18-year-olds out there, it's still no contest. Which may explain why, after putting out calls to some of the major online programs, I could turn up only one student who was awarded an undergraduate diploma online. Tasha Overton, 23, got a B.S. in computer programming last year from the University of Maryland University College. The primary interpersonal connections she says she made were in her sorority, which she joined during the semester she spent on campus at Tennessee's Austin Peay State University: "I was interested only in getting through my classes, and I didn't go to college to meet people. For me, online education meant the freedom from ever having to set foot in a classroom."

However, even the staunchest backers of online learning would   16
curtail that freedom. According to Geteducated.com's Phillips, "Colleges will always exist as we know them as social rites of passage. People don't only go off to college to learn Plato, but to come of age." And they do so not just by hearing an inspired literary mind render *Hamlet*, but also by spending the first day of class dazed and confused in a field of tombstones.

Examining the Reading

Finding Meaning

1. Describe the author's previous experiences with first days of school.
2. Why did Morse choose Berkeley for her online course?
3. Why did Morse choose to study Shakespeare?

4. What is the author required to do for her online class?
5. What is the asynchronous format and how well did it work for Morse?
6. What differences does the instructor find between her online and traditional students?
7. Why does online education work for Marilyn McKay?
8. Why won't online education replace actual colleges and universities?

Understanding Technique

1. Review the first paragraph. What is its tone? Why does Morse include it? How does it relate to the last paragraph?
2. Morse actually enrolled in an online course. How does her personal involvement add to the article? How else could she have gathered information for her report?
3. Evaluate the author's use of topic sentences.

Thinking Critically

1. Why was it a relief for Morse to start her online class?
2. Why has online education become so appealing?
3. Why did Morse wait until the end of the course to tell her professor she was a journalist?
4. How important is "class unity"? Why is Morse concerned about it?
5. If Morse were taking the course just for her article, then why did she care so much about her grade?
6. Why should institutions offering online courses want to foster "class unity"?
7. What is Morse's final evaluation of online education?

Writing About the Reading

A Journal Entry

Write a journal entry about how you feel on the first day of school.

A Paragraph

1. Computers are everywhere. Write a paragraph explaining the most important task or tasks that computers perform for you.
2. Many people struggle with the decision to continue their education after high school. Write a paragraph explaining your most important reason for attending college.
3. Write a paragraph describing how classmates can affect your learning experience.

An Essay

1. Write an essay explaining what there is to college life besides academics. Why are these other aspects so important?
2. Write an essay discussing the advantages and disadvantages of on-line courses.

A Creative Activity

Some courses would not work online. Name and describe some examples.

Inventing the Future

▸ Thomas J. Frey and Darby L. Frey

In this essay from The Futurist, *the authors discuss several techno-logical advances that are expected to become realities in the future.*

Reading Strategy

After you finish reading this essay, prepare a vertical, two-column list. In the first column, list the future inventions that were discussed. In the second column, list the primary use for each invention.

Vocabulary Preview

profound (1) deep; intense
emerge (1) come out; happen
interjecting (4) including; adding
pundit (4) critic; commentator
leverage (5) advance; take advantage of
dormant (7) inactive; closed down
algorithms (8) step-by-step procedures
formulations (11) ideas; plans
mammalian (11) like warm-blooded animals
spherical (14) having the shape of a globe
itineraries (14) travel plans; routes

*A*t the DaVinci Institute, our goal is to forecast future inventions, many of which will have a profound effect on our lives. We do not make value judgments as to whether or not these technologies should be pursued. Our belief is that these unborn technologies will emerge someday with or without our blessing. We believe it is in society's best interest to thoroughly understand the concepts and be forewarned of the changes that lie ahead.

High-Impact Inventions

Here are snapshots of a few highly probable inventions that our research tells us are likely to have a profound effect on the future:

Personality services for computers.   The day is coming when we will be able to hold an intelligent conversation with our computer. But the novelty of a talking computer will quickly give way to the need for a more complicated humanlike interaction. This need will give birth to a new industry: computers equipped with personality services.

Most people will subscribe to more than one online personality service, adding a new dimension to the human–computer interface. If, for example, you were to subscribe to a David Letterman personality service, suddenly your computer voice would start sounding like David Letterman, interjecting jokes and wild comments. If your choice was a political pundit personality such as Rush Limbaugh or Geraldine Ferraro, you would be able to hold a stimulating conversation about current political topics. If you wanted to ask your computer about the news of the day, you could subscribe to a Tom Brokaw or Peter Jennings personality. 4

Personality services will be an interesting market to watch as celebrities leverage their name recognition even further and relative newcomers offer unique personality services at bargain prices. 5

Controlling the brain. When a person's liver stops working, does it stop because the liver gives out or because the person's brain tells it to stop? This question is currently being debated by theorists in the medical community. We suspect that the answer lies somewhere in the feedback loop of impulses between the brain and the liver. 6

Many medical researchers believe that the brain has an override capability that can keep an organ functioning in spite of a "shut-down" order. Possibly this brain function could become subject to conscious human control. One can speculate about possible ways to upload the brain's version of a batch file or lines of code to force the brain to override a shut-down signal and restart a dormant body function. 7

In the past, controlling the brain has always been accomplished through the use of drugs. Chemicals introduced into the body produced a chemical reaction to create the desired effect. In the future, this could be accomplished with medical algorithms, which means sending direct impulses to the brain to trigger the necessary override changes to a given body function. The advantage of algorithms over drugs is that there are no chemical side effects. 8

Uses for medical algorithms could include curing physical maladies such as color blindness or hearing loss, controlling appetite or desire for sweets, controlling addictions or illicit drug use, and improving stamina, memory, or reaction time. 9

Meat grown from plants. Researchers continue trying to develop hybrid plants to serve as meat substitutes, but a more direct breakthrough could soon yield pork, chicken, and beef plants. 10

In Boulder, Colorado, a company called Somatogen is in a competitive race to produce the first FDA-approved artificial blood product. Plants grown using this blood as the primary source of nutrition 11 (instead of water) could begin to exhibit a mammalian type of growth. There may also be other bio-cloning formulations that will accomplish the same thing. And there is definitely a ready market for plant-grown beef among vegetarians and cardiac patients.

Overlooked Ideas

There are also a number of significant technologies already invented   12
but generally overlooked. Some concepts are already being developed; others may be tied up in legal or funding battles. Here are two ideas that are within the scope of current technology and have the potential to reshape the thinking in several industries:

Spherical-shaped computer display.   Computers come in different   13
colors and sizes, but all computer displays are limited to the same basic shape: the rectangular screen. This configuration hasn't substantially changed since Philo Farnsworth's invention of the television was commercialized in the 1950s. Some would say that operating a computer program with our present monitors is like trying to watch a baseball game through a knothole.

A spherical display will have unique applications for computer   14
users who need to observe the surface of the earth or some other planet. Travel agents will easily plan and display complicated international itineraries by means of a true-shaped image of the earth. Meteorologists will broadcast a real-time global view of weather patterns that will appear on a globe sitting on your desk.

Computers that read aloud.   Systems already exist for visually track-   15
ing eye movement; at the same time, talking computers are making inroads. It won't be long before we have a device that combines these technologies in order to pronounce words as a reader reads them. Such devices will have tremendous value in teaching students to read and to understand foreign languages. They will also create a multisensory learning experience for anyone reading a book, vastly improving levels of information retention.

Examining the Reading

Finding Meaning

1. What are the goals of the DaVinci Institute?
2. What are some of the DaVinci Institute's predictions for future computers?
3. How might the brain be controlled without the use of drugs?

4. List several medical applications of brain control.
5. What would be the advantages of meat grown from plants?

Understanding Technique

1. This essay lacks a conclusion. Write a conclusion that could be added to the essay.
2. How do the authors make future inventions clear and understandable to readers who lack a background in technology?

Thinking Critically

1. How do you think medical algorithms can be used to treat alcoholism?
2. What other uses might be developed for artificial blood?
3. How is the technology described in the "Computers That Read Aloud" section different from systems that already exist, such as computers that recognize and pronounce text for blind people?
4. What do the authors mean when they say, "operating a computer program with our present monitors is like trying to watch a baseball game through a knothole"? How will spherical displays be an improvement?
5. What additional information about one or more of these future inventions do you wish the authors had included?

Writing About the Reading

A Journal Entry

Imagine that you are a college student fifty years in the future. Write a journal entry describing a typical day at school.

A Paragraph

1. The authors describe how the brain might be controlled to treat certain physical problems. Write a paragraph describing another way this type of technology might be used.
2. Technology advances rapidly. Write a paragraph describing an example of a major technological change you have experienced since your childhood.

An Essay

1. As computers become more and more humanlike in the future, how do you think relationships between people will be affected? Write an essay describing some possible changes.

2. Write an essay describing a technological advance you would like to see in your lifetime. Explain how this invention would benefit humanity.

A Creative Activity

Suppose you could subscribe to a computer personality service. Whom would you choose for your computer's personality? Write the dialogue of a conversation you might have with your computer.

Dr. Dolphin

▶ **Richard Blow**

Scientific research often leads to life-saving discoveries. This reading explores the fascinating use of dolphins as therapy for humans. Blow's essay appeared in Mother Jones *magazine.*

Reading Strategy

When you have finished reading, list the potential benefits of swimming with dolphins. Then write a brief explanation of how these benefits occur.

Vocabulary Preview

cadre (2) tightly knit group
proponents (3) supporters
black holes (5) regions of space-time from which nothing
　　　　　　can escape
visionaries (5) people who develop ideas that seem unlikely
　　　　　　but prove true
simulate (6) imitate
obviating (6) doing away with
prototype (7) original model; first of its kind
ambient (7) surrounding; encircling
sonar (20) method of locating objects using sound waves
echolocate (20) use sounds that are reflected back to
　　　　　　determine the direction and location of objects
resonates (21) echoes; vibrates
bolster (24) support; make stronger

David Cole knows that people consider him a little odd. Cole spends   1
much of his free time swimming with dolphins, and he has enough perspective to realize that this makes him, by most people's standards, eccentric. He doesn't mind.

　　Cole, a 28-year-old computer scientist, lives about half an hour   2
south of Los Angeles. With excitable gray eyes and long brown hair in ringlets, he looks a little like a youthful Michael Bolton. Cole works for a computer hardware manufacturer, but in his spare time he heads the AquaThought Foundation, a cadre of computer wizards, doctors, and naturalists researching "dolphin-assisted therapy."

For about two decades, physical therapists and psychologists have   3
argued that swimming with dolphins can help the sick and handi-
capped. Dolphin-assisted therapy seems to accelerate the vocal and physical development of autistic and mentally retarded children, for example.
Some researchers claim that dolphin swims also boost the human immune system. Most proponents of the therapy say it helps patients'
psychological well-being; the dolphins distract them from their suffering.

But Cole doesn't buy this conventional wisdom. He rejects the idea   4
that dolphins make humans feel better simply by making them happy.
That's what clowns are for. Cole believes that swimming with dolphins
can have a profound *physiological* effect on humans. The health of
your immune system, the state of your brain, the makeup of your
cells—these things, Cole believes, can be radically altered by dolphins.

To the layperson, all this might sound a little nutty. (Acquaintances   5
who knew I was working on this article kept making "Flipper" jokes.)
But then, black holes and cloning and artificial intelligence seemed
nutty, too—except to the people who believed in them, and who turned
one day from daydreamers into visionaries.

Cole asks me to try Cyberfin, a "virtual reality interaction" he in-   6
vented to simulate swimming with dolphins. Eventually he hopes to
make Cyberfin realistic enough to substitute for the real thing, helping
humans who can't afford a dolphin swim and obviating the need for
captive dolphins.

Cole has fashioned his prototype from a converted flotation tank in   7
his garage. Three-D goggles strapped around my head, I lie down on a
water mattress inside the tank. Directly overhead is a television monitor; ambient, surreal music pulses from speakers. I feel a little silly, like
I'm about to fight the Red Baron, but I try to keep an open mind.

The screen lights up, and suddenly I'm floating in a pool. Two dol-   8
phins cavort in the water, zipping by one side of me, a stream of bubbles
in their wake. Their whirs and clicks surround me. As I watch, my skep-
ticism fades into curiosity and wonder. One of them swims directly up
to my face, and instinctively I shake my head, thinking I'm about to be
bumped. Then, with a flip of its tail, the dolphin disappears.

Ordinarily, I would never admit this. But I find myself hoping that   9
it will come back soon.

Cole grew up in Winter Park, Fla., not far from NASA. After graduating   10
from the University of Central Florida in 1988, he founded a software
company called Studiotronics. A year later, Cole hooked up with a
group that was conducting dolphin-assisted therapy with cancer patients. They told Cole that the dolphins seemed to have a profound effect on the mental states of their patients; Cole offered to perform
neurological tests to see what was going on.

"At first I thought our equipment was not working," Cole remem- 11
bers. "We were using a fairly conventional statistical evaluation of
EEG—'This is your brain, this is your brain on dolphins.' The level of
change was like nothing I'd ever seen."

Essentially, Cole found a far greater harmony between the left 12
and right sides of the brain after a subject swam with dolphins—
a crude suggestion that the brain is functioning more efficiently
than normal.

When Cole studied the medical literature to try to explain this phe- 13
nomenon, he couldn't find anything. So in 1991 Cole sold Studiotronics to a Japanese company called Chinon, moved to California, and
founded AquaThought with a colleague. Though he now works for Chinon, the company gives him all the time he needs to pursue his dolphin
research. To facilitate that research, he and a colleague invented a device called MindSet. Looking like a bathing cap with electrodes attached to it, MindSet translates brain waves into real-time images; the
fluctuating brain waves are projected onto a computer screen, and the
resulting picture bears some resemblance to a lava lamp. The pair created the device because they couldn't afford a $75,000 EEG.

Three years after founding AquaThought, Cole thinks he has fig- 14
ured out why dolphins have beneficial effects on humans. He warns,
however, that a lot of people aren't going to believe what he has to say.

Cole isn't the first freethinker to be obsessed with dolphins. He's a dis- 15
ciple of futurist writer and scientist John Lilly, who in 1975 founded
the Human/Dolphin Foundation to explore the possibility of inter-
species communication. (Lilly himself believed he was following in the
footsteps of Aristotle, who had an interest in dolphins.) The dolphins
he was studying, Lilly wrote in his 1978 work "Communication between Man and Dolphin," "would do anything to convince the humans
that they were sentient and capable."

The field of dolphin-assisted therapy was probably started by Dr. 16
Betsy Smith, an educational anthropologist at Florida International
University. In 1971 Smith, who was researching dolphin-human interaction, let her mentally retarded brother wade into the water with two
adolescent dolphins. "They were pretty rough dolphins," Smith remembers. But not with her brother. "The dolphins were around him,
still, gentle, rubbing on him." Somehow, they knew he was different.

There are now 150 dolphin-assisted therapy researchers world- 17
wide, and there seems little doubt that dolphin swims can help humans
with disabilities such as Down's syndrome, autism, depression, attention deficit disorder, muscular dystrophy, and spinal cord injuries.
Mentally retarded children who swam with dolphins, for example,
"learned their lessons two to 10 times faster than in a normal class-

room setting," says Chris Harre of the Dolphin Research Center in Grassy Key, Fla.

18   Other researchers have found that swimming with dolphins boosts the production of infection-fighting T cells. The generally accepted theory is that swimming with dolphins increases relaxation, which helps stimulate the immune system.

19   Such vague psychological explanations drive Cole crazy; he calls them "horseshit," though he's not a very good swearer. Cole doesn't deny that relaxation helps T cell production. ("I could send you to Tahiti for a week, and your T cell count would probably go up," he says.) But Cole believes that relaxation can't explain the changes in brain waves and blood chemistry in humans who've swum with dolphins.

20   Cole thinks these changes are caused by dolphins' sonar, which they use to scan the water around them. The sonar is incredibly precise; dolphins can "echolocate" a shark half a mile away in the ocean and determine whether its stomach is full or empty—and, consequently, whether it might be feeding.

21   "The dolphins produce an intense amount of echolocation energy," Cole says. "It resonates in your bones. You can feel it pass through you and travel up your spine."

22   Cole's theory is too complicated to do justice here, but it goes basically like this: A dolphin's sonar can cause a phenomenon called cavitation, a ripping apart of molecules. (You see it in everyday life when, for example, you throw the throttle of a speedboat all the way down, but the boat doesn't move; for that second, the propeller is cavitating the water.)

23   "It's very possible that dolphins are causing cavitation inside soft tissue in the body," Cole says. "And if they did that with cellular membranes which are the boundaries between cells, they could completely change biomolecules." That could mean stimulating the production of T cells or the release of endorphins, hormones that prompt deep relaxation.

24   Someday, Cole says, scientists may be able to replicate dolphin sonar and use it in a precise, targeted way to bolster the immune system. But for now, he says, "the dolphin is a part of the experience."

25   In the cloudy water, I hear the dolphins before I see them: whirs, clicks, and buzzes fill the water.

26   To find out what it's really like to swim with dolphins, I have come to Dolphins Plus in Key Largo. It's a family-run place, surprisingly small, a suburban house that borders a canal with several large holding pens fenced off. (The dolphins can swim in the canal, but they always return to the pens.) Half an hour in the water costs $75, but before we can take the plunge we are given some guidelines. We are asked not to touch the dolphins; if they want to, they will touch us. We should swim with our hands at our sides, and avoid swimming directly

at or behind the dolphins, which they might interpret as hostile. Dolphins generally like children best, women after that, and men last.

Equipped with flippers, mask, and snorkel, I slide off the dock. I   27
can see only a few yards in the murky water. I am so nervous that I worry I won't be able to breathe through the snorkel, but my breath eventually settles into a steady rattle.

Quickly come the dolphin noises, seeming to feel me out. Still, I   28
see nothing. Suddenly, there is a flash of white and gray to my side; a few moments later, a dolphin passes below me. It looks even larger in the water than it does on the surface.

The next time one passes, I dive down. As instructed, I try to make   29
eye contact; for a few seconds the dolphin and I are swimming eye to eye, looking at and—I would swear to it—thinking about each other. These are not just cute, lovable puppy eyes; there's an intelligence here.

More dolphins swim by me, moving too fast for me to keep up. As   30
they swim, huge yet graceful in the water, I am acutely aware of my human clumsiness, and grateful that these animals are letting me swim with them. I can't resist the temptation to wave slowly, hoping that they'll understand the gesture. (This is not so bad: One woman sang "Happy birthday, dear dolphin" through her snorkel for her entire half hour.)

The dolphins swim so close that I'm convinced I'll bump into them,   31
but somehow they always keep an inch, two, three, between us. The temptation to touch them is great, yet resistable. Corny as it sounds, I want them to like me. To touch them would be like coughing at the opera.

At one point I am swimming with a mother and calf; the mother   32
makes eye contact with me, and suddenly I feel it: the zap of the dolphin echolocating me, almost like an electric shock. This, I decide later, is what telepathy must feel like: You hear a sound in your head, but it didn't get there through your ears. It startles me, and I stop swimming. The dolphin opens her mouth, seeming to smile, and she and her calf dart away.

When I get out of the water after 30 fleeting minutes, I feel an in-   33
credible calm. I wonder if there is a purely psychological explanation—the magic of the experience affecting me. But it feels deeper than that. Somehow, my body feels different. At this moment, I think David Cole is right.

A woman who was swimming with me sits down. She puts her face   34
in her hands and begins sobbing quietly. "I thought I would be all right," she says to a companion. I never do find out what she means.

Not everyone likes the idea that swimming with dolphins helps hu-   35
mans. Animal rights groups are concerned that such a theory could lead to an explosion in the number of captured dolphins. "We don't feel it's right," says Jenny Woods of People for the Ethical Treatment of Animals. "The animal has to be caged for the program to work."

Cole and other dolphin researchers share this concern. Betsy Smith,   36
for example, has given up swimming with captive dolphins and now
only swims with dolphins in the wild. (One concern of Smith's is that
echolocation is less common among captive dolphins. When I tell her
that I was echolocated, she says the dolphin must have found something about me interesting. "That's flattering," I remark. "Not necessarily," she says. "It may have been a tumor.")

For his part, Cole is trying hard to perfect Cyberfin, so people can   37
virtually swim with dolphins.

Smith and Cole may be racing against time. As more and more   38
people hear of dolphins' therapeutic effects, the desire to exploit the
animals for a quick buck will spread.

But to Cole, this is not a reason to stop working with dolphins. He   39
wants to establish a permanent dolphin research facility, something
that doesn't exist right now. "We're not looking for a magic bullet," Cole
says. "We're looking for ways of interfering with the progression of disease. It's virgin territory."

And if it means that people think he's a little odd—well, David Cole   40
can live with that.

Examining the Reading

Finding Meaning

1. What does the term *dolphin-assisted therapy* mean?
2. To what do most professionals attribute the positive effects of
   dolphin-assisted therapy?
3. According to Cole, how do dolphins make people feel better?
4. According to researcher Dr. Betsy Smith, dolphins may be able to
   help people with what disabilities?
5. Cole believes that swimming with dolphins has physiological effects
   on humans. After the author swims with dolphins, what does he
   conclude about the effect? What effects have occurred in others?
6. What is Cyberfin?

Understanding Technique

1. Evaluate Blow's sentence structure. How does he use it to add variety and interest to the essay?
2. The middle portion of the essay is written in the first person (I, me),
   while the first and last sections are written in the third person (he,

Cole, etc.). Usually a writer uses one point of view consistently throughout the essay. What is the effect of not doing so?

Thinking Critically

1. Discuss why animal rights groups don't like the idea of people swimming with dolphins (or don't like Cole's research).
2. What is Cole's real (or long-range) goal in conducting his research?
3. What does the author mean when he says this about swimming with dolphins: "To touch [dolphins] would be like coughing at the opera."
4. What does the article imply about the effect of relaxation on the immune system? Explain your answer.

Writing About the Reading

A Journal Entry

Generate a list of questions you would like to ask David Cole about dolphins and their behavior.

A Paragraph

1. Imagine that you get paid to invent products and services that would help people who have physical or mental disabilities. Write a paragraph describing what you would like to invent and how it would be beneficial to people.
2. Write a paragraph explaining how you think Cole would react to a proposed federal law that would ban all animal research.

An Essay

1. The author makes a point of reminding the reader that certain scientific theories that originally seemed "nutty" ended up being factual. He cites black holes, cloning, and artificial intelligence as examples. Did you or a family member ever have an idea that other people thought was "nutty" but that turned out to be reasonable? Write a story that explains your idea and the reaction it received.
2. Assume that further research discovers that swimming with dolphins can cure certain types of cancers. What types of problems do

you see? What types of rules and regulations would be needed? Write an essay exploring potential problems.

A Creative Activity

Assume that you are an animal rights activist who is opposed to the use of dolphins for research and therapy. Write a letter to David Cole outlining your objections.

The Case for Selling Human Organs

▸ **Ronald Bailey**

Ronald Bailey describes the current organ shortage and proposes a financial solution. His article originally appeared in Reason Magazine Online (**www.reason.com**) *in 2001.*

Reading Strategy

As you read, highlight the elements of Bailey's argument, including important background information.

Vocabulary Preview

registry (5) a list or catalog
salutary (6) beneficial; good; wholesome
hasten (8) quicken
taboo (9) forbidden
euphemisms (9) expressions used in place of ones that might
                    be offensive
compensate (10) pay; offer financial reward
bereaved (11) having lost a loved one through death
coercion (14) force
psychosocially (14) related to both social and psychological
                        factors

National Organ and Tissue Donor Awareness Week is, by order of   1
Congress, celebrated this week [April 20–26]. It's been 34 years since
Dr. Christian Bernard performed the world's first heart transplant in
Cape Town, South Africa, but the modern era of organ transplantation
essentially began when the anti-rejection drug cyclosporin was intro-
duced in 1981.

In 2000, 22,827 organs were transplanted in the United States.   2
Since 1990, a total of 185,347 organs have been transplanted into patients in the U.S. That's the good news

The bad news is that, according to the nonprofit United Network for   3
Organ Sharing (UNOS), there are now 75,863 men, woman, and children on the national organ transplantation waiting list. That's up from
20,481 a decade ago. Cadaveric donors—that is brain-dead donors—

increased from 4,011 in 1989 to 5,984 in 2000, according to the U.S. Department of Health and Human Services (HHS). An average of 3.6 organs for transplant were taken from cadaveric donors. Meanwhile living donors surged from 1,918 in 1989 to 5,532 in 2000.

Despite these increases, an average of 15 people still die every day while waiting for an organ that could have saved their lives. "With the success and acceptance of organ transplantation, it has become routine therapy for many diseases," UNOS President Patricia Adams says. "We have the know-how to save tens of thousands of lives. What we don't have are enough donated organs to make it possible." 4

HHS Secretary Tommy Thompson announced plans to address the organ shortage by exploring the idea of creating a national online registry where people can officially record their desire to be organ donors after they die. Thompson has also launched a campaign to get corporations to discuss becoming donors with their employees. Finally, Thompson wants to create a national medal to honor the families of organ donors. 5

All of these are decent, salutary goals. And they will do absolutely nothing to end the shortage. 6

The normal way to handle shortages is to let prices rise to the market-clearing price. With organs, it might work this way: A cadaveric donor's family might be able to sell their dear departed's organs to patients who need them. Better yet, consenting living donors would be able to bargain with transplantees or their insurance companies for the sale of, say, a kidney or a piece of liver (both can be surgically removed without causing much permanent harm to the seller). But there is nothing resembling a market in human organs in the United States. 7

Why? At the very beginning of the organ transplant era some people feared that their doctors might hasten their deaths in order to obtain transplantable organs. Others worried that people living in rich countries might pay poor people living in developing countries for their organs. These fears have given rise to one of the most durable urban legends of all time: the one about the guy who goes to Spring Break in Florida and wakes up 3 days later in a hotel room with a hole in his side through which someone has extracted one of his kidneys. 8

The taboo topic in the organ transplant community is payment for organs. When it is discussed, euphemisms like "rewarded gifting" or "compensated donation" are used. 9

In 1983, Dr. Barry Jacobs publicly suggested that the U.S. government consider setting up a fund to compensate the families of cadaveric donors. Dr. Jacobs also proposed to set up a business that would buy kidneys from living donors for transplantation in American patients. Spearheaded by U.S. Reps. Henry Waxman and Al Gore, Congress rushed 10 the passage of the National Organ Transplantation Act in 1984 to ban the sale of human organs from either dead or living donors.

National Organ and Tissue Donor Awareness Week is an appropriate time to rethink this policy. In the long run, the organ shortage may be solved with biotech miracles like transplantable animal organs genetically tailored to match individual human immune systems, or by repairing damaged organs using human stem cells. But in the short run, monetary incentives will matter. As one transplant physician pointed out to me years ago, everybody else in the transplant business—from doctors to hospitals to pharmaceutical companies—gets paid. And, of course, the recipient gets something far more valuable than money. Given all that, it seemed reasonable to him that the bereaved families of brain-dead donors should be paid something, too.

But what about compensating living donors? It should be noted that in the United States we already have robust markets for blood, semen, human eggs, and surrogate wombs. Extending markets to include nonvital solid organs such as kidneys and pieces of liver, which can be obtained with reasonable safety from living donors, is not such a stretch. Keep in mind that of the more then 75,000 people on the waiting list for organs, 48,639 need kidneys and 17,413 need livers.

The Journal of the American Medical Association published its "Consensus Statement on the Live Organ Donor" in its December 13, 2000, issue which offers this guidance for determining when living organ donations are appropriate:

"The person who gives consent to be a live organ donor should be competent, willing to donate, free from coercion, medically and psychosocially suitable, fully informed of the risks and benefits as a donor, and fully informed of the risks, benefits, and alternative treatment available to the recipient. The benefits to both donor and recipient must outweigh the risks associated with the donation and transplantation of the living donor organ."

All of that is quite reasonable; the emphasis on true donor consent gets around the grisly reality in communist China, where organs are harvested from prisoners without consent. For the transplant recipient, the hoped for benefits are clear—they are freed from dialysis, their health improves, they avoid dying. But how can doctors and ethicists be certain that the benefits outweigh the risks for the living donor? One good way to make sure that the "benefits to both the donor and the recipient must outweight the risks" is to offer appropriate monetary compensation to a living donor for a kidney or a piece of liver.

When that happens, it will finally be time to celebrate National Organ and Tissue Donor Awareness Week.

Examining the Reading

Finding Meaning

1. What organizations keep statistics on donors and recipients?
2. What plans does Tommy Thompson have for increasing organ donations?
3. What does Bailey propose for a solution to the shortage?
4. Why are people afraid to be organ donors?
5. What did Dr. Barry Jacobs propose to increase donations? What happened in response?
6. How are some organs obtained in China?
7. What does the author feel would be a true reason to celebrate National Organ and Tissue Donor Awareness Week?

Understanding Technique

1. Identify Bailey's thesis. How does he support it?
2. With what tone does the author treat the subject of organ donation? How effective is this tone?
3. Bailey includes the *Journal of the American Medical Association* guidelines for living organ donations. What does this contribute to the article? How else could he have provided this information?
4. The author begins and ends the article with mention of National Organ and Tissue Donor Awareness Week. What do these references accomplish?

Thinking Critically

1. Why do you think there is such a shortage of organ donors?
2. Why does the author feel that Tommy Thompson's plans will not end the organ shortage?
3. Why is the organ trade such a taboo subject?
4. Why was there such opposition in Congress to Dr. Jacobs's suggestion?
5. Do you think organs should be bought and sold? Why or why not?
6. Why doesn't Bailey think the benefits of organ donation currently outweigh the risks? Do you agree with him? Explain.

Writing About the Reading

A Journal Entry

Create a list of words describing your feelings about organ donation.

A Paragraph

1. Write a paragraph explaining what may motivate people to donate their organs.
2. Some people feel that money solves all problems. Write a paragraph describing a situation that cannot be changed with money.
3. Write about a time you gave or received a priceless gift.

An Essay

1. Are you registered to donate your organs upon your death? Write an essay giving your reasons for your position on this issue.
2. Bailey mentions that his suggestion is a "taboo topic." Write an essay describing several other important subjects that Americans feel uncomfortable discussing.
3. Write an essay explaining and justifying what you would do in the following situation. A costly experimental medical treatment may save your child's life. You have exhausted all appeals to have the treatment covered by your health insurance. You learn that in another country you can sell one of your kidneys for an amount of money that would cover the experimental treatment. Doctors have told you that one of your kidneys is below normal functioning. Would you sell your kidney?

A Creative Activity

Create a conversation between an organ donor and the recipient.

Human Interaction

▸ **Christine Choi**
Student Essay

*A college student explains how people are interacting directly
with their computers more than with other people.*

Commercials and catalogs everywhere advertising faster Internet con-   1
nections, wrist pads, screen covers, and contoured "therapeutic" mice
indicate that we are being drawn into an age of computer efficiency,
spending longer hours at glowing screens extracting more information
while expending less effort. Services like America Online's Instant Messenger allow us to communicate virtually and instantly with friends all
over the world. At the same time, we sit in our swivel chairs, buy CDs
online, complete assignments online, self-diagnose our illnesses online,
and even date online. But while computers today have the ability to ful-
fill virtually every human need, actual social interaction is still important and necessary during the course of a day's computing.

AOL Instant Messenger (AIM) is easily one of the leading causes of   2
the decrease in human interaction. Particularly on college campuses, it
is easier to click on one's "Buddy List" and check if "Webwombat"
wants to meet for dinner than it would be to look up his number, pick
up the phone, punch in each of the digits, and actually talk to him.
Phone usage also deprives us of such luxuries as posting an "away message" that says "brb" (be right back)—stunningly efficient communication in just three convenient letters. But AIM can be addictive, causing
the user to forget that direct, face-to-face conversation still remains an
option. I once "IM'ed" my friend Amy to ask if a friend of ours was in
his room. She replied that his screen name was idle, that his away message wasn't up, and that I should therefore wait until his name
changed color from light gray to black again, indicating that he was
back online. Despite her advice, I followed a hunch and called him. He
was there. This demonstrates how the convenient little world of chim-
ing pop-up windows may not accurately reflect the real world. There
are people out there whose names don't appear on our buddy lists, and
there are alternative, more gratifying ways of interacting with them
outside AIM.

Computer technology offers ways to substitute not only real con-   3
versations, but also basic activities such as shopping for clothing or

food. Popular web sites like Peapod.com allow their users to fill their virtual grocery carts with everything from Turkish apricots to eyelash curlers with mere clicks of a mouse. Customers are even granted the freedom to personally select between green or ripe bananas, rolled or loose mints. Why sift through piles of fruit at the market, sniffing, squeezing, checking for brown spots, when one can simply click on "ripe"? Also through the Internet, crowded malls and shops can be avoided completely, and shoppers can instead double-click on a 1" × 2" photo of an anonymous pair of legs wearing cotton-blend cropped pants, available in lavender, shale, or moss. The advantages of shopping from the still-warm swivel chair are apparent, especially to the busy and tired. But with the number of big-name online shopping services growing rapidly, it is easy to forget that shopping for things we need, despite our busy and important lives, has its own value. Do we really want to trade in the pleasure of trying on clothing and feeling textures of fabrics, for those few extra hours of typing? Leaving the house once in a while to smell a peach or try on leather sandals is refreshing and provides an excellent opportunity to be with friends or family, to exchange smiles, gestures, and dialogue—to interact with real people.

The world of real human interaction also offers opportunities for 4 learning that could not be achieved as effectively through interaction with a small glowing screen. Increasingly, professors are posting their syllabi, grades, announcements, and lectures on the Web, and encouraging inter-class "chat" among students through e-mail, inviting them to log in more hours of their day blinking at computers. The fact that some courses are taught completely online excites some and frightens others. While these online courses enable a student to roll out of bed and "attend class" in a shamelessly rugged, pajama-clad state, they restrict opportunities for actual hands-on learning and helpful student discussions. Furthermore, while the routine greetings we exchange on the walk to class may seem trivial, losing them is a small step toward the extinction of social interaction. Even outside the classroom, the Internet is full of "do-it-yourself" web sites where one could learn to do everything from self-diagnose medical symptoms, to build his or her own aquarium—all without having to budge from the swivel chair.

While new computer technology does not necessarily force people to 5 become moles, it does allow people to turn away from good old interpersonal interaction and head toward a world in which speaking and gesturing is replaced by soft clicking. When technological opportunities are new and exciting, it is easy to be lured by the pressure to take advantage of what is available. At the same time, it is important to stop and ask ourselves if the long hours we spend sending Instant Messages to a friend two doors down or purchasing produce from a laptop is really necessary.

Examining the Essay

1. What is Choi's thesis? What types of evidence does she use to support it?
2. Highlight and evaluate Choi's topic sentences.
3. Examine the descriptive language used by the author. How does it strenghten her essay? Highlight several particularly effective examples.
4. Evaluate Choi's introduction and conclusion.

Writing an Essay

1. Write an essay evaluating your degree of dependency on computers and whether it limits your social interaction.
2. Technology has changed American life drastically in the past 100 years. Write an essay explaining the pros and cons of one form of technology.
3. Write an essay that examines how today's children may be affected by growing up with computers. How are their lives different from that of their parents due to computer accessibility?
4. Choi considers shopping in real stores as a worthwhile experience. Explain whether shopping is important or unimportant to you and how you approach it. Do you prefer online or real store shopping?

 ## Making Connections

1. "Stepping Through a Computer Screen, Disabled Veterans Savor Freedom," "Log to Learn," and "Human Interaction" are all concerned with the use of computers. Compare the ways in which computers are used in each of these readings.

2. Reconsider the following articles: "Dr. Dolphin" and "Inventing the Future." In each article, the author discusses new or future directions for the application of technology. Write an essay explaining how feasible you feel each new use of technology to be. Make projections about which applications will be in widespread use in twenty-five years and which will not.

3. Can there be too much technology? Consider the messages of "The Seven Sustainable Wonders of the World," "Inventing the Future," and "Human Interaction."

Internet Connections

1. How much do you know about the Internet? Find out by trying some of the quizzes at **http://www.netsurfquiz.com/**. Summarize what you learned about the Internet, one of our newest and most influential technologies.

2. Read the information about some of the inventors on this site: **http://www.invent.org/book/book-text/indexbydecade. html**. Write a paragraph about the individual who made a technological contribution that you found to be the most interesting.

3. Visit the web site for Community Voice Mail at **http:// www.cvm.org/index.html**. Write an essay evaluating this program and suggesting other ways in which we can use technology to help the less fortunate members of our world.

   (If any of these web sites are unavailable, use a search engine to locate another appropriate site.)

Glossary

analyze To examine carefully and closely; to determine why something has happened or can be expected to happen.

annotate To write notes or comments in response or reaction to what you read.

argument A set of ideas that states a position (or claim) and offers reasons and evidence in support of that position.

biased One-sided; prejudiced.

brainstorming A method of developing ideas by writing a list of everything that comes to mind about the topic.

chronological sequence A method of organizing ideas according to the order in which they happen.

compare To discover how two or more persons or things are alike and how they differ.

conclusion The ending of an essay that draws it to a close and often reemphasizes the thesis statement; a decision, judgment, or opinion reached by reasoning.

describe To provide a picture or account of something in words.

details Specific information that explains a topic sentence; particulars.

develop To make bigger, fuller, or more complete by providing greater detail.

dialogue Conversation between two or more people.

discuss To consider many aspects of a topic; to talk over.

evaluate To consider the worth, value, or importance of something.

evidence Facts that show why something is true or not true; proof.

highlight To mark important information using a wide-tipped pen.

illustrate To make clear or to explain using stories, examples, comparisons, etc.

implied thesis A thesis that is suggested but not directly stated in the essay.

imply (implied) To suggest, but not to state directly; to mean without saying so.

introduction The opening of an essay that identifies the topic and often presents the thesis statement. It may also interest the reader.

justify To demonstrate that something is correct or right; to give reasons for or to defend.

opinion A belief; what one thinks about something.

organization The arrangement or sequence of ideas in a paragraph or essay.

point of view The perspective from which a story is told; the relationship between the narrator of the story and the story itself.

sentence structure The arrangement or order of the parts of a sentence.

structure Arrangement or order of ideas.

subject A general or broad topic.

summarize To express only the main points.

technique The method, skill, or system a writer uses to compose and express ideas.

theme A statement that a piece of literature seems to be making about its subject.

thesis statement The main point of an essay; a sentence that identifies and explains what an essay will be about.

tone The attitude of the author toward the subject matter (examples: serious, apologetic, humorous, angry).

topic sentence A sentence that states the main idea of a paragraph; the one idea that all the details in a paragraph explain.

transitions Words or phrases that connect ideas within a paragraph or essay.

Acknowledgments

JOSEPH TOVARES "Mojado Like Me" by Joseph Tovares, *Hispanic* Magazine, May 1995. Reprinted by permission of *Hispanic* Magazine; BARBARA EHRENREICH Barbara Ehrenreich, "What Are They Probing For?," *Time* Magazine, June 4, 2001. © 2001 Time Inc. Reprinted by permission.

Chapter 4 KIM MCLARIN "Primary Colors" by Kim McLarin, *The New York Times Magazine*, May 24, 1998. Copyright © 1998 by Kim McLarin. Reprinted by permission of Witherspoon Associates; ROBERTO SANTIAGO "Black *and* Latino" by Roberto Santiago, *Essence* Magazine. Roberto Santiago is the editor of *Boricuas: Influential Puerto Rican Writings—An Anthology* (Ballantine/One World Books, 1995). Reprinted by permission of the author; JADE SNOW WONG "The Fifth Chinese Daughter," from *The Immigrant Experience* by Thomas C. Wheeler. Copyright © 1971 by Doubleday, a division of Bantam Doubleday Dell Publishing Group, Inc. Used by permission of Doubleday, a division of Random House, Inc; ALFONSO ORITZ "Through Tewa Eyes" by Alfonso Oritz, *National Geographic*, October, 1991, pp. 6–7, 11–13. Alfonso Oritz, Professor of Anthropology, University of New Mexico, Albuquerque, NM 87131. Reprinted by permission of the author; LARS EIGHNER Lars Eighner, "Dumpster Diving." Copyright © 1993 by Lars Eighner. From *Travels with Lizbeth* by Lars Eighner. Reprinted by permission of St. Martin's Press, LLC; RICHARD P. APPELBAUM AND WILLIAM J. CHAMBLISS Source: *Sociology*, by Richard P. Appelbaum and William J. Chambliss, ScottForesman/Addison Wesley, 1995, p. 369.

Chapter 5 CAROL FLEISCHMAN "Shopping Can Be a Challenge with Curious Onlookers, Puzzled Clerks and a Guide Dog" by Carol Fleischman, *Buffalo News*, February 24, 1998. Reprinted by permission of the author; BILL COSBY From *Love & Marriage* by Bill Cosby. Copyright © 1989 by Bill Cosby. Used by permission of Doubleday, a division of Random House, Inc; ALLISON BERNARD "Our Wounded Hearts" by Allison Bernard. Reprinted with permission from *Health*, © 1998; MARIO CUOMO From *Diaries of Mario M. Cuomo* by Mario M. Cuomo. Copyright © 1984 by Mario M. Cuomo. Reprinted by permission of Random House, Inc; LESTER SLOAN Lester Sloan, "Planting Seeds, Harvesting Scholarships: Food from the 'Hood." From *Newsweek*, May 29, 1995, © 1995 Newsweek, Inc. All rights reserved. Reprinted by permission; MICHAEL SCHALLER, VIRGINIA SCHARFF, AND ROBERT D. SCHULZINGER Source: From Schaller, Michael, Virginia Scharff and Robert Schulzinger, *Present Tense: The United States Since 1945*, 2/e. Copyright © 1996 by Houghton Mifflin Company. Used with permission.

Chapter 6 DEBORAH TANNEN "Oprah Winfrey," by Deborah Tannen, *Time* Magazine, June 8, 1998, copyright Deborah Tannen. Reprinted by permission; PATRICE GAINES From *Laughing in the Dark* by Patrice

Index of Authors and Titles

"Advertising: Institutionalized Lying," Donna Woolfolk Cross — 202

Anderson, Siu Wai, "A Letter to My Daughter" — 64

Appelbaum, Richard, and William J. Chambliss, "Silenced Voices: Deaf Cultures and 'Hearing' Families" — 147

"Arming Myself with a Gun Is Not the Answer," Bronwyn Jones — 25

Bailey, Ronald, "The Case for Selling Human Organs" — 253

Bernard, Allison, "Our Wounded Hearts" — 165

"Bill Gates: Computer Wizard," Michael Schaller, Virginia Scharff, and Robert D. Schulzinger — 178

"Black *and* Latino," Roberto Santiago — 130

"Blind to Faith," Karl Taro Greenfeld — 77

Blow, Richard, "Dr. Dolphin" — 245

"Breaking Glass," Jonathan Rosen — 73

"Can TV Improve Us?" Jane Rosenzweig — 206

Case, David, "Mr. Mom's World" — 91

"The Case for Selling Human Organs," Ronald Bailey — 253

Chambliss, William J., and Richard Appelbaum, "Silenced Voices: Deaf Cultures and 'Hearing' Families" — 147

Chartrand, Sabra; "Working Students Need to Look for Career Experience" — 97

Choi, Christine, "Human Interaction" — 258

"The Chosen One," Laura Cunningham — 20

Cosby, Bill, "The Promised Land" — 161

Cross, Donna Woolfolk, "Advertising: Institutionalized Lying" — 202

"Cultural Education in America," Jonathan Wong — 151

Cunningham, Laura, "The Chosen One" — 20

Cuomo, Mario, "Poppa and the Spruce Tree" — 170

Dawson, George, and Richard Glaubman, "Life Is So Good" — 29

"Desert Storm and Shield," Scott Stopa — 85

Dickman, Jennifer S., "Saying Good-Bye to Eric" — 35

Diez, Colleen, "Sporting the Fan(tasy) of Reality TV" — 217

"Disney's Head Trips," Jane Keunz — 105

"Do unto Others," David Polmer — 182

"Dr. Dolphin," Richard Blow — 245

"Dumpster Diving," Lars Eighner — 143

Durning, Alan Thein, "The Seven Sustainable Wonders of the World" — 223

Ehrenreich, Barbara, "What Are They Probing For" — 116

Eighner, Lars, "Dumpster Diving" — 143

"Evan's Two Moms," Anna Quindlen — 39

"The Family Farm," David Mas Masumoto   101
"Fifth Chinese Daughter," Jade Snow Wong   134
Fleischman, Carol, "Shopping Can Be a Challenge"   157
"Food from the 'Hood," Lester Sloan   174
Frazier, Ian, "To Mr. Winslow"   69
Frey, Darby L., and Thomas J. Frey, "Inventing the Future"   240
Frey, Thomas J., and Darby L. Frey, "Inventing the Future"   240
Gaines, Patrice, "My First Story"   193
Gard, Carolyn, "Music 'n Moods"   197
"The Gift of Sacrifice," Blanca Matute   47
Glaubman, Richard, and George Dawson, "Life Is So Good"   29
Greenfeld, Karl Taro, "Blind to Faith"   77
"Hello, Goodbye, Hey Maybe I Love You?" Joshua Kurlantzick   43
"How Much 'Reality' TV Can We Survive?" Todd Leopold   211
"Human Interaction," Christine Choi   258
"Inventing the Future," Thomas J. Frey and Darby L. Frey   240
Jones, Bronwyn, "Arming Myself with a Gun Is Not the Answer"   25
Keunz, Jane, "Disney's Head Trips"   105
Kleinfield, N. R., "Stepping Through a Computer Screen,
    Disabled Veterans Savor Freedom"   227
Kurlantzick, Joshua, "Hello, Goodbye, Hey Maybe I Love You?"   43
Leopold, Todd, "How Much 'Reality' TV Can We Survive?"   211
"A Letter to My Daughter," Siu Wai Anderson   64
"Life Is So Good," George Dawson and Richard Glaubman   29
"Log to Learn," Jodie Morse   233
Masumoto, David Mas, "The Family Farm"   101
Matute, Blanca, "The Gift of Sacrifice"   47
McLarin, Kim, "Primary Colors"   126
"*Mojado* Like Me," Joseph Tovares   109
Morse, Jodie, "Log to Learn"   233
"Mr. Mom's World," David Case   91
"Music 'n Moods," Carolyn Gard   197
"My First Story," Patrice Gaines   193
"Oprah Winfrey," Deborah Tannen   188
Ortiz, Alfonso, "Through Tewa Eyes"   138
"Our Wounded Hearts," Allison Bernard   165
Polmer, David, "Do unto Others"   182
"Poppa and the Spruce Tree," Mario Cuomo   170
"Primary Colors," Kim McLarin   126
"The Promised Land," Bill Cosby   161
Quindlen, Anna, "Evan's Two Moms"   39

"Ragtime, My Time," Alton Fitzgerald White 59

Rosen, Jonathan, "Breaking Glass" 73

Rosenzweig, Jane, "Can TV Improve Us?" 206

Salinas, Marta, "The Scholarship Jacket" 53

Santiago, Robert, "Black *and* Latino" 130

"Saying Good-Bye to Eric," Jennifer S. Dickman 35

Schaller, Michael, Virginia Scharff, and Robert D. Schulzinger,
    "Bill Gates: Computer Wizard" 178

Scharff, Virginia, Michael Schaller, and Robert D. Schulzinger,
    "Bill Gates: Computer Wizard" 178

"The Scholarship Jacket," Marta Salinas 53

Schulzinger, Robert D., Michael Schaller, and Virginia Scharff,
    "Bill Gates: Computer Wizard" 178

"A Seafood Survey," Robert Wood 120

"The Seven Sustainable Wonders of the World," Alan Thein Durning 223

"Shopping Can Be a Challenge," Carol Fleischman 157

"Silenced Voices: Deaf Cultures and 'Hearing' Families,"
    Richard Appelbaum and William J. Chambliss 147

Sloan, Lester, "Food from the 'Hood" 174

"Sporting the Fan(tasy) of Reality TV," Colleen Diez 217

"Stepping Through a Computer Screen, Disabled Veterans
    Savor Freedom," N. R. Kleinfield 227

Stopa, Scott, "Desert Storm and Shield" 85

Tannen, Deborah, "Oprah Winfrey" 188

"Through Tewa Eyes," Alfonso Ortiz 138

"To Mr. Winslow," Ian Frazier 69

Tovares, Joseph, "*Mojado* Like Me" 109

"What Are They Probing For?" Barbara Ehrenreich 116

White, Alton Fitzgerald, "Ragtime, My Time" 59

Wong, Jade Snow, "Fifth Chinese Daughter" 134

Wong, Jonathan, "Cultural Education in America" 151

Wood, Robert, "A Seafood Survey" 120

"Working Students Need to Look for Career Experience,"
    Sabra Chartrand 97